'MY STYLE OF GOVERNMENT'

The Rt. Hon. Nicholas Ridley, M.P., was born in 1929 and educated at Eton and Balliol College, Oxford. After a career in industry he entered Parliament as M.P. for Cirencester and Tewkesbury in 1959, and he kept this seat throughout his parliamentary career. He was Parliamentary Private Secretary to the Minister of Education (1962–64), and Under-Secretary of State at the Department of Trade and Industry (1970–72), before resigning from Edward Heath's government. Under Mrs Thatcher he was Minister of State at the Foreign and Commonwealth Office (1979–81), Financial Secretary to the Treasury (1981–83), Secretary of State for Transport (1983–86) and for the Environment (1986–89). He was Secretary of State for Trade and Industry (1989–90). In these posts, as one of Margaret Thatcher's staunchest supporters, he has been at the centre of shaping government policy on privatization, the Poll Tax and Europe, the issue on which he resigned from the Government.

Nicholas Ridley is a keen amateur painter. He is married and lives in Gloucestershire.

NICHOLAS RIDLEY

'My Style of Government'

The Thatcher Years

Fontana
An Imprint of HarperCollinsPublishers

Fontana
An Imprint of HarperCollins*Publishers*
77–85 Fulham Palace Road,
Hammersmith, London W6 8JB

Published by Fontana 1992
9 8 7 6 5 4 3 2 1

First published in Great Britain by
Hutchinson 1991

ISBN 0 00 637822 6

Set in Plantin

Printed in Great Britain by
HarperCollinsManufacturing Glasgow

CONTENTS

ILLUSTRATIONS

1

THE BEGINNING

ONE AFTERNOON TOWARDS the end of 1974, I met Sir Keith Joseph in the Members' Lobby of the House of Commons. I asked him whether he was firm in his intention to challenge Edward Heath in the coming contest for the leadership of the Conservative Party. He replied that he had decided not to do so 'for personal reasons'. I was aghast. At last the opportunity had come to break with the miserable years of the past and secure a change of leader, and it was widely believed that it would be Keith Joseph who would make the challenge.

'I think Margaret will stand,' he said.

I was amazed, because the news that Margaret Thatcher might stand hadn't reached my ears before. But I was relieved; at least there was a challenger.

I walked off to ponder the news and immediately met Margaret Thatcher in the Long Corridor which runs up to the Speaker's Office.

'I hear from Keith that he is not going to stand and that you are,' I said. 'Is that right?'

'Yes,' she said, 'I will stand.'

I told her I would do everything I could to help her.

On 11 February 1975 Margaret Thatcher was elected Leader of the Conservative Party.

On 26 November 1990 I went to lunch at Number 10 Downing Street. It was the last lunch Margaret Thatcher gave as Prime Minister. John Major became Prime Minister on 28 November. At her right-hand side was Keith Joseph, who had sponsored her bid for the leadership some fifteen years before. There were about thirty of her parliamentary colleagues there, who had all been faithful to the last. It was one of the saddest, most moving occasions of my life.

It was the end of her fifteen-and-a-half-years of leadership of the party, and eleven-and-a-half years as Prime Minister. All my first thoughts were for her personally – how dignified she was in the face of rejection, how loyal to those who were loyal to her, how brave in facing adversity. What would she do now? Where would she live? How would she react to her brutal rejection? What contribution would she make to world, or European, or national politics? Or would she leave the high political stage as abruptly as she had entered it?

Second thoughts quickly follow first thoughts. What has Thatcherism achieved, and in what ways is the nation changed? Have those eleven-and-a-half years made any permanent change in the fortunes, the character and the attitudes of the British people? Is the remarkable economic upsurge of the 1980s to hold firm and continue, or was it remarkable because of its uniqueness? Had she found a new international role for Britain, or was it all just the brilliance of a star which was eventually snuffed out?

That it was a unique period in the recent history of Britain is indisputable. Many would say it was a uniquely bad one. Many others would say it was a renaissance, a transformation, a decade of inspired political leadership. History alone will decide, but I am in the latter camp. It was an inspiration to see it all happening at first hand, and to have been part of it.

It was an extraordinary achievement to remain leader for some fifteen years, to win three elections in a row, never to lose one and, more important, to achieve so much during her period of power.

But Thatcherism's ending has to be explained too. Otherwise it might seem as if it was a gigantic experiment, which ultimately failed – like some vast science fiction concept which missed out one vital consideration and was never heard of again.

I was disappointed that February afternoon that Keith Joseph had decided not to stand for the leadership. I admired him. He was a great thinker, and at that time the only leading Tory to show the courage of his convictions. I was desperately unhappy with the way the Tory Party had been led off course by Edward Heath from 1970 to 1974. Keith Joseph seemed to be signalling a return to replacing socialism, not adapting it for electoral convenience.

I had decided to go into politics in my twenties because of my experiences under the Attlee Government of 1945–51. I wanted to see socialism decisively reversed – no less.

One of the reasons was my dislike of nationalization. During my Oxford days, when I first began to think about politics, the Attlee Government was busy nationalizing all the basic industries. I developed an ideological objection to it. Later, when I was working with Brims & Company, building shipyards on the banks of the Tyne, I found practical experience confirmed my objections. There was a sloppiness about the way public corporations behaved: early on I realized they were dominated by their workforce, not their customers. Service was on a 'take it or leave it' basis. I resented having to contribute to making up their losses and raising their capital through my contribution to taxation. My political objection to public ownership seemed to be confirmed by my experience of the very real drawbacks of it in practice.

Another reason was my dislike of trade union power – which rampaged unrestrained at that time. As I could see for myself in the Tyne shipyards, it was used to maintain demarcation rules and restrictive practices, which did far more to damage the long term interests of the workers than any wage increases they obtained did them good.

Lastly, I resented the high level of taxation which the Chancellor, Sir Stafford Cripps, imposed on us all at that time.

If I emerged from Oxford University a confirmed Tory, eight years of working on Tyneside made me a radical one. I wanted to see the nation's industry and economy properly run. I wanted socialism defeated for ever.

I fought the 1955 election against Alfred Robens in Blyth, Northumberland, and was beaten by some 23,000 votes. In 1959 I secured the candidature for Cirencester and Tewkesbury and was elected in the General Election of that year. There were 104 new Tory MPs elected in 1959. By the end of 1990 there were only three of them left still representing the same seats in Parliament. They were Sir John Farr, Margaret Thatcher and myself.

All through the 1960s I had pressed for the Tory Party to be firmer in its resolve to restore the market economy and to roll back the frontiers of socialism. I had found Harold Macmillan unsatisfactory in respect of his acceptance of consensus government, and had been much more attracted by the economic views of Enoch Powell than by those of any of the other Tory leaders. However, it was Ted Heath whom the Tories chose as their leader in 1965, not Enoch Powell, for whom I had voted. Ted Heath nevertheless seemed mildly promising. When he took his Shadow Cabinet to the Selsdon Park Hotel in Surrey for a weekend in 1969 and produced the new policies on which he would fight the election, I became enthusiastic. He promised to stop subsidizing industry, to reduce taxation, and to return some nationalized industries to the private sector. He even asked me to chair the small policy group he was setting up to work up the privatization policy. Our small group met frequently, and we soon had a report, which after much fine-tuning I presented to Ted Heath. I attended a Shadow Cabinet meeting at which it was approved, with one or two deletions and additions. Suitably disguised, the policy went into the Manifesto. We won the election of June 1970 and Ted Heath became Prime Minister. I was appointed Parliamentary Under-Secretary at the Ministry of Technology. Geoffrey Rippon was Secretary of State. All seemed set to embark on the privatization programme and the dismantling of the socialist state.

In the end, the Government of 1970–4 succeeded in denationalizing only two small concerns: Thomas Cook, the travel agent, and the state-owned pubs in the Carlisle area. The pubs were apparently nationalized during the First World War, as they had served their customers too well, rather to the detriment of the output of the armaments factories in the area. These two small businesses seemed but a token of good intentions towards the privatizing policy, after which it was quietly dropped. Indeed, later the Government went on to nationalize Rolls-Royce when it got into severe financial difficulties.

Ted Heath's Government actually enlarged the public sector. Perhaps there is a touch of irony in the fact that it was the public sector, in the form of the coal miners, that finally brought about his downfall.

Rising unemployment in 1970–1 had led him to abandon the Selsdon Park policies upon which he had been elected. He went on to inflate the economy massively and quickly and tried to deal with the resulting inflation by legislating to prevent prices and incomes rising. It had all come to grief when he took on the miners who were demanding a large pay rise. He tried to 'beat them' at the polls – and lost. If he had won, I don't know how he thought it would have stopped the miners' strike. They wanted the money, and legislating was not going to stop them.

Earlier he also produced the famous Industry Bill of 1972, which gave the Government power to distribute large sums of public money to ailing private companies. It was prepared behind the backs of the junior industry ministers, of whom I was one.

I could stand it no more. Ted Heath sent for me in April 1972 when he had a reshuffle. I was on an official visit to Lisbon, and had to fly back in the middle of the night. He tried to move me sideways and asked me to become Minister for the Arts. I refused: I said I wanted to have no more to do with his Government. It was my first political resignation. It was a lonely experience.

I was later very glad to have had nothing to do with the Government of 1972–4 and I used my freedom to the maximum advantage. I managed to get myself elected Chairman of the Conservative Back-bench Finance Committee. It was at this time that I first met Alan Walters. He was Professor of Economics at the London School of Economics, and was an expert on monetary policy. He and a few academic friends had become deeply concerned about the direction Ted Heath's economic policy was taking and he had begun issuing stern warnings in the press and elsewhere. He was no politician: indeed, he was a person who despised politics. He it was who led me to define an economist as 'a politician who doesn't have to be elected'. Nevertheless, Alan Walters turned to that minute band of politicians who were trying to articulate the massive changes in policy that were required. He cared desperately about the plight of the British economy. In 1972 there were few of us who felt strongly, and we were all junior backbenchers. The ringleaders were John Biffen, Jock Bruce-Gardyne and myself. We had all been in Parliament for some time and had shared the same feeling of disillusionment about Ted Heath's disastrous U-turn. John Biffen is a Somerset farmer's son, and Jock Bruce-Gardyne was a Scot who in his early career had been a journalist with the *Financial Times*. Our mutual friendship became reinforced by a common determination to try to get the Tory Party back on course.

Our first foray was to oppose the Report Stage of the Industry Bill, keeping the debate going until 11.30 pm on a Friday night – an unprecedented event. We could not stop the Bill passing, but we made our point.

Jock Bruce-Gardyne and I, both then officers of the Finance Committee, asked Alan Walters to help us prepare a paper on how to control the economy by using monetary policy. Our paper was scorned by the backbench members of the Committee and when we took it to Anthony Barber, the Chancellor of the Exchequer, he scorned it even more. It was about the frostiest meeting I can remember. The officers of the Finance Committee and the Chancellor failed to agree about any one aspect of economic policy.

We struck a greater 'blow for freedom' when Ted Heath produced his Bill to control prices and incomes in 1973. John Biffen and I both spoke during the Second Reading Debate in terms unusually mild for us, and we voted for it. This was a ploy to get ourselves made members of the Standing Committee to consider the Bill in detail, which followed directly. The Committee of Selection, who appoint members to Standing Committees, are obliged to ensure a Government majority on every bill; we both qualified to be included since we had not opposed the principle. When we got there the two of us represented the Government's majority and we proceeded gaily to carry a whole series of amendments, with the support of the Labour Opposition. The main one we succeeded in carrying reduced the life of the powers in the Bill to one year. The Government was alarmed. A standard had at last been hoist in Parliament against them by Tory members. Although they more or less reversed the amendments at the Report Stage, battle had been joined and the press became aware of it. The struggle for the soul of the Tory Party had begun.

Margaret Thatcher was Secretary of State for Education. No doubt her main preoccupations at that time were with running that department. She first broke her silence about the wider disasters going on around us one evening in the Division Lobby. She came up to John Biffen and me and said how much she agreed with our stand over the Prices and Incomes Bill. 'I wish I could join you in your battle,' she said. 'You could', we replied, 'if you resigned and joined us.' She didn't. I don't think at that time she realized the gravity of the situation, and also to her it would have been 'disloyal' to leave Ted Heath's Government.

If she was slow to move against Ted Heath in 1973, she was quick to declare for Keith Joseph in 1974, after the disastrous February election when the Tories lost office. She rallied to Keith Joseph's intellectual lead.

We greatly admired Keith Joseph. He had a fine intellect and was exceedingly brave in stating his opinions. I think that he was right not to offer himself for the leadership. I think that even he would admit that he was less incisive in taking action than Margaret Thatcher turned out to be. He could never quite bring himself, as a minister, to embark on the brave courses upon which he had called on us to embark. If he had become Prime Minister instead of Margaret Thatcher, I am sure he would not have had the strength and the resolve to carry through the programme which he had been proclaiming, like John the Baptist, in the wilderness. In a series of speeches around the country in 1974, he articulated the policy of the free market – or the 'Social Market', as he called it. Socialism had failed, was his message. 'We have inherited a mixed economy which has become increasingly muddled as we tried our best to make semi-socialism work,' he said. He set out the case for replacing demand management with money supply control. He advanced the policy of public expenditure control, lower taxes, and privatization. He railed against collectivism and prices and incomes policies. He got across publicly what a small number of us in the Tory Party had been trying to say ever since Ted Heath's U-turn in 1972.

Margaret Thatcher and Keith Joseph both remained members of the Shadow Cabinet, but from the moment the 1974 election was lost, they felt free to articulate the policies of the 'Social Market'. The 'Social Market' meant free markets, but with the State still providing the essential underpinning of things like social security, free health care and free education. 'Social' spending was, however, to be much more closely targeted on those in need than had been the case hitherto. The 'Social Market' not only was what we believed was right, but it was also an essential safeguard against the current Labour jibe that in a free market the poorest go to the wall.

Between February 1974 and February 1975, Keith Joseph was the undisputed leader of the rebel group. Margaret Thatcher added such weight as she had – but she was not then a crusader for monetarism. She had probably not thought much about economic policy during her years on the front bench, where she had handled various portfolios since she first got there in October 1961. She was soon converted to the logic of Keith Joseph's argument, and she set about acquiring a full knowledge of the monetarist theory straightaway. She learned from two teachers in particular: Alan Walters and Alfred Sherman.

Alan Walters was always happy to advise politicians – he gave Keith Joseph and Margaret Thatcher the benefit of his advice, as well as helping our small team on the Backbench Finance Committee. He remains a vital adviser to Margaret Thatcher to this day, although the relationship became both intermittent and more contentious later on.

Alfred Sherman was once a Communist, who became converted to the market economy, and, like all converts, believed in it with a passion that bore the crusade forward, perhaps too fast.

He was both outspoken and radical, impatient with the compromises and fudges of the political process, like Alan Walters. Alfred Sherman's zeal certainly contributed to the radical purism of the new philosophy and to the enthusiasm with which the new leaders espoused it, but his blunt and critical manner eventually succeeded in alienating most of his admirers. He eventually obtained a knighthood for his services, but his period of influence was not long-lived.

Keith Joseph and Margaret Thatcher managed to raise a substantial sum of money from the growing number of businessmen who shared their despair at the Heath legacy. They set up a think tank – 'The Centre for Policy Studies' (CPS) – in June 1974. In a draft statement of goals, one of the co-founders, Simon Webley, encapsulated the new politics: '. . . to meet the needs and expectations of society wealth must be created by the efficient use of scarce resources. This can only be achieved by a vigorous, efficient and well-motivated private sector, producing a surplus profit, a proportion of which goes to sustain and develop welfare "services", in their widest sense.' Alfred Sherman was installed as Director of Studies at the Centre for Policy Studies. For a while he became one of the driving forces behind the new policies and a close colleague of Margaret Thatcher and Keith Joseph. He helped with speeches, wrote pamphlets, organized conferences and a series of study groups to draft policies to put the new economics into effect in government. The CPS became the furnace in which the new economics was forged. Margaret Thatcher and Keith Joseph were also helped by two other think tanks: the Institute of Economic Affairs, founded in the 1950s by Ralph Harris and Arthur Seldon, and later the Adam Smith Institute, founded in 1977 and directed by Madson Pirie. Nonetheless, it was the CPS which was always closest to Margaret Thatcher and Keith Joseph, and from where many of their most formidable allies were drawn, such as Sir John Hoskyns and Alan Walters, both introduced to Keith Joseph, and then Margaret Thatcher, by Alfred Sherman.

Margaret Thatcher had a piece of good fortune at this time. Ted Heath had made Robert Carr his shadow Chancellor, but had appointed another Shadow Cabinet minister to lead the assault on the Labour Government's 1974 Finance Bill. This was a person with knowledge of tax law and an abrasive style in opposition. It was none other than Margaret Thatcher. Throughout the period that she was standing as a candidate against Ted Heath, she was the party's gladiator fighting against the Labour Government's tax proposals as put forward by the Chancellor, Denis Healey.

Denis Healey had promised to tax the rich 'until the pips squeak' and proceeded to do so. There were plenty of targets, therefore, for her assaults: revamped and draconian taxes on capital gains and capital transfers; the disallowing of relief on interest paid; tax increases all round; and a whole rag-bag of technical and complicated tax refinements that the Treasury had seen fit to insert into the Finance Bill while Denis Healey was busy fulminating about how best to make 'the pips squeak'. She took her opportunity. In those Finance Bill debates she shone. When Denis Healey referred to her as 'La Passionara of Privilege' on one occasion, she retorted by saying, 'Some Chancellors are micro-economic. Some Chancellors are macro-economic. This one is just plain cheap. . . . If this Chancellor can be Chancellor, anyone in the House of Commons can be Chancellor.' The Party was entranced. In 1974 the Conservative Party had lost its way: it was beaten and humiliated. Here was a senior figure who didn't seem beaten at all; she exuded confidence and certainty. She made a lot of converts.

The other politician who was very close to her at the time was Airey Neave. He was MP for Abingdon and had a very distinguished war record, escaping and organizing others to escape from prisoner of war camps. He was skilled in organizing undercover operations – a skill he put at Margaret Thatcher's disposal. He organized her campaign for the leadership, and he did it superbly well. He knew from his canvass that she was fairly close to winning the vote against Ted Heath – but he instructed his helpers to move round the Palace of Westminster on the eve of the ballot with long faces. Once MPs got the feeling that she was doing badly, more of them resolved to vote for her as the only way of forcing a second ballot. There was a good majority against Ted Heath and Airey Neave's tactics delivered it all in the shape of votes for Margaret Thatcher. He became a very close associate. She rewarded him with the shadow portfolio for Northern Ireland after she had won. It was a tragedy when Airey Neave was killed by the IRA when a car bomb blew him up in the House of Commons car park. She grieved greatly at his loss: perhaps she never quite got over it.

When the ballot was held on 4 February 1975, there were only three candidates: Ted Heath with 119 votes; Margaret Thatcher with 130 votes; and Hugh Fraser with 16 votes. No one quite knew why Hugh Fraser had stood. Edward du Cann, who kept threatening to throw his hat into the ring, eventually kept out. All the other members of the Shadow Cabinet who might have been inclined to stand felt that their duty of loyalty to Ted Heath effectively prevented them. I was never quite clear why. So she had the field virtually to herself.

When it came to the second ballot – which was necessary under the rules, the votes having been cast as they were – Ted Heath decided to withdraw and his colleagues felt that they were free to stand themselves. Willie Whitelaw, Geoffrey Howe and Jim Prior all threw their hats into the ring, together with an outsider, John Peyton. The voting was: Thatcher 146, Whitelaw 79, Howe 19, Prior 19 and Peyton 11. She was the undoubted winner, with well over half the votes.

During the first half of February 1975, Margaret Thatcher had to spend long hours on the Standing Committee on the Finance Bill. I was also a member. It met at 4.00 pm on Tuesdays, Wednesdays and Thursdays, and sat through until well after midnight on most days. Tuesday, 11 February was the day of the second ballot. Margaret Thatcher remained in her place until the news of her victory came through. When it did, the Chairman of the Committee interrupted the proceedings to congratulate her. She made a short speech in reply, which began: 'I am most grateful to you, Mr Crawshaw. I think that, due to circumstances beyond my control, I have been called to higher things and, therefore, may not be with the Committee very much longer . . .' We were left to argue about tax until 2.55 am. She was left with her victory, her joy, her opportunity. It was a moment when the course of history was changed.

Willie Whitelaw, who might well have been Ted Heath's successor in a more normal leadership election, had failed to come near to beating her. This was partly because he was perceived as not having had the necessary courage to challenge the incumbent, whom most wanted to get rid of, and partly because the party at that time was looking for a change of leadership, a change of style and, more important, a change of policies. Margaret Thatcher and Keith Joseph had begun to articulate the way ahead. He had provided the thinking. She had shown the new style: she had shown the courage to enter the fray in a determined manner. She it was they rewarded with the crown.

It is hard to analyse precisely why such an outsider had won the leadership. Partly it was because she had behaved directly and decisively in mounting the challenge. But more important, the new emphasis had appealed to a majority in the parliamentary party. They were fed up with the humiliations of 1974 and realized that a new direction, a new vigour, was needed. Thatcherism had by no means been fully articulated at that time – if it had been, it might have put some of them off. Nevertheless, I think most people in the party had come to a conclusion that the drift, not only of Ted Heath's Government, but of the last thirty years, required a decisive change of direction. She was also full of confidence and all other senior figures in the Tory Party lacked it in 1975.

In fact, there were over four years to go before the General Election of 1979. There was a lot to do and she set about doing it with alacrity.

Her first task was to establish herself as firmly in charge of the Tory Party. This was a formidable enough task in itself. She was a woman – the first woman leader of a political party in Britain. There was plenty of prejudice in the Party on this account alone. She was almost unknown. Outside the world of education, of which she had been Secretary of State, few knew anything of her. She had made enemies by challenging and then defeating Ted Heath. The Tory hierarchy was sceptical of her. She was on probation. The country was astonished by the choice. My own constituency party were 80 per cent behind Ted Heath at the time of her challenge, just as they were 80 per cent behind her when Michael Heseltine challenged her in 1990.

She could not afford to make enemies at that time. She kept many of Ted Heath's Shadow Ministers in her Shadow Cabinet. She kept many of them in her first Cabinet. She seemed always to rely on her own ability to get her way, rather than seeking to build in majorities of her own supporters. The business before her was opposition: she had no need to strike out on detailed new policy statements at that time. Opposition consists of criticizing the Government, while giving away little of detailed policies to come, other than their flavour and their tone. The hallowed phrase is 'We want to create a society which . . .' It is still being used today.

She also proved a formidable opponent in the House, first to Harold Wilson, who resigned in 1976, and then to Jim Callaghan. She always concentrated on attacking the Government, and rarely released hostages to fortune in the shape of policy positions of her own. From later experience I know what a godsend to governments Opposition policy statements are. It is possible to concentrate debate on the inadequacies of the Opposition, rather than on those of the Government. Twice weekly she took on the Prime Minister, at Prime Minister's Questions, and she came to be feared by them both in turn. A small group used to meet her before each Question session, to discuss and devise the best strategy for the day for harassing the Prime Minister and to think up the punchlines. Nigel Lawson and Norman Tebbit were members of this group and I joined it towards the very end of the period. The sole purpose of the group was to devise the most awkward and pertinent line of attack for the day.

The Opposition of 1975–9 was formidable in more ways than one. It was enormous fun. Fury and reason, wit and irony, ingenuity and ambush, were all employed. The Labour Party is bad at opposition. It is basically lazy and goes home too early at night. Humour is virtually absent: their rhetoric is all righteous indignation and humour doesn't fit with that. They read out too many briefs – and briefs provided by trade unions are particularly dull – as well as easy to spot. Tory Oppositions are better at keeping the House late and mounting surprise attacks in the early hours. They have less of the 9.00 to 5.00

attitude, perhaps through having more experience of London night life. They tend to be much funnier. If the Government has to be tortured, at least Tories try to make it amusing and not just unpleasant.

Among the best fora for the Opposition were the annual debates in the Finance Bill Committees, right from that first one in 1975 through to the end of the Parliament. Most of the stars of future Tory governments were to be found on these committees. Nigel Lawson, Norman Lamont, Patrick Jenkin, John Cope, David Howell, Peter Rees, John Biffen, Jock Bruce-Gardyne, Cecil Parkinson, Tony Newton, John MacGregor and many others were all to be found there for most of the summer months. Joel Barnett was the Chief Secretary to the Treasury, whose job it was to take the Finance Bill through for the Government. He was affable, competent, tolerant and effective. He was assisted at the beginning by the Financial Secretary, Dr John Gilbert, whom we especially relished as a target.

The hours were long, the debates were fierce, but there was good humour. Ted Graham, the Labour Member for Edmonton, made a long speech moving an amendment concerned with the capital taxation of the owners of stately homes. 'Those who contribute to our national heritage,' he said, 'should be able to live in modesty and comfort.' Nigel Lawson interjected, 'In my experience, such people live in immodesty and discomfort.'

These lighthearted touches should not conceal the fact that the Finance Bill debates of the 1970s was the forum where the major tax reforms of the 1980s were conceived and tested in debate. Neither Margaret Thatcher nor Geoffrey Howe was there – but I am sure it was then that Nigel Lawson first began to think seriously of the major tax reforms that he was later to bring in. It was also extremely discomforting for the Government to be under such heavy and continuous intellectual assault against their confiscatory plans for egalitarianism through taxation.

The assault upon the Government was maintained equally effectively upon the floor of the House. We defeated them occasionally in late-night votes. We kept them up late, tiring ministers who had a busy programme next day. We wore them down with constant pressure to make them argue their case, to answer our questions and to stick to the minutiae of procedural propriety. Robin Maxwell-Hyslop, an energetic and contentious barrackroom lawyer from Tiverton, even succeeded in getting the Speaker to declare the Aircraft and Shipbuilding Nationalization Bill a Hybrid Bill. This caused enormous consternation in the ranks of a frightened Government.

I am convinced that the Opposition of 1975–9 effectively weakened the Government in the House of Commons. In a way, this is a vindication of our parliamentary system. Naturally, it is unpleasant when the same tactics are used against one, as they were against Margaret Thatcher's Government of the 1980s. The only difference, in fact, was that we damaged them, while the Opposition never damaged Margaret Thatcher's Government. They weren't as good at it as we were.

I don't think the Labour Government's failures in themselves were enough. I think it needed the determination, the confidence, even the moral fervour that the Opposition under Margaret Thatcher brought to its task to persuade the electorate to make a change in 1979. They were not invited to switch to a government with clearly spelt-out superior alternative policies. Margaret Thatcher was careful not to articulate them too closely in public for two very good reasons. First, she was not at all assured of her colleagues' support for what she wanted to do. Second, it is never wise, as I have said, for an Opposition leader to expose his or her detailed policies to the possibility of ruthless dismemberment by the Government.

I think she was conscious of both these good reasons for keeping her ambitions for Britain's future close to her chest. I think she had a third reason too. She didn't feel any doubt about what she wanted to do. She did not need research organizations and study groups and policy committees to work out policies for her. She knew where her priorities lay, and she didn't want others to tell her where that was – she knew. Nor was she then strong enough fully to reveal her plans – so she concentrated on establishing her personal position within the party and on harrying the Government in order to make sure she actually got to Number 10.

Thus, the full nature of 'Thatcherism' was not known to the electorate in 1979. Nor was it fully understood within the parliamentary party. To the extent that people knew of Margaret Thatcher's policies, many thought that she would be pushed off them by the old hands still in her Cabinet. Her basic beliefs were clear enough: sound money, reform of the trade unions, targeting welfare where it was needed, low taxation, rebuilding Britain's position in the world. What was not understood was that she meant to deliver. Few, indeed, realized that the 1979 election was to be the start of a long period of rigorous reform.

She confirmed Keith Joseph in his job of formulating policy. He pursued his remit with enthusiasm and set up study groups on many aspects of policy. But the results of all this work were not always accepted by her and the Shadow Cabinet, and very seldom released into the public domain. I think she saw all this more as an exercise to keep the young turks happy than a serious contribution to what she would do on becoming Prime Minister. Nothing is more cheering to a young aspirant to office than being asked to chair a study group into some area of policy. It is the invitation which flatters – what happens to the conclusions is of secondary importance. There were perhaps three areas of policy where things were not quite so simple. They were industrial relations, the sale of council houses and privatization.

Margaret Thatcher and Keith Joseph asked Jim Prior to work up the policy on industrial relations. Jim Prior had been a prominent member of Ted Heath's Cabinet, whom she kept on as Shadow Employment Secretary and for two years as the real thing in her first Cabinet. Why she kept him on has always eluded me: he was a landowner and farmer, a patrician Tory, very much on the wet side of the Party and not at all in sympathy with her views. He was later quite open in his criticisms of her throughout her prime ministership. After a spell at the Northern Ireland Office, he left politics to become Chairman of the General Electric Company (GEC) in 1984. When Lord Weinstock, the Managing Director, came to ask Margaret Thatcher whether she would release Jim Prior from her Government to become Chairman, she is alleged to have replied, 'I wouldn't like to stand in his way.'

Jim Prior had no intention of carrying out any serious reforms of trade union law, despite the fact that the trade unions were clearly holding industry to ransom owing to the privileges and immunities they had been allowed under the law. Not even the Grunwick dispute, when violent pickets attacked the police during a particularly bitter strike in 1977, nor the 1978 Winter of Discontent itself, persuaded him that serious reform was desirable. He had inherited the legendary mantle of Sir Walter Monckton, Winston Churchill's Minister of Labour, who believed that Tory governments had to do business with union leaders or else they would make the country ungovernable. He thought it would be a serious error to offend them. Two previous attempts to reform trade union law had been made: one by Barbara Castle during the Labour Government in 1968, and one by Geoffrey Howe during Ted Heath's Government in 1971. Both had been overturned, although for different reasons, and the myth remained strong that it was both impossible and undesirable to do anything serious. Trade unions were like the weather: they were part of our environment and we couldn't change them.

The result of Jim Prior's policy work was a document entitled *The Right Approach to the Economy*. It promised no changes in the law, but conceded that trade unions did not have to be consulted about everything, as had been the case under the Labour Government. Beer and sandwiches at Number 10 were to end, but that was as far as it went.

What Margaret Thatcher thought of this, history does not relate. She was later in office to make Jim Prior push through a reforming bill, and to follow it up with three further bills. The combined effect of these four statutes was to push the trade unions firmly back within a very tightly restricted framework of law. This policy most certainly worked and there was no backlash or general strike. Jim Prior had simply been wrong in his assessment of the position. Presumably she was content, while still in Opposition, not to stir up either the trade unions or Jim Prior. She could wait to attain office to work out the details. Also it was not an issue which she judged had electoral appeal. She just let Jim Prior carry on being his own emollient self and did not expose her true intentions until she had the power to implement them.

The exception to her tendency to keep her major policy intentions under wraps was the sale of council houses. The idea was produced by Michael Heseltine, who was her Shadow Environment Secretary. He conceived of it as a good piece of popular capitalism, a vote-catcher. She took it up eagerly, perhaps more because it would create large numbers of extra homeowners, transferring property and wealth from the State to individuals, moving them to the private sector and away from what she saw as the dependency culture – that condition whereby people were made dependent on the State because they had no practical choice. It turned out to be a huge success and over 1 million council houses were later sold. It went into the Manifesto.

When Keith Joseph asked me again to lead a small group to plan the privatization policy for 1979 I was delighted, but a bit sceptical. I accepted. I told him that I had done this once before for Ted Heath and that nothing had happened. I feared history might repeat itself. 'It will be different this time,' he said. I am not sure I believed him, but I set about it with relish. It was not difficult to provide the policy; my report was almost identical to the original 1970 one, suitably updated. But this time it really was implemented, and more.

Privatization was a popular policy among Tory MPs in 1979. The experiences of the nationalized industries hitherto had convinced nearly all that, as a system, nationalization was riddled with flaws. Privatization was by then accepted as the only way to deal with the problem. Most people believed, like me, that the new Government wouldn't actually do it, just as Ted Heath had not done it earlier. But having another go didn't cause any qualms in the Party.

Much of my report was concerned with tighter disciplines for running the nationalized industries – which would be needed for a while before privatization took place – and for the utilities, which I put bottom of the list as candidates for privatizing. I also suggested breaking up many of the industries into smaller units before selling them. In the event, all the candidates I identified were in fact privatized, and so were gas, electricity and the water authorities, which I believed then were too difficult. In addition, of course, numerous minor concerns, which had seemed too small to identify at the time, left the public sector during the 1980s.

With the advantage of hindsight, I believe we should have broken up more of the industries into smaller units before selling them, in order to achieve more competition. I also believe I was wrong about the public utilities, which were natural monopolies – as I shall come to later.

The report was cleared by the Shadow Cabinet, after a certain number of changes, and found its way into the Manifesto in general form. This time it was implemented.

There were, of course, many other policy groups. As I have said, I don't think they played a very important part in shaping the policies which were later to be implemented. They were all there in Margaret Thatcher's head, and rather than wanting detailed blueprints for office, she wanted more ideas. It was natural that only those ideas which had electoral appeal found their way into the public domain.

If we are not to find in the policy groups the source of the policies that Margaret Thatcher put in place as Prime Minister, what background influences, apart from her 'gut instincts', were important in forming the ideas that crystallized in her head? How did her thinking develop during her four years in Opposition?

This is not a biography of Margaret Thatcher, but rather an analysis of what she achieved seen through the eyes of a colleague. I was with her throughout, but I only became close to her for the last five or six years after I joined her Cabinet. I always admired her, but it was some time before I really understood the force of her character. It was her immense conviction about the rightness of certain basic ideas which carried her through. She had at the same time an acute political understanding of the prides and prejudices of her fellow countrymen, many of which she shared. This combination of knowing instinctively how millions of people in the country would react, together with her iron determination to achieve something, or to stop something, but never to fudge, was all-powerful. It was the fudging to which she had to resort in her last three years which led to her eventual downfall, not her positive 'Iron Lady' characteristics.

She had immense energy and excellent health. She needed very little sleep and she had great courage. I never saw her daunted by or frightened of any challenge she faced. Her spirit remained with her to the end.

She didn't find it difficult to articulate her beliefs and the policies she wanted to pursue. She knew them already, almost as of instinct. Of course, the detail had to be worked through, but that could be done when she was in office. She believed in sound money and good housekeeping so far as the economy was concerned. She believed in rolling back the frontiers of the State. She believed in minimum public expenditure leading to minimum taxation. She hated the 'dependency' culture and she wanted social welfare to be for the genuinely needy alone.

Her attitude to Europe was in the mainstream of British opinion – she wanted a Europe of member states, cooperating and working together, but she did not want to hand over one inch more sovereignty than was necessary to secure free trade and fair competition throughout Europe.

Over and above these simple political beliefs, she had strong views of a more moral nature. She believed strongly in the importance of trustworthiness – not so much blind loyalty, as the concept of mutual respect and honourable dealing between individuals. If a colleague was trustworthy, she would repay with personal loyalty. She disliked intensely those who operated behind her back – she would describe such manoeuvrings as 'treachery'. She expected of her colleagues total commitment – both of physical and intellectual effort. She did not suffer fools gladly, unless she wanted something out of them.

She was scrupulously honest. I don't believe she ever told a lie – though often in public life one cannot reveal the whole of a truth. She would never have abused her position for money or advantage.

Her private life was without blemish. It was remarkable that throughout those fifteen years no single piece of dirt that was dug out by the press even remotely stuck, eager though they no doubt were to find some. On the rare occasions when they tried, they were shown to be wrong.

She was brought up a Methodist, becoming more attracted to the

17

Church of England later in her life. I doubt if she was a very religious person in terms of strong beliefs, but she believed passionately in the Christian morality and practised that morality in her dealings with others. She had very good manners, showed great charity to the sick, the unfortunate and the bereaved. She was not vindictive, but she was firm in her resolve to resist or dispense with those who opposed her. There was a touch of 'an eye for an eye and a tooth for a tooth' in her. She believed that the punishment should fit the crime: she consistently voted in favour of the restoration of the death penalty. Despite her strong sense of right and wrong, she was remarkably uncensorious of others who fell by the wayside over sexual misadventures, or other similar deviations from her own high standards.

What troubled her was her need to prove that there was a close relationship between the Christian faith and her politics. She wanted to categorize socialism as definitely conflicting with the faith, and Toryism – at least her sort of Toryism – as being the purest political distillation of Christianity. Thus it infuriated her when later a number of Church of England bishops began to preach against the policies she pursued as Prime Minister. I believe she was over-ambitious in trying to make this direct link between Christian morality and her political beliefs. She went further than I would go in claiming there was no comfort for egalitarians in the Scriptures, or that the parable of the talents was a direct call by Christ for the entrepreneurial society. She was a bit inclined to treat evidence from the Old Testament with the same respect as evidence from the New Testament: to my mind, the Old Testament was no more than a fascinating glimpse into the history and habits of some particularly savage and primitive middle-eastern tribes, long before the birth of Christ. The New Testament contains some of Christ's doctrines which were extraordinarily advanced for His time, about how human beings should behave towards each other in a society. But I would not seek to justify my views about economic or social or foreign policy on the back of Christ's teachings. Where I agree strongly with Margaret Thatcher is that I don't think the Anglican Church should seek to criticise such policies on the grounds of Christianity either.

She was on safer ground with Victorian values: hard work, good housekeeping, thrift – 'neither a borrower nor a lender be' – private charity, birth in wedlock, condemnation of violence and rioting and the mob, and freedom under the law. Critics, of course, tried to add sweated labour, harsh punishments and the Poor Law as other examples of Victorian values. But that was not what she meant. She was recalling all those qualities that had made the country so successful in Victorian times, and trying to extol their virtues in the very different circumstances of the 1980s. She arrived on the scene following a period of highly permissive society – which she thought had become a bit too permissive. She strongly disapproved of those who deliberately planned to have a 'single parent' family, both on the grounds that children should have fathers, and on the grounds that such people were making themselves dependent on the taxpayers' largesse, when they could easily have earned their own living.

'Freedom under the rule of law' was the most important single concept to Margaret Thatcher. She would use that phrase as Prime Minister in relation to countless oppressed peoples overseas, as well as nailing it down as the main plank of her political philosophy at home. It exactly encompassed her view of permissiveness – as well as discipline. She acknowledged the freedom of all to do as they like, provided they respected the constraints of the law. It was for the lawmakers to decide where the frontiers lay.

She did not approve of substantial inherited wealth any more than she did of the poor who would not try to better themselves. She was not impressed by the landed gentry with large estates. She admired self-made men, but she was exasperated by managers of large companies and yuppies who paid themselves inordinately large salaries. 'Good housekeeping' required this money to be ploughed back into the business and, besides, she thought it set a bad example. She was in no sense egalitarian – quite the reverse: she believed passionately in incentives and rewards. But she strongly believed that money should be earned and disapproved of those who got their money either from their fathers, or social security, or from some sinecure position. She resisted always increases in the pay of MPs and ministers; she thought they were well enough paid. She even abated her own salary later as Prime Minister and drew only a cabinet minister's salary.

Above all, she wanted to give leadership. Like very many, she abhorred the muddle and drift of the 1960s and 1970s – the endless stop-go, the nationalizing/denationalizing farce, the crippling strikes culminating in the Winter of Discontent, Britain's ailing industrial performance, Britain's continuing decline. But unlike those very many, she was determined to change what was wrong and to lead Britain back to prosperity and success and enhanced prestige in the world. She had the iron will to do it; she knew instinctively how to do it. She was convinced that every attempt would be made to blow her off her course – and she was determined that they should fail. It was this certainty and this unshakeable resolve which made her unique among post-war politicians.

There were many circles she frequented in the late 1970s in order to derive inspiration and ideas, as well as to broaden her base of support among opinion-leaders. The Centre for Policy Studies was a major one. Another was a dining club called the Conservative Philosophy Group. Run by Jonathan Aitken, this group dined a number of notable intellectuals – historians, economists and philosophers – who gave their views to the group about the shape of the new Conservative philosophy they wanted to see arise out of the ashes left by the Heath Government.

Another was the Economic Dining Club. I had originally started this group in 1972 with the object of trying to anchor Enoch Powell into the Conservative Party. He eventually left the party, on the ground that he could not accept our membership of the European Community. He left the Club too, and entered into that strange last phase of his extraordinary career as the Member for South Down.

The Economic Dining Club continued and thrived through the 1970s. We discussed economic policy, and what later came to be called supply-side policies. Membership was limited to twelve Tory MPs and we dined once a month, in different members' houses by rotation. I have two cherished memories. The first was the evening that Peter Hordern dined us in his Club in Mayfair. We talked late, and eventually found that the staff had left and we had been locked in. The only way out was through the window and down a drainpipe. I will never forget the sight of Enoch Powell climbing down the drainpipe, wearing his black overcoat and black homburg hat. The second was one evening much later when the Club dined at my flat. I was a bachelor at the time and had prepared the meal. I was just letting Margaret Thatcher in through the front door when the entryphone rang. It was a girlfriend who had got the wrong night to come and dine. Margaret Thatcher was highly amused and teased me mercilessly.

She joined the Club in about 1977 and was a regular attender. Most of its members later joined her Cabinet at one stage or another. I like to think that we influenced her and ourselves in plotting out the directions in which policy was to go. I think the major change in the role of the Department of Trade and Industry, over which I eventually presided in 1989, was first hatched in the Economic Dining Club.

This was the background to the Tory leader who won the 1979

General Election. The other part of the background was the record of the last months of the Labour Government.

During the course of the late 1970s, the minority Labour Government's grip on power became increasingly tenuous. Labour had only been able to remain in power since May 1977 due to a pact with the Liberal Party led by David Steel. In May 1978 the Liberals, disappointed with their lack of influence on the Government, announced that they would end the pact at the end of the parliamentary session. Jim Callaghan was thus widely expected to call an election in the autumn, but, to everyone's intense surprise, in a speech to the TUC Conference in September 1978 he vowed to carry on, relying on the uncertain support of the Scottish and Welsh Nationalists in the House of Commons to maintain the Government's majority. In March 1979 this fragile coalition, based on Jim Callaghan's promise to submit Scottish and Welsh devolution to regional referendums, fell apart and on a Motion of No Confidence, the Government lost by one vote. Jim Callaghan called a General Election for 3 May.

The campaign was thus fought at a time of Margaret Thatcher's choosing, not the Government's. This was crucial, since if Jim Callaghan had gone to the country in the autumn of 1978, he would have had a small lead in the opinion polls and an economy which was making some small steps towards recovery. The International Monetary Fund had moved in in 1976 and insisted on heavy cuts in spending as the price for a standby loan. The cuts caused fury and resentment from backbenchers and trade unions alike. Despite this inflation began to accelerate. The Government resorted to the same failed policy that Ted Heath had tried of seeking to control wage and price rises by legislation. The Election of May 1979 was thus conducted in the wake of the notorious Winter of Discontent which followed and which completely discredited the Government. Jim Callaghan had staked his Government's reputation on maintaining a 'pay norm' (as it was called in the jargon of the day) of 5 per cent for the round of pay bargaining that occurred every winter. However, in the winter of 1978–9, the unions flagrantly ignored this figure, allegedly because they felt betrayed that Jim Callaghan had refused to call an election in the autumn. And so the winter brought a long series of strikes for higher pay which resulted in industrial output falling to its lowest levels since the three-day working week of 1974. Unions demanded wage increases of up to 25 per cent and to enforce their demands, union picketing swiftly brought the country to a halt. The dustmen's strike left piles of garbage on the streets, while a strike of school caretakers caused millions of children to be kept at home. The television cameras had a field day and the public were treated to daily images of NUPE (National Union of Public Employees) officials turning patients away from hospitals and the dead piling up in disused premises in Liverpool owing to a gravediggers' strike. In the middle of all this, Jim Callaghan returned from a summit meeting in Guadeloupe, tanned and fit, and declared that 'I don't think other people in the world would share the view that there is mounting chaos.' the *Sun* newspaper memorably summed up his air of indifference with the headline: 'Crisis? What crisis?' The Government seemed out of control and out of touch. Ironically, the Government was being brought to its knees by its very own supporters, the public sector unions.

The Winter of Discontent bore out all of Margaret Thatcher's warnings about the evils of trade union power and the need for an entirely new, 'free market' approach to the economy. Against the background of the Winter of Discontent, the election was almost a foregone conclusion, as Labour's claim that they alone could control the unions was shown to be utterly bankrupt. A new approach was needed. On 3 May the Conservatives won 399 seats, a net gain of 55, to give them an overall majority of 43 in the House of Commons. The first woman Prime Minister in British history moved into Number 10 Downing Street.

2

'MY STYLE OF GOVERNMENT'

O<small>N</small> 31 O<small>CTOBER</small> 1989, following Nigel Lawson's resignation, the officers of the 1922 Committee came to lunch at Number 10, together with Kenneth Baker, then Party Chairman. After the luncheon, he told the press waiting outside, 'Yes, people did say "Get your act together". There are times when the Government is looking disunited on policy.' He went on, 'But she is a strong leader, and if you are expecting her to stop being a strong leader, you are wrong.'

I happened to be with Margaret Thatcher on other business immediately afterwards. 'They wanted me to change my style of government, Nick,' she said. 'Why should I change my style of government? I am not going to.'

She never changed her style of government, thank goodness. It was splendid and it was an essential part of her. She not only had ambitions of substance to achieve in 1979, but she wanted to achieve them in style, even with panache. The style was an essential part of it – both for its own sake, and for the purpose of prosecuting the policies.

Although she governed with superb style, carrying every war into the enemy's camp, seeking to destroy, rather than contain the Opposition, and determined to blaze a radical trail, she never let power corrupt her; nor did she ever fail to be compassionate and kind as a human being. She made mistakes, but the record is a dazzling one of achievement, both of substance and of style. This chapter is about her style.

She was the first British woman Prime Minister ever, and many didn't believe she would have the guts and the stamina to prevail. Moreover, her Cabinet was full of the old Tory hierarchy, who were ever-watchful of this untried, radical woman. She made Peter Carrington Foreign Secretary, Jim Prior Employment Secretary, Peter Walker Minister of Agriculture, Mark Carlisle Education Secretary, Francis Pym Defence Secretary, Ian Gilmour Lord Privy Seal – as number two in the Foreign Office he was the Foreign Affairs spokesman in the Commons. Norman St John Stevas was Leader of the Commons and Minister for the Arts. In addition, she reinstated Christopher Soames to deal with the Civil Service. None of these great men believed in radical reform, none had understood the message of monetarism, and all of them were determined to keep her on the straight and narrow path of traditional consensus conservatism. She had a few 'believers' in her policies in the shape of Geoffrey Howe, John Biffen, Keith Joseph and John Nott. But there was a large majority in her Cabinet in 1979 who were not so much against her, as against too radical a programme.

The one exception, indeed, the enigma in her first Cabinet, was Willie Whitelaw. On every normal assessment he was a 'wet'; he was a patrician Tory, the least radical man I ever knew. After a splendid war record, he entered politics in 1955 as Tory member for Penrith and the Borders. He rose easily through the ranks of the Tory Party to become first Chief Whip and then Ted Heath's Deputy Prime Minister. Margaret Thatcher defeated him in the leadership election in 1975, but he resolved not to resent that, and to give her his full support. He became the linchpin of her first Government and an invaluable element in the stability of the Government until his sad retirement due to a minor heart tremor. His huge contribution was twofold – first, he was the advocate of the concept of a sort of military loyalty to the Commander-in-Chief, the more fiercely promoted the rougher the going got. Second, he was possessed of almost supernatural political antennae. He knew exactly when to warn Margaret Thatcher that a situation was approaching the breaking-point. He knew even not to do it until it was necessary. Although he had been the defeated candidate when Margaret Thatcher challenged and overcame Ted Heath, he nevertheless resolved to transfer his loyalty and his energies to her cause. He never wavered and he was even prepared to accept the consequences of the 1981 monetary squeeze in supporting her although in his heart of hearts I suspect he was uneasy.

It was a great loss when ill-health forced him to retire, although I am sure he continued to give Margaret Thatcher the benefit of his advice from outside. It is a remarkable achievement to have succeeded as number two to both Ted Heath and Margaret Thatcher, and to have left the scene with the admiration of nearly every person in politics. I myself at first saw him as a 'wet' and a conservative (small 'c'), who could not see the need for radical Toryism. I later saw him as an essential pourer-of-oil on troubled waters, no matter who had troubled them, and a very wise man, a confidant and a good friend. He was the opposite of an intellectual, yet as nimble on his feet as it was possible to be. I remember when as Home Secretary he was reading out some long and boring speech at the opening of a Home Office debate, a Labour MP interrupted him to point out that he was reading a page of his speech a second time by mistake. 'Of course I am,' he retorted. 'Don't you realize that this is by far the most important page of my speech?'

I suspect that Willie Whitelaw's support for Margaret Thatcher in the early period of her premiership was vital to her survival. Later his influence was crucial in some of the most difficult moments, such as the Westland crisis and the Libyan bombing decision.

To me, and to my friends, it was always inexplicable why she appointed to her first Cabinet so many people who didn't share her ambitions or believe in her analysis of the nature of the cancer eating into the heart of Britain. I confess to being bitterly disappointed at finding myself dealing with the problems of Latin America and the Caribbean from the Foreign Office, where she sent me in 1979, while the Cabinet was packed with supporters of the old consensus, Heathite policies. For the whole of her time as Prime Minister she put more than their fair share of her opponents into her Cabinet. The people she selected from the backbenches for Junior Ministerial office always contained a minority of 'believers', and so did those who were promoted from Junior Minister to Minister of State. Thus, the ranks of Minister of State, from among whom Cabinet Ministers are chosen, never contained sufficient 'believers'.

No doubt in part this was because she did not want to exclude her opponents. She felt her opponents could do her more harm out of her Government than in it. She also liked to appear generous with those who did not agree with her. She wanted to carry all sections of the Party with her. Also, in part, I think she felt she could achieve her objectives despite having a majority who were not of her persuasion in her Cabinet. She didn't believe the Cabinet should decide on contentious issues; she never took matters there to a vote. She believed her will-power and her certainty would prevail and the alternative course of promoting a majority of her supporters was the most dangerous since it would leave too many powerful people and points of view unrepresented and on the backbenches.

She probably did not actually choose those who were to be promoted from the backbenches herself. She could hardly have known enough about them. She left this job to the Chief Whip. Her first Chief Whip was Michael Jopling, a northern farmer, who later became Minister of Agriculture. He was a protégé of Willie White-law's, very much an orthodox Tory, and hardly likely to push forward a number of dangerous young Tory radicals. Her successive Chief Whips were John Wakeham, David Waddington and Tim Renton. Between them all they produced a continual paucity of Ministers of State who shared her views and from whom to choose future Cabinet Ministers.

In choosing her first Cabinet in 1979, she probably felt up against force majeur. Many of the great men of the 1970s were still around – indeed, she had had them in her Shadow Cabinet. She was far from well-established in the party. She needed the support of the hierarchy, and she probably consulted Willie Whitelaw as to how to get it. In many respects, it was Willie Whitelaw's Cabinet which she first appointed.

So she had the Cabinet that circumstances, and Willie Whitelaw, dictated. She was, however, going to make sure she got her way. That was why she had been elected, first as leader, and then as Prime Minister. She wasn't going to be diverted by a Cabinet not of her persuasion. I remember hearing Peter Carrington on a radio programme at the time being asked the question, 'Who would succeed Mrs Thatcher now if she was run over by a bus?' 'Oh, the bus wouldn't dare,' he replied. She was unstoppable.

As a result, it was this aspect of her Prime Ministership about which she has been much criticized: her conduct of cabinet government. There were three dramatic resignations from her Cabinet, those of Michael Heseltine, Nigel Lawson and Geoffrey Howe. They all, as I shall show, cited her conduct of Cabinet business as at least part of the reason for their discontent. It became a theme of journalists and other detractors that she was autocratic in Cabinet, that she didn't allow important issues to be discussed, and that she reduced the Cabinet to a sort of rubber stamp. This charge took hold and it became eventually an established fact in the minds of the press and the British people. An opinion poll in February 1991 recorded that in September 1990, 57 per cent believed that the Tory Party was too dominated by its leader, whereas in February 1991 only 11 per cent felt this about John Major.

What is the nature of cabinet government in Britain? Did she abuse it? How did these charges arise? Who made them and were they well-founded? It is essential to answer these questions in the pursuit of an understanding of Margaret Thatcher's long period of supremacy. The answers shed light perhaps upon the reasons for the length of her rule, and even perhaps upon the reasons for its coming to an end.

The United States Constitution is quite explicit in stating that the Executive consists of one person – the President. Cabinet secretaries are hired and fired; their only function is to serve him and assist him. He is solely responsible for proposing both policy and action – he had the responsibility to act and he takes the responsibility for things that go wrong. The Legislature – the Congress – is separate and performs a separate function, as in Britain. But the Executive consists of one person with supreme power and supreme responsibility. Many nations have followed the USA in vesting supreme power in just one person – a President.

Britain's practice is not so very different. The constitutional position is that the Monarch asks that person to form a Government who seems to be the most likely person to command a majority in the House of Commons. In practice this means the leader of the party which has the parliamentary majority. The chain of responsibility is thus that the Monarch appoints a Prime Minister, on the grounds that he or she is the person who can best maintain a majority. The Prime Minister holds office only at the pleasure of the majority. Thus, when there is a Tory majority, the party can decide to switch to another leader, as was demonstrated at both the beginning and the end of Margaret Thatcher's period of leadership.

Thus, the Prime Minister alone carries the responsibility of the Executive, just as the President of the USA does. The difference is that the Prime Minister can be changed by the Party, whereas the President can only be changed at a Presidential Election.

Another difference is that in Britain ministers are members of one or other of the Houses of Parliament. They don't have to be, but in practice they always are. In America they cannot be so. So British prime ministers appoint to their cabinet and government those of their colleagues, from both Houses, whom they judge to be supportive, and both experienced and skilled at conducting the Government's business. Thus ministers in Britain, like their counterparts in America, are 'hired and fired' by the person in whom the power of the Executive is vested. They do not have positions in their own right. Whether or not they prosper is in the hands of the Prime Minister. It is obvious that selecting backbenchers to become ministers, and ministers to become Cabinet ministers, is of vital importance, not only for the careers of the lucky ones, but also to the Prime Minister in acquiring a Cabinet of the necessary talents.

The Prime Minister, however, carries the full responsibility: an error by a minister is the Prime Minister's responsibility, just as much as the minister's. The Prime Minister is also First Lord of the Treasury, symbolizing the Chancellor's role as the minister charged with assisting in running the nation's finances. Thus, Cabinet ministers have no status or independent positions: they are there to help the Prime Minister, and at the Prime Minister's pleasure.

In practice, the Cabinet has acquired a greater status than its precise constitutional position would suggest. The minutes of its meetings are kept for posterity's benefit. Its proceedings are fairly formal, and are supposed to be entirely confidential. Every member is expected to be present at every meeting, and only a convincing excuse, usually on account of illness or foreign travel, is ever accepted. Decisions by the Cabinet seem to carry greater weight than the decisions of a single person. It is seen as the top decision-making body of the land, and naturally enough a certain aura attaches to Cabinet ministers.

It is for each Prime Minister to decide how to run his or her Cabinet. In an interview with Kenneth Harris of the *Observer* newspaper just before the 1979 election, Margaret Thatcher had talked of Cabinet government: 'When the time comes to form a real Cabinet, I do think I've got to have a Cabinet with equal unity of purpose and a sense of dedication to it. It must be a Cabinet that works on something much more than pragmatism or consensus. It must be a "conviction" government . . . We've got to go in an agreed and clear direction. As Prime Minister, I couldn't waste time having any internal arguments.' Margaret Thatcher saw the Cabinet as very much a formal body. She did not see it as a body to take decisions, except for decisions of the very greatest importance. She saw it as the forum in which all important activities of government were brought together and reported upon. She saw it as the body to approve individual ministers' policies. She used it as a tactical group to discuss the immediate problems of the day.

It was also the 'Court of Appeal' to which any Cabinet minister could take a disagreement with his Cabinet colleagues, and have it decided by his colleagues. During my six years in Cabinet, I only recall this happening twice. The first occasion resulted in Michael Heseltine's resignation. The second concerned Quintin Hailsham's disagreement with his colleagues in a Cabinet Committee over the breaking of the monopolies of barristers and solicitors. I well remember the Committee meeting when he was outvoted. He banged his walking sticks on the table, stormed out, and drove home, where he promptly ran into a brick wall. He ran into a brick wall at Cabinet too, and the legal monopolies were duly broken.

Margaret Thatcher was going to be the leader in her Cabinet. She wasn't going to be an impartial chairman. She knew what she wanted to do, and she was not going to have faint hearts in her Cabinet stopping her. Francis Bacon wrote, in his Essay *On Counsel*: 'A long table, and a square table, or seats about the walls, seem things of form, but are things of substance; for at a long table, a few at the upper end in effect sway all the business; but in the other forms, there is more use of the Counsellors' opinions that sit lower.' Margaret Thatcher definitely preferred a long table.

The Cabinet is also the forum to which the structure of Cabinet Committees reports. There are large numbers of these – some permanent, and some ad hoc, set up to consider certain transient problems and then stood down. The permanent Cabinet Committees deal with the main aspects of policy – like defence and overseas policy, home affairs, legislation, and economic policy. Of these, the one dealing with economic policy called 'E' – acquired a certain notoriety. Jim Prior made much of the fact that he was allowed to remain a member of 'E' when he was switched to Northern Ireland. Its members were the economic and industrial ministers, and it was alleged that they were dictating the new economic polices behind the backs, as it were, of the Cabinet itself. To make this allegation is to ignore the point that 'E' reported to the Cabinet. It also happened that there were very few wets on 'E' Committee. I attended 'E' on many occasions, and I failed to see anything sinister about it.

Margaret Thatcher extended the Cabinet Committee system by setting up small groups consisting of those ministers most closely concerned. The composition of each group depended on the subject, but on the whole she preferred the least possible number of ministers to be present. When the decision concerned spending money, it was usually the Prime Minister, the Chief Secretary and the spending minister only who attended. There was nothing wrong with this – it seemed eminently sensible to me. There was no more need for me to be present as Environment Secretary when the subject was, say, defence, than there was a need for the Defence Secretary to be present when the subject was environmental. All decisions of importance were reported to the Cabinet, except those which were market sensitive, or just plain 'sensitive'. There was thus an opportunity for anyone who wanted to do so to reopen a question if he didn't like a decision. It did sometimes happen, but only rarely. For the most part, Cabinet ministers were so busy that they were only too thankful that other people's complex problems were sorted out without their having to be involved.

Cabinet business came under four headings – Parliamentary Affairs, Home Affairs, Foreign Affairs and Community Affairs, in that order. Any special topic was taken at the end. One could raise any matter that troubled one, or that one thought one's colleagues should know about. It was judged courteous, though not essential, to warn Margaret Thatcher of any item one might be going to raise. That too was eminently reasonable.

She disliked having votes in Cabinet. She didn't see it as that sort of body. Nor was it suitable to decide matters by vote in view of the constitutional position. She was Prime Minister, she knew what she wanted to do, and she didn't believe her policies should be subject to being voted down by a group she had selected to advise and assist her. Just as an American President would never allow himself to be outvoted by his Cabinet, so too did Margaret Thatcher believe she had every right to retain the initiative as head of the Government. Anyone who did not like her policies could resign. Indeed, she had the power to dismiss those who were not likeminded. I can remember only one occasion when a formal vote was actually taken in Cabinet – on a relatively minor and specialized matter. Since some of us knew little of the background to this decision, it could well be that we got the answer wrong.

Thus, I myself have no complaints to make about the way Margaret Thatcher ran her Cabinet. She carried the responsibility, so she was going to be in a position to discharge it. That was why she disliked Royal Commissions; she never appointed a single one. She was not going to be put in the position where someone else was given an official licence to tell the elected head of the Executive what the policy was going to be.

There seem to me to be two important points to make, however. The first is that I accepted without question the constitutional position – it was necessary that everyone should do so if cabinet government was to be harmonious. She was Prime Minister and the rest of us were not. The trouble started when some did not. Nigel Lawson said, after his resignation in 1989, that the Prime Minister 'must appoint ministers he or she trusts, and then leave them to carry out the policy'. I do not agree with that. The Prime Minister is also responsible for what the policy contains. She can only leave them to carry it out if she is completely satisfied with the policy.

The second point is that she had to have colleagues in her Cabinet who were sympathetic to her aims, and were there to support her, rather than there to try to change her or her policies. Where a Cabinet colleague chose to do neither, trouble was likely to ensue, as indeed it did.

There is a feeling in the Tory Party that each strand of opinion in the Party should be represented at Cabinet. This feeling is magnified into the proposition that such representatives should be in Cabinet almost as of right, as leaders of some important group or faction, and that they have a political position of their own, as a result of their powerbase in the Party. This feeling gave some a sense of being more important than they were. It also made them harder to dispense with, lest they go back to their powerbase on the backbenches and cause real trouble. Although I believe such people greatly overestimate their power, it always caused Margaret Thatcher much concern.

Margaret Thatcher was always immaculately turned out herself. She dressed smartly, was well-groomed and expected other people to be so as well. During the 1987 election Nigel Lawson appeared on television with his hair in need of a trim; he got a complaint from next door. She wanted to set an example of high standards in all things, and for her example to be followed by others. She wanted 10 Downing Street to become renowned as a place of quality entertaining. She arranged for it to be redecorated in the mid-1980s with style and much gold leaf. It was transformed into a very grand and elegant house for entertaining the great and the good. It was adorned with good pictures from the national collections – one room contained a particularly lovely group of Turners. She entertained a lot. She saw to it that the food and wine, the flowers and the service, were of the highest quality. Quality was the keynote – not extravagance. Whenever the programme of a visiting foreign dignitary allowed, she would give a dinner for him. These dinner parties were glittering occasions. Important and interesting people were asked; she also liked to have plenty of pretty and well-dressed women among the guests. She expected people to rise to the occasion, and they did. Her speech after the dinner was always a model of fluency, erudition and courtesy. She was a master of the impromptu speech. Some of her speeches when the East European leaders came to London were particularly moving. It seemed to cause her no nervousness or bother when she had to make a speech after dinner. This was not the case with some of her principal guests. I remember being fortunate enough to sit next to President Havel of

Czechoslovakia when he dined there. Margaret Thatcher was on his left, and she talked to him for most of the meal. When my turn came, he hastily picked up his speech notes to make last-minute improvements. My attempts to engage him in conversation were dashed by Margaret Thatcher saying to me across him, 'Can't you see, Nick, he's trying to finish his speech.'

In addition to official dinners, she gave frequent receptions – for party workers, or a visiting overseas delegation, or for scientists, artists, musicians or entrepreneurs. She also held lunch and dinner parties at Chequers at weekends, particularly when an overseas visitor was staying there. I remember one particular lunch, given for Lech Walesa, the Polish Leader of Solidarity. He was very conscious of Poland's debt to her and of all her help and encouragement. But that didn't stop him calling for a lot more in his very effective after-luncheon speech. There was a strange affinity between the fiery Polish shipyard trade unionist and the high-principled British Tory Prime Minister – two people as different as they could be. It was because they both believed in freedom and in democracy with an equal passion that they were in alliance; not so much friendship, as a common cause to fight.

Sometimes groups of colleagues would be invited to lunch. It was after some such lunch that she resolved, after a long conversation with Nigel Lawson, Patrick Jenkin and myself, that another attempt must be made to replace the domestic rates. This was the day that she decided to start the studies which eventually led to the Community Charge.

She held a Boxing Day lunch every year to which family, friends and loyal supporters, both inside and outside politics, were bidden. It became a little too famous, and the press would find out who was there and who was not, trying to speculate as to who was 'in' and who was 'out'. It was difficult for her to keep any part of her life private. She always used to ask to this and other parties those acquaintances who had been widowed, or had been ill, or had suffered some misfortune, as well as her friends.

She was neither an egalitarian nor a puritan. From the way she entertained, it could hardly be said that she believed in a 'classless society'. She believed in equal opportunity for anyone to qualify to receive an invitation to one of her dinners; but once achieved, this was a distinction in a class of its own.

She liked to drink a little, although never too much. She preferred whisky and rarely did justice to the excellent wines that adorned the

Number 10 dinner table. Government hospitality over the years had procured for Number 10 wines from the finest vineyards of France, and her predecessors cannot have done much damage to the stocks. The wine was always both excellent and adequate in quantity. One of the disappointments of my leaving office was no longer to be able to drink some of the clarets from the 1970s. I doubt if her successor will make many demands on them either. She was entirely tolerant of those who had had one too many, unless they were proposing to drive themselves home. She often asked people before they had a drink whether or not they were driving and was very strict about this. One evening she unexpectedly visited the Whips Office in the Commons late at night. One of the Whips in the Lords happened to be there. He was considerably inebriated, but he thought he would go undetected if he stayed put where he was standing, and hung onto the table firmly. 'Why don't you sit down,' she said. 'You look far too drunk to stand up.'

She wanted to extend the acknowledgement and enjoyment of success to others. She awarded honours quite liberally. She reversed Ted Heath's earlier decision never to create another hereditary peerage, and created three – two viscounts, Willie Whitelaw, and George Thomas, who had been Speaker from 1976 to 1983. She also maintained the earlier tradition that former Prime Ministers are entitled to an earldom when she gave one to Harold Macmillan. She bestowed a peerage on every one of her Cabinet ministers who left the Commons, with the exception of John Nott. I suspect she thought that he had transgressed by leaving politics before he had served for long enough – a sort of dereliction of duty. When many of these ennobled ex-colleagues were reported to have voted against the Government in the Lords, she used to be surprised. 'I sent them there to support me: they ought to know better,' she would say. So she created many other peers who would be more reliable. Even some of them were to transgress. Indeed, in the mid-1980s the Lords became quite troublesome, amending bills and forcing votes against the Government which were unwelcome. She particularly resented being defeated in the Lords when the result increased public expenditure: the Commons alone could, in theory at least, vote extra public spending. Their Lordships seemed to find ways round this. At one point, before the 1987 election, she certainly considered reforming the powers of the House of Lords. Rightly, discretion became the better part of valour over this: it wouldn't have been worth the effort. After all, by then there was no discernible opposition to the Government in the Commons.

She also distributed four or five knighthoods a year to senior and loyal backbenchers in the Commons – the traditional way of rewarding them for their loyalty, and also *'pour encourager les autres'*. Some say she saturated the market in this respect and devalued the prized honour by creating too many. *'Les autres'* were not always *'encouragés'* as a result. She would also reward with honours those who worked loyally for her – from civil servants down to personal assistants. She made sure that those who gave their time or money to charities and those who contributed excellence to art, sport, science and the professions, were properly rewarded. So too were those who worked for or helped the Conservative Party. She used the honours system to the full for the many purposes of which a Prime Minister has to take account.

Despite the fact that she was accused endlessly of not 'caring', she took immense trouble when someone was sick, or a tragedy befell them. In her later years, she became very concerned about the plight of Harold Wilson when he became ill. When George Thomas, later Viscount Tonypandy, was once very ill she visited him several times in hospital. I remember being with her one day when she left to go to see him. Her diary for that day was appalling, but nothing would put her off going. She was particularly keen to help the widows of those of her friends who died – two as a result of IRA murders. She agonized over the sadness of these friends who she felt had been widowed while their husbands had been in her service. She never failed to send flowers to sick friends and always remembered to ask after sick members of the family when she knew someone had been ill.

Nor was this genuine concern reserved only for her friends. Whenever there was a major disaster – like that at Manchester Airport, or the *Marchioness* tragedy, the Lockerbie disaster, or the Zeebrugge ferry catastrophe, she would drop all her plans and visit the site of the tragedy and its victims in hospital. She often had to return home early from an overseas visit or holiday in order to do so. Unlike so many of her critics, she didn't believe 'caring' meant helping at other people's expense. She was resolute in visiting Northern Ireland regularly, despite the great personal risks involved, in order to give strength to the population and sympathy to the victims of terrorism. She had to live her life with strict security controls because of the threat from the IRA. She grieved very much when there was another senseless killing perpetrated by them. Their crude brutality only served to strengthen her resolve to give not one inch of ground to them in her handling of the Irish question. With her, as with all British Prime Ministers, the IRA's campaign was counterproductive. But she felt the grief they caused their victims deeply. Her poise after the Brighton bombing, from which she only narrowly escaped, showed her enormous courage and her resolution against the pressures of terrorism.

She was often accused of being 'bossy'; on occasion, she most certainly was. In her bad moods, she would interrupt people halfway through their contribution, and she would often repeat her view on a situation over and over again during a discussion. Sometimes she resorted to this mood when she was tired, sometimes it was her way of fighting a rearguard action: when she knew she had lost an argument she would go on arguing her case, and grudgingly concede when she summed up.

Her beratings came to be known in the press as 'handbagging'. She always carried a smart leather handbag, and it became famous – almost the symbol of her authority. I remember a Cabinet Committee meeting when we were all assembled, but she, unusually, was late. Her handbag, however, was on the table at her place. 'Why don't we start?' I said. 'The handbag is here.' When she visited Washington for George Schultz's farewell party upon retiring, he presented her with a brand-new handbag. 'You are the only person so far to whom has been awarded The Order of the Handbag,' he said. She joined in the general mirth merrily. She was always able to laugh at herself.

She did not always choose people well. Nor was she always good at disposing of them. She seemed to lose her otherwise acute political instincts when it came to selecting people. She failed to promote early enough many of the bright young members who would have supported her; she instead promoted many who were antipathetic to her views.

Later on she sacked John Moore, a man of total integrity and dedication to her cause, and a very able man as well. He was later to help her unstintingly in the leadership contest of 1990. But she could never bring herself to sack Nigel Lawson or Geoffrey Howe, although they had become out of sympathy with major elements of her Government's aims, and were later actively working against her, although they wouldn't resign. They were not prepared to accept the meaning of cabinet government. She kept Peter Walker in her Cabinet until ten years later when he retired from politics, although he too was not always working in the same direction. She though he would be more troublesome out than in. The answer can only be that she saw these latter three as too powerful to reject, whereas John Moore was extremely unlikely to raise the standard against her from the backbenches; indeed, he never did.

Sometimes it seemed as if she simply took insufficient trouble to find out about people. A chance speech that she read, or a good parliamentary performance one evening when she was in the Chamber, or a successful contribution towards a speech that she had to make; these chancy, transient achievements could result in people suddenly finding themselves in the Cabinet. I do not want to belittle those who can do such things: David Hunt and Chris Patten were two such happy beneficiaries. But rapid promotion to the highest positions in government requires wider and deeper qualities, which have to be tested over periods of time and assessed in the light of many different circumstances. I remember often being surprised and rather disappointed myself when some colleagues who I knew were far from being supporters – some even who disliked her as well – were suddenly shot into the Cabinet, while equally able people who only wanted to support her were left languishing in junior posts for years. I used to remonstrate with her about this: but she didn't seem to realize that she was doing it, perhaps because she didn't know who was which.

One such attribute that has to be assessed is loyalty – not loyalty of a blind and unquestioning nature such as is required of military men; but loyalty of the sort that if you do join an army you do it because you believe its cause is a just one, for which you are prepared to fight. Political 'loyalty' is not required to be absolute, but one should not join a Government, let alone a Cabinet, in order to sabotage it. If that is the objective, you should neither join, nor be asked to join it. Margaret Thatcher frequently overlooked the need to take this precaution, and to appoint 'ministers she trusted', in Nigel Lawson's words.

One quality which attracted her admiration was being good at 'presentation'. Those who got a consistently good press, or who excelled on television, found their futures assured, no matter that sometimes the press praised them for apparently having different views from hers. When as time passed and the press were more and more critical of her, she clutched at those who could still get a good press, recruiting them to her service. Kenneth Baker's successful demolition of Ken Livingstone in a face-to-face television debate about the abolition of the Greater London Council was one such event: John Moore was promoted, so we were told, for a good election broadcast. It may be that she felt that presentation was not one of her greatest skills and that these performers merely filled a need which the

Government had. She could be very competent on television, but was never relaxed or humorous and came across as very stern and rather bossy. She said to me once, 'Neither you nor I are very good at presentation.' Yes, but we were better at doing the right things, I thought to myself. Politics is about more than presentation, except in the very short term.

One of Margaret Thatcher's difficulties in operating the system of Cabinet government was the endless 'leaks' which came out of her Cabinet. A few of these leaks were probably due to officials – some were successfully traced to individuals. Others were never traced and it must be concluded that some, at least, came from her Cabinet colleagues. 'Leaking' continued throughout her time in office, indicating that there was a copious supply of 'leakers', since those who were in a position to do so came and went.

Francis Bacon, in the essay alluded to earlier, also wrote: 'And as for Cabinet Councils, it may be their motto, "plenus rimarum sum". (I am full of leaks). One futile person, that maketh it his glory to tell, will do more hurt, than many that know it their duty to conceal.' The 'hurt' in this case meant that Margaret Thatcher couldn't trust her Cabinet to keep matters to themselves. No wonder many things could not be discussed there: too often what was discussed appeared accurately in the newspapers next day. It was the members of her own Cabinet who reduced their influence and importance by simply not being sufficiently trustworthy for her to have confidence in them. Can it be any wonder she preferred small groups from which the leakers could be successfully excluded? This continual problem was one of the main reasons for her style of government. Towards the end, she was reduced to announcing all important decisions on Thursdays. She would clear the decisions through Cabinet at the weekly morning meetings, and have them announced that afternoon in the House. That way the leaks pre-empted little or nothing becoming less worthwhile and therefore less frequent. The irony is that some of those who complained about her style of government were almost certainly among the leakers.

The leaks were also damaging because of their frequency. The descriptions of what took place were always twisted and described as 'furious rows' or 'bitter disagreements' by the press. They gave an impression of rampant disunity within the Cabinet, which was not apparent to those who at the time were members of it. I don't intend to write down the names of those who I suspect were guilty of these leaks – although I could – but I might be wrong and would malign some innocent people. But whoever they were, why did they do it? What were their motives?

The answer must be in two parts in order to cover the two main periods of Margaret Thatcher's political ascendancy. The first period – up to about 1983 – was when the Tory hierarchy still had pretensions of guiding her in the directions in which they wanted her to go. They leaked in order to try to head her off. One such major leak was of a document prepared by the Government's own think tank – the Central Policy Review Staff – in November 1982. It proposed extravagantly savage cuts in public spending for the future, based on imperfectly worked-up plans to transfer burdens from public to private spending in health, education and the social services. Some member of the Cabinet – and a name has been publicly suggested as to who might have done it – leaked it to *The Economist* in order to have it publicly squashed. The tactic succeeded, but it is a tactic which makes rational discussion of options in private impossible. The 1983 election ended that period; burgeoning economic recovery discredited them, and most of them left office.

The second period was in the later years, when it began to appear as if Margaret Thatcher was permanent. Those who wished to inherit her mantle grew restless. Her self-confidence gave them no hope that they could make her change her policies, and her reign seemed to be without end. In a mixture of resentment and disagreement, some started leaking in order to destabilize her. There were many such leaks. I was the victim of one in April 1988 when a Number 10 minute was leaked reporting the outcome of a discussion about how to pay for the extra concession on the Community Charge Rebate scheme which we had agreed. It contained the unfortunate words 'claw back', suggesting that some poor people would have money extracted from them. What it actually meant was 'clawing back' the money from the total of the Government's grant to local authorities. It caused quite a stir at the time and we never traced the leaker.

Such is the nature of the political profession. Life at the top is a never-ending vigil for the leader to safeguard himself or herself from leaks and plots and conspiracies and attempts to destabilize. It was ever thus: for medieval kings, for 18th, 19th and 20th-century prime ministers, for leaders the world over and throughout all history. The miracle was that she managed to outwit her enemies for so long – for eleven-and-a-half years she dominated an establishment of clever and ambitious male politicians, in an era of instant media communication and comment. In the aftermath, let us not begrudge her the use of all the legitimate means of staying in power and achieving her objectives. She never used illegitimate ones. She was constitutionally always in the right. Power never corrupted her. So impregnable did she become that her enemies had to build up myths about her abuse of the system of cabinet government, myths which were eagerly taken up by the media. There was no other way to undermine her. But many of those who complained about abuse of Cabinet Government were the ones who lost the arguments.

In retrospect, it may be said that she made the traditional mistake of the successful in outstaying her welcome. Certainly in the end she was forcibly removed. A combination of circumstances in 1990 made her position vulnerable, unfortunately, before she herself was ready to depart. I am convinced she intended to win a fourth General Election and then retire gracefully from the scene. She was troubled by the question of who should succeed her. She was fully aware of the need to groom her successor, but she was far from successful in doing it.

Perhaps I should make it clear that I was never a candidate myself. I didn't want the job. My ambition was to reach the Cabinet, which I achieved. I don't think I wanted to give the total commitment which the top job required: too many other things in life claimed my time and attention. Besides, I couldn't have done it well, I knew: not least because I was not a good communicator. That was one of the qualities she looked for in choosing an heir apparent.

Her first choice of an heir apparent back in 1983 was Cecil Parkinson. Cecil Parkinson was a close friend and associate of both hers and mine. He was a dedicated supporter of hers, a member of the inner circle of believers, of the Economic Dining Club, and of numerous Finance Bill Committees in the days of Opposition. He was not a prime mover in the thought processes which went into the making of the philosophy; he was in no sense an intellectual, but he was an extremely good communicator. He rose quickly through the ranks. He was Minister of State for Trade from 1979 to 1981 when she made him Chairman of the Party, with a seat in the Cabinet and the task of winning the next General Election. He became a very close associate of Margaret Thatcher's, and as Party Chairman she invited him to join the Falklands War Cabinet. He was ideally suited to the job of Party Chairman, and with his excellent Deputy Michael Spicer and Treasurer Alistair McAlpine, a superb team was formed which inspired the loyalty of the staff at 32 Smith Square. But perhaps his prime contribution to winning the 1983 election was his television appearances. They were relaxed, affable and incisive all at once. She had made a very good appointment.

After the 1983 election she promoted him again to the important job of Secretary of State for Trade and Industry. Sadly he had to resign four months later, which put paid to any idea of his inheriting her mantle. I was the lucky beneficiary from his misfortune, taking his place in Cabinet on becoming Transport Secretary. I had been a Minister of State at the Foreign Office from 1979 to 1981 and Financial Secretary to the Treasury from 1981 to 1983. I finally reached the Cabinet in October 1983.

Her second choice of heir apparent was John Moore. He followed me as Financial Secretary to the Treasury when I became Transport Secretary, and again followed me to become Transport Secretary when I went to the Department of the Environment. As Financial Secretary to the Treasury he devoted much of his time and energies to a succession of vigorous speeches on the merits of privatization. He also took part in a highly successful television programme during the 1983 election. The clarity and purity of his communication skills reached Margaret Thatcher and she quickly promoted him in 1986 to Transport Secretary, and then in 1987 to Secretary of State for Health and Social Security. Later, when that Department was split into its two constituent parts he retained the Social Security portfolio. In 1989 she suddenly sacked him altogether from her Government. I never understood why she did this. He was not the best of performers in the House of Commons; he had difficulty raising his voice high enough when the House was in a noisy mood. It might have been right to give him an easier job with less exposure; but to sack one of her best supporters, and an able man at that, was a sad misjudgement. That was the end of the second heir apparent.

The third heir apparent was John Major himself. He first came to prominence in 1989. She believed he shared all her views. He was highly competent and very pleasant. He did not come from the patrician wing of the party. I don't think that any particular speech or television appearance or especially dazzling episode prompted her to let her mantle fall upon him. But I do remember her saying to me at the time, 'He is another one of us.' She elevated him first to Chief Secretary, then to Foreign Secretary, then to Chancellor. He was then elevated to Prime Minister. For once she had picked the winner, even if not in quite the way she intended.

These tales demonstrate an uncertain touch in selecting, promoting and dispensing with people at the highest level. This was her chief weakness. She hated sacking people, and seemed to take too little care in selecting them. She listened too much to the views of others, who had prejudiced motives, often being uncertain in her own judgement. Perhaps this was one of the difficulties she had as a woman, when the people she had to deal with were almost all men. Her instincts were too often to select men she liked for promotion but to leave the more humdrum appointments to others. She wasn't too concerned about this because she relied more on her own drive and determination than on the help of others. Her Press Secretary, Bernard Ingham, was alleged by the press to drop hints about those ministers she favoured and those she did not. I doubt this: it is by no means clear who really dropped such hints, but once a name was in the 'public domain' as destined for dismissal, that poor individual suffered grievously. It became impossible for her to retrieve the situation; she could not give him any public endorsement, if it was in conflict with her intentions.

She was a paragon of loyalty to her personal staff. One of the apparent paradoxes about her was her dislike of and antagonism to civil servants in general and her fierce admiration for, in particular, those who worked closely with her. It was like those who say they detest America but like Americans. Her prejudice against the Civil Service probably sprang from some unhappy experiences when she was a junior minister, or even from the period when she was Secretary of State at the notoriously 'dreadful' Department of Education and Science. There is no doubt that junior ministers often find civil servants obstructive, usually because a civil servant's prime loyalty is to the Secretary of State, with whom junior ministers may be in conflict. There are some obstructive civil servants high up in the Service. A cabinet minister can move them out of the way. In my view, a good cabinet minister can always get what he or she wants out of the Civil Service. Margaret Thatcher's experiences must have left her with a certain animus against them in general – but she was loyal to them as individuals. She rightly saw civil servants as being in a very different category from ministers. Civil servants could not defend themselves from public attack, whereas politicians could. She was always fierce in her defence of her staff against Opposition attack. Over the years, two men in particular came to be very close to her and were vital advisers: Bernard Ingham, her Press Secretary, and Charles Powell, her Foreign Office Private Secretary. It is the custom for able civil servants in the main government departments to be seconded to the Prime Minister's office for two or three years, after which they return to their department, and are usually promoted. Bernard

Ingham was an official in the Energy Department in 1979 when he was suddenly summoned to Number 10 and given the job of Press Secretary. Why she picked him – she barely knew him beforehand – history does not relate, but he stayed in that post until the end, retiring from the Civil Service as Sir Bernard at the end of 1990.

He is a bluff, blunt Yorkshireman, with a growling voice and he looked the least likely person to be able to manipulate the press. Yet he proved invaluable to her, and his regular press briefings at Number 10 became famous, both for what he did tell them and for what he did not. Probably his best remark was the one he made after John Biffen argued in a television interview for a 'more balanced leadership'. 'He is only a semi-detached member of the Cabinet,' said Bernard Ingham. Later in his book, he regretted this indiscretion.

Margaret Thatcher certainly needed a good press officer. After a few years the press turned strongly against her, particularly the left-wing 'heavies'. The *Guardian*, in particular, seemed to pursue a relentless personal vendetta against her and all her works. Even the *Independent*, which prides itself on fairness, frequently did the same. The way she commanded the loyalty of the British people winning three elections and remaining in power for eleven-and-a-half years, was more than the intelligentsia could stand. They couldn't destroy her politically, so they tried to destroy her personally. Bernard Ingham protected her from the full horror of these onslaughts by letting her have only a summary sheet of the day's press each morning. Some say she became out of touch with public opinion as a result. But in truth, I think to have exposed her fully to this uncaring hate campaign might have been more than she could have borne. When my wife once talked to her about my own sufferings at the hands of the press, she replied, 'Tell him not to read it; if I read all they write about me, I couldn't carry on.' I think the truth is that Bernard Ingham enabled her to 'carry on' without inflicting unnecessary hurt on her, but without denying her the knowledge she needed to have about what was being said about her.

I found Bernard Ingham to be an entirely honest and fair servant of his mistress. He had no axe of his own to grind. He was entirely straight. It is not easy to handle the press relations of such a radical, iconoclastic person as Margaret Thatcher in the face of the sour and turgid hostility of frustrated intellectuals making a staged retreat from socialism. In their desperation, they simply tried to shoot the messenger.

The other work relationship which was equally successful was with Charles Powell. He was seconded from the Foreign Office in 1983 to be one of her Private Secretaries. He too stayed with her until the end, when she made him Sir Charles. When his tour of duty would normally have been over, he just stayed on and on and on. She wouldn't let him go and he didn't want to go. Although nominally not the senior Private Secretary, he came to be her right-hand man on all matters, and her confidant and close adviser. He shared her views and policies on most things, particularly on foreign policy, where his greatest expertise lay.

Some have wondered what were the qualities he brought to her service that enabled him to achieve such a special relationship. He was tireless in his devotion to working for her; his output was enormous and he worked long hours. He was skilled at drafting speeches and briefs. He was entirely loyal as well as discreet. These qualities surely are enough to explain the reason for his prominence.

Margaret Thatcher travelled abroad a lot. To begin with, she had to get to know all her foreign counterparts. Soon she became more positive, pursuing active policies and relationships. She very early struck up a close and lasting relationship with President Reagan; and later on with President Gorbachev. She became a heroine in Eastern Europe, giving encouragement to the nascent independence movements there as the iron grip of Russia began to relax. She came to be one of the most formidable figures on the international scene. Yet she never forgot the importance of meeting people. One night flying back from Japan, her aeroplane had to refuel at a remote airbase in Siberia. They arrived at 3.00 am. While the aircraft was being refuelled, all the local Russian party officials came to see her, together with an interpreter, and she gave them a lecture on the importance of democracy and freedom under the law. A spectacularly good debate on political philosophy took place for an hour and a half. They were all amazed.

Charles Powell accompanied her on all her foreign visits and helped her with briefs and speeches on foreign policy. With his help she took direct control of foreign policy, conducting it personally as she travelled from capital to capital.

Hers was certainly a most unorthodox technique. She never liked the Foreign Office – she regarded the senior officials there as pussyfooting and lacking in 'guts'. She always felt, with some justification, that the Foreign Office wanted to sell Britain out over European union. She also thought they were soft over sanctions against South Africa, and not sufficiently adroit in pursuing the thaw in the Cold War.

Her foreign policy achieved some remarkable successes, despite the unorthodox way in which it was conducted. Much credit is due to Charles Powell for the help he gave her. She did not choose the easiest way of running foreign policy, but the main result of her approach was a foreign policy that actually had a major impact on the world.

Margaret Thatcher's relationships with her political colleagues were variable – they depended on her fancy and upon who was 'one of us' and who was not. Her relationship with the Civil Service was not easy either, at least until she came upon civil servants who were both capable and loyal as individuals; these received her entire support and trust – but she was suspicious of the general body of civil servants. For both groups the test was, 'Are you here to help or to hinder?' It seems to me a reasonable question for the Head of Government to ask, but perhaps she asked it too obviously.

Another group of people with whom she had to deal were senior industrial managers. It was vital to find good people to manage the nationalised industries – both before they could be privatized and during the process of privatization, and for those that remained in public ownership. It was also in her eyes important to identify, support and recognize those managers who were effective in managing private-sector companies. Among these business managers too there was a select band of people she knew and trusted and respected. This band of people had access to her whenever they wanted. Nearly all of them ended up as peers, or at least knights.

She relied on this small group for selecting top managers for the industrial jobs that were within her gift. These were mainly the chairmanships of the dwindling number of nationalized industries. She seemed to rely on a few men – such people as Sir Michael Edwardes, Lord King, Lord Haslam and Ian MacGregor – to fill these posts, excluding others.

Sir Michael Edwardes was the man chosen initially to run British Leyland. He left in 1982 and went back into the private sector. Ian MacGregor, another manager with a first-rate reputation, was put forward by Keith Joseph to take over the British Steel Corporation. He was rightly seeking a manager in the international class. Margaret Thatcher agreed, although it was necessary to pay the merchant bank with whom Ian MacGregor was currently working compensation of £1,825,000. She saw the point that if you want the best, you must pay what it costs. He was a success at Steel; he began to turn it round very quickly. She is alleged to have described him as 'the only man she knew who was her equal.' When the time came to find a successor for Lord Ezra as Chairman of British Coal, it was to Ian MacGregor she immediately turned.

Sir Robert Haslam was chosen by Ian MacGregor as his Deputy at the Steel Corporation. He later went on to become its Chairman and in due course he succeeded Ian MacGregor as Chairman of British Coal.

She recruited John King in 1981 to take on British Airways, which by then had got into deep financial trouble. John King had made his way up to become Chairman of Babcock and Wilcox – and to make a success of it. He was the sort of man she admired, a tough and determined bully, but very successful. By 1983 he had turned BA round so that eventually it could be privatized in 1987. The long delay was due to the need to sort out some particularly difficult antitrust lawsuits in America. Instead of waiting patiently for this to be completed, John King decided to mount a prolonged press campaign against me for 'dragging my feet' over privatization. Were I to have given the true reason for the delay, BA's case in the lawsuit would have been weakened. He even went so far as to ask for a meeting with Margaret Thatcher in order to complain about my 'obstructionism'. He was surprised to find me sitting with Margaret Thatcher as he entered her study. He could only fill in the half hour allotted with pleasantries. She was very supportive in never undermining her ministers by letting businessmen get at her behind their backs.

There was a small number of businessmen in the private sector whom she also trusted and admitted to the magic circle: people like Lord Sterling, Lord Palumbo, Lord Hanson, Lord Laing and a few others. Some of these were helpful on the Party side of life, but mainly she admired them for the way they had built up successful companies. It was her way of honouring a new generation of good managers in British industry, good managers having been so rare before.

There are many examples of Margaret Thatcher taking over a subject about which she felt strongly or because she had a lack of confidence in the views of the minister responsible for it. One could spot these subjects immediately when the press reported that she was 'taking a special interest' in some topic or other. One important example was the handling of the miners' strike, and another was her preparation of the policy for the Health Service reforms. With both of these she 'took a special interest', appointing a small group of the ministers involved, including sometimes an outsider or two, and chaired regular meetings for as long as was necessary. This could well be justified on the grounds that such operations needed coordinating, and it was right for her to do it on subjects as important as these. It didn't always follow, however, that she was the only person who could do the coordinating. Both Willie Whitelaw, and after him Geoffrey Howe, could, and did, fulfil that role. But she wanted to have subjects in which she 'took a special interest' firmly under her own control, and she wanted to make sure the answers came out in the end as she wanted. She was determined to avoid being faced with a decision or a policy from a small group with which she did not agree. If she had strong views on a subject, it was not a bad way of working. I never found it irksome. I participated in many such small groups – from the miners' strike, through education policy, football hooliganism, to small matters like trying to attract a film studio to settle in Rainham Marshes in Essex. Sometimes she took a special interest in matters which were really too minor to be worthy of her attention and time.

One subject in which she came to 'take a special interest' was Westland, a British company which made helicopters, and which was approaching bankruptcy in 1985. The Board of Westland still hoped, as the only UK helicopter manufacturer, that they would be in a special position which would enable them to get some money out of the Government, although industrial rescues had been abandoned ever since the Government came to power. The answer was, correctly, in the negative – no money was forthcoming. They were told that the Government would be neutral in relation to any foreign company that might take them over. By the end of the year, it appeared that the American company Sikorski was likely to be the White Knight, and negotiations reached an advanced stage. Leon Brittan, then Secretary of State for Trade and Industry, remained neutral and content with this solution.

Michael Heseltine was the Defence Secretary at the time. He first entered Parliament in 1966. He had earlier made a huge fortune out of publishing magazines. He was intensely ambitious. A story is told of how he had sketched out his career on the back of an envelope while an undergraduate at Oxford: a fortune by 30, Parliament by 35, Cabinet by 40 and Prime Minister by 55. Soon after he arrived in the House, the Labour Government produced a small Bill to regulate the activities of employment agents. Two of us, Jack Page and I, took exception to this Bill. We believed it to be unnecessary. We recruited Michael Heseltine to our aid and decided to try to stop it. We eventually succeeded in doing so, carrying out a filibuster on the Report Stage throughout one whole Friday. Michael Heseltine made speeches of inordinate length and great fluency. We couldn't have succeeded without his help. I congratulated him afterwards, and he replied, 'Thank you very much; I'm not at all sure that I don't agree with the Bill, all the same!'

He climbed rapidly up the ranks, not quite making the Cabinet in Ted Heath's Government, but reaching the threshold as Minister of Aviation. Margaret Thatcher made him her Shadow Environment Secretary in 1975, and in 1979 the real thing.

In 1981 she appointed him Defence Secretary. For some unaccountable reason he came to the conclusion that Westland should not be rescued by Sikorski, but by a European consortium, although no such consortium even existed at that time. This was intervention on a truly 'Bennite' scale and would have involved taking unto the Government powers which it did not have (and should not have.) to instruct private shareholders as to whom they should sell their shares. His motive was said to be to make it clear that Britain's military and industrial future lay with Europe and not America. (How unwise this policy was came later to be demonstrated by the Gulf crisis.) He barnstormed round Europe in order hastily to get assembled a rival European consortium, together with the backing of the relevant governments. He got a rudimentary consortium organized although they never came near to getting their act together. The Westland Board was furious; they believed their future was their business, not his.

Margaret Thatcher was furious too. It immediately became a subject of 'special interest', and quite right too. She had to ensure that the view of all the Cabinet (with the exception of Michael Heseltine), that Westland should be allowed to determine its own future, prevailed. A small group was formed (I was not a member, obviously, since I was then at the Department of the Environment and had no departmental interest in this topic). The small group reaffirmed the policy that the Government was neutral, and said so.

Michael Heseltine behaved in an extraordinary way. Outnumbered 20 to 1 by his colleagues, ridiculed by informed commentators, and pursuing a policy which was technically impossible (since the Government lacked the necessary powers to put it into effect even if it had wanted to), he went public on the issue and made speech after interview after broadcast extolling the case for the European solution, the details of which had still not materialized.

The general view of Michael Heseltine at the time was that he was a mercurial, dynamic, but erratic fellow. At the time I came to the conclusion that he was obsessed by his desire for the European solution. I now think I was wrong. I think in retrospect he was determined on taking a course of action that would lead to a spectacular resignation, and that this was the best issue he had been able to find. The Government was in the usual 'mid-term blues' situation at the time. I believe that he thought the next election might well be a disaster, and he wanted to go out on a matter of high principle, in order to distance himself from what he expected to be a sinking ship. The difficulty was that no real issue of principle was around, so he decided to elevate Westland into one.

As soon as the 1985 turkey and Christmas pudding were eaten, he returned to the fray in the media, giving interviews, making press statements and demanding that his colleagues fall into line with his minority point of view. Margaret Thatcher was exasperated. Her authority was being openly and daily flouted – nor was it just her authority; in the Cabinet he had not one single ally, not even his own junior ministers supported him. And still there was no comprehensive offer on the table to the Westland shareholders from the European consortium.

I have a clear memory of the first Cabinet in 1986 after the Christmas recess, on 16 January. The Westland issue came up early. Margaret Thatcher proposed that the Cabinet should adhere to the policy that we should all remain neutral and that no one should advocate either the case of Sikorski, or the case of the European consortium. Those who wanted to make public pronouncements on the subject should clear their statements through the Cabinet Secretary, Sir Robert Armstrong. We all agreed, except Michael Heseltine, both with the policy, and with the requirement to clear anything we were minded to say through the Cabinet Office. None of us wanted to say anything anyway, so it was no great sacrifice to us. But in theory such an agreement effectively limited Michael Heseltine. That was its purpose, as conceived by Margaret Thatcher.

It was the only way to reimpose collective responsibility, which Michael Heseltine had been daily flouting in public. He gave us his interpretation of the Prime Minister's request that all statements be cleared through the Cabinet Secretary: it was to apply to all of us but not to him. This was too much for me. I immediately challenged him on the lines that if we who held one view were to conform, surely he who held the opposite view should conform too? Michael Jopling came in behind me, and then I pressed him a third time. Twice he refused to agree. At the third time of asking, he closed his Cabinet folder and said, 'I cannot accept this decision. I must therefore leave this Cabinet.' He stormed out, and announced his resignation to some startled journalists waiting in Downing Street.

The Cabinet issued the following brief statement: 'The Cabinet have reaffirmed that it is the policy of the Government that it is for the company to decide what course to follow in the best interest of Westlands and its employees. Cabinet discussed how this decision should apply in practice to ensure that collective responsibility was upheld. It was agreed that during this period when sensitive commercial negotiations were in process, all statements by Government Ministers should be cleared inter-departmentally through the Cabinet Office to ensure that all answers given by the Government were consistent with the policy decided by Cabinet. Mr Heseltine found himself unable to accept this procedure and left the Cabinet. The Prime Minister expressed her regret at his decision.'

It was one of the most extraordinary events I have ever witnessed. It seemed that Michael Heseltine was committing political suicide; a whole career wrecked by a sustained and brazen defiance of the doctrine of collective responsibility. His decision to resign could hardly have been an entirely emotional reaction: he had been riding for a fall for weeks and he must have realized that his refusal to accept the verdict of his colleagues that all statements had to be cleared left the Prime Minister with no alternative but to dismiss him. Maybe emotion overcame him, maybe it was a calculated strategy that he was following. It is all the more ironic, therefore, when one thinks of his criticism of Margaret Thatcher five years later when he wrote to his constituents: 'The Tories could lose control of the nation's destiny unless the Cabinet faced up to Mrs Thatcher and asserted its collective judgement on European policy.' He was not prepared to accept its 'collective judgement' himself in the matter of Westland.

I have heard it said that she nearly dismissed Michael Heseltine before Christmas. When asked later by an interviewer why she had not done so, she replied, 'Had I done that . . . I know exactly what the press would have said: There you are, old bossy-boots, at it again.' After he stormed out of the Cabinet, I said to her that I had decided to challenge his refusal to accept the will of his colleagues because it was more than I could take. She replied that she understood that, but that she feared the consequences. It was her familiar fear of the dangers of having powerful figures loose on the backbenches. On this particular occasion, her fears were perhaps later justified, although I believe that Michael Heseltine was determined upon resignation in January 1986 anyway.

Margaret Thatcher appointed George Younger as Defence Secretary in his place, and Malcolm Rifkind as Scottish Secretary in George Younger's place. The new member arrived and only twenty minutes later Cabinet resumed and completed the rest of business.

I have left the tale of the Solicitor General's letter out of the main story of Michael Heseltine's resignation, in order not to confuse the two issues and complicate what would have been, by itself, a fairly straightforward and harmless matter. But the parallel events surrounding the leaking of the Solicitor General's letter brought Leon Brittan down and came close to bringing Margaret Thatcher down. It became a major political 'storm', although like all such storms, there was no substantial matter of policy underlying it. There were allegations of dirty work at the crossroads. They are the stuff of which political storms are made.

The story itself was simple enough. At one point after Christmas, Margaret Thatcher had written a public letter to the Chairman of Westland reaffirming the Government's policy, and pledging that the Government would do its best to prevent any discrimination against Westland by European Governments in their ordering policy, in the event that the company went to Sikorski. Soon after, Michael Heseltine, determined to challenge her authority, arranged for the European consortium's merchant bank to write to him, as a pretext for his reply, which contradicted hers and stated that a Westland Sikorski marriage would render 'incompatible' any further involvement by them in certain European military projects. He released both letters to the press. Naturally, Margaret Thatcher was furious and with complete justification. Apart from sacking him then and there, she was powerless. But she questioned the validity of his reply. She consulted the Solicitor General, Sir Patrick Mayhew, and in due course he advised her that there were 'material inaccuracies' in Michael Heseltine's letter. His arguments could not be sustained by the contractual position between Westland and the various European governments. On her suggestion, the Solicitor General wrote to Michael Heseltine, and said that he should publicly correct various of these 'material inaccuracies' in his letter. That letter from the Solicitor General was in the hands of the press that evening. It is one of the firm rules of the law, both in and out of government, that legal advice is never made public, nor can a Court force it to be produced in evidence, nor a Select Committee of Parliament. Everyone is entitled to receive secret legal advice and legal advisers are entitled to their advice being kept secret. It was unthinkable that a law officer's advice should be published.

So the question was, who leaked it, or rather, who authorized the leaking of it? We know that the Department of Trade and Industry (DTI) Press Officer, Ms Colette Bowe, gave it to the press, but on whose authority? Leon Brittan's private secretary had telephoned the contents of the letter to him while he was out at lunch. He replied that it should 'go into the public domain,' but only 'subject to the agreement of Number 10.'

History does not relate exactly what was said in the exchanges between Number 10 and the DTI as a result of this instruction. Number 10 – in the shape of Bernard Ingham – certainly refused to leak it themselves. He speaks for himself in his book where he said that it shouldn't be leaked at all. He feared that his message did not get across in terms that were sufficiently clear and adamant. There was probably a misunderstanding. The cock-up theory is always more likely to be true than the conspiracy one. In any event, Ms Bowe gave the substance of the letter to the press that evening.

There was just enough doubt about precisely what had happened for it to be possible for her enemies to accuse Margaret Thatcher of authorizing the leak and then denying it. That was the chink of light her detractors needed in order to launch a witchhunt into a matter which put in question her propriety – even her integrity. It was just the sort of opportunity they had so completely failed to find hitherto. That fact alone makes it extremely unlikely that she had personally authorized the leak – it just wasn't the sort of thing she would ever do, and had never done. Her integrity was absolute.

She was fully aware that the Government's legal advice should never be made public, while Leon Brittan had made it clear, in that famous telephone conversation, that he had 'forgotten' the sanctity of legal advice and had no scruples about taking such a course of action. On top of all that, Bernard Ingham says that she may not even have known about the dramas that were taking place that afternoon. Prime ministers are busy people who do not sit around waiting to react to everything that happens.

I think the most likely explanation is that 'Downing Street' in the persons of Bernard Ingham and Charles Powell, and not including the Prime Minister, were not averse to the fact that there were 'material inaccuracies' in the letter reaching the 'public domain', but never authorized the leaking of the actual letter. There were plenty of ways of doing this in due course. Michael Heseltine could have been forced to publish a letter retracting the 'material inaccuracies' in his earlier one, or Margaret Thatcher could have published one contradicting it.

Any such device would have been acceptable. Owing to some misunderstanding, however, the whole letter was leaked forthwith.

The whole affair, of course, took off in the press and in Parliament with the intensity of a Zinoviev Letter or a Profumo affair. Editorials thundered, Parliament moved votes of censure, and Select Committees set to work. The Opposition tried to make it stick on Margaret Thatcher, but the real pressure came on Leon Brittan. The 1922 Committee on 23 January bayed for his blood. He resigned the next morning. It must be for the reader to judge whether the punishment fitted the crime, indeed whether there was any crime at all.

Margaret Thatcher, with her usual sense of loyalty to a colleague, had tried to save him. She refused to say anything which would have incriminated him. This in turn made her own position more vulnerable. She came under intense pressure. As she went to the House of Commons to defend herself against a Vote of Censure, she is alleged to have said, 'This may be my last day as Prime Minister.' Neil Kinnock mishandled the attack, which was typical but fortunate. She carried the vote without difficulty.

I could not believe that so much trouble could have come out of so minor an affair. She seemed to be in a bog: the more she struggled the more bogged down she became. It was because her personal integrity could for the first time be questioned that her enemies pressed the attack so relentlessly. It was because I believed in her personal integrity that I myself never had any doubts over the Westland affair.

She set up an enquiry under the Cabinet Secretary, Sir Robert Armstrong, which came to no new conclusions. None of the parliamentary enquiries revealed anything new. The affair rumbled on for a long time, and although in the end it disappeared into the slipstream of history, it left her weakened. For the first time her integrity had been under question, and she hadn't been quite able to prove her innocence.

That she mishandled the whole affair is self-evident. There was no great issue of policy, no split in the Cabinet and no need for the matter to have got so grossly out of hand. If she had asserted her authority on the issue of collective ministerial responsibility and dismissed Michael Heseltine when his behaviour had become insupportable, the whole affair would have been avoided. I also suspect that her attempts to save Leon Brittan from his eventual fate greatly increased the difficulties she had over the Solicitor General's letter. Her dislike of sacking her colleagues and her high sense of loyalty towards them had, for the first time, endangered her position. These same admirable qualities later contributed to her downfall.

3

THE SUPPLY SIDE

MARGARET THATCHER'S FIRST priority in achieving power in 1979 was to liberate the wealth-creating sector of the economy. Unless we could earn more as a nation all her other goals would be unobtainable. This chapter is about her policies for the 'supply side' of the economy.

I think this term originated in the United States. It refers to all those activities within the economy which produce tradeable goods or services – and which are therefore the source of earnings. In this chapter I discuss Margaret Thatcher's policies to boost the supply side – the City, services and manufacturing industry.

Over a long period services, as opposed to goods, have been increasing as a proportion of Britain's total output. It might be said that we have been fortunate to have such a vigorous service sector since our manufacturing sector declined. Indeed, we have almost talked ourselves into believing that our manufacturing industry is destined to continue to decline, and that we will never be able to match the Germans and the Japanese and the Pacific Rim countries. Measured over a long period of time, it is undoubtedly true that we have lost world market share in manufactures continuously over a period of about a hundred years. Socialists see the cure for this malaise as spending more public money on industrial investment, research, development, technology, training and anything else that is trendy. Nationalization is the ideal way of doing this; the Government can just spend money on nationalized industries without bothering where it goes: publicly owned industry must surely spend money 'in the public interest'?

Traditional consensus Tories were sceptical of this judgement: up to 1970 they couldn't think of anything else to do to arrest the decline, but they didn't like the socialist solution, and it was very expensive. When in power they just stopped the process going any further: they froze the industrial budget, and they stopped nationalizing any more industries. Ted Heath in 1970 actually set out on a policy to improve the supply side. He started off wanting to reform trade unions and to reduce industrial subsidies, and even planned a privatization programme. But when the going got rough, he performed his famous U-turn and restored a policy closer to the socialist one even than to the traditional Tory one.

Margaret Thatcher, prompted by Keith Joseph in 1975, believed that there should be no subsidies to industry, that it should all be returned to the private sector in a competitive environment, that corporate taxes should be reformed and lowered, that restrictions and petty regulations should be swept away, and that world markets should be opened into which it could sell. It was vital to weaken the grip of the trade unions. In this way, they believed, industry would be 'set free' to put its house in order and get on with the job of winning back world market share.

Margaret Thatcher's Government set out to achieve all these 'supply side' goals in 1979. Over time she succeeded in most respects in freeing up the supply side.

In 1979 she made Keith Joseph her Industry Secretary. He started to phase out direct industrial subsidies straight away. By 1989, when I arrived in that job, the only direct subsidy left was 'launch aid' for new aircraft, an anomaly which for various reasons neither I nor my predecessors were able to get rid of. There remained a programme of regional aid, designed to attract investment to the less fortunate industrial areas of Britain. The cost of this too had been drastically reduced over the decade. There were various small programmes designed to encourage research, and to bring consultants' services to the attention of firms and to assist with preparing for the Single Market in Europe. The Department spent 81 per cent less in real terms in 1989–90 than it did in 1979–80. Direct subsidies to industry were done away with.

A vital element in supply-side policies is to increase competition. Competition policy was progressively tightened. Competition was given a higher priority than company size. The concept of allowing large industrial companies to form so that they could become successful competitors on the world industrial scene was abandoned. What such companies actually did was to merge with all their domestic rivals, and then seek to exploit the British market from a monopolistic position. In theory international competition was available, but it was hard to mobilize it because political lobbying was employed to prevent an overseas company securing a major British order. 'British jobs are at stake' or 'We cannot buy foreign-made defence equipment' were telling pressures, especially when the order came from the Government or a nationalized industry. Most large companies did not prove themselves to be star performers on the world scene.

The policy of maintaining as much domestic competition as possible was not always achieved. GEC (General Electric Company) and Siemens were eventually allowed by the Monopolies Commission to take over Plessey, and so was British Airways allowed to take over British Caledonian Airways. Both these decisions were wrong, in my view, but it was not possible for the Secretary of State at the time to go against the decisions of the Monopolies Commission whose job it was to arbitrate in such matters.

Competition was introduced into many areas of the service sector where it had been effectively suppressed before. Opticians, barristers, solicitors, consulting engineers, conveyancers, funeral directors, even the City of London itself, were all made to open up their activities to competition in one way or another.

Industries which were privatized were often put into the private sector in a form which created some competition. The bus industry was one that I privatized myself when I was Secretary of State for Transport between 1983 and 1986. I insisted on selling the National Bus Company split into 72 different companies, against violent opposition but with, I believe, wholly beneficial results. I was less successful with the British Airports Authority (BAA), which I wanted to privatize by selling off as many as possible of the airports separately. My colleagues decided to sell it as one, which was not the most competitive solution. Gas and Steel too were sold as monoliths, although the gas industry could have been split up more. Happily, the greatest degree of competition possible was achieved in the electricity sale. For British Telecom (BT) a competitor was promoted and nurtured in the shape of Mercury. Telecommunications is an industry which used to be seen as a natural monopoly. Now there are at least four methods of establishing communications between two different points, and soon it will be a highly competitive industry. The problem here was managing the transition to the new situation.

I think the sum of all those activities was to induce a considerably greater degree of competition in the domestic economy than there had been before. A climate was created where monopolies and cartels were discouraged. Many firms started up and entered previously protected markets. There is much more to do, but I do believe that the more competitive atmosphere which the Government created over the decade contributed much to the improvement of the supply side.

Another impediment to be tackled was excessive red tape and regulation of businesses. The case for controlling the activities of industry and commerce is unanswerable. Health and safety legislation, fire precautions, anti-pollution regulations, laws against monopoly and cartels, and laws to protect intellectual property, consumers, shareholders and creditors are all vital. They are the essential legal infrastructure of a developed market economy. At one time they were collectively described as 'quality control'. But many regulations in 1979 were not about 'quality control' but 'quantity control'. They were about protecting markets, excluding would-be competitors and some were about preserving the position of public suppliers of goods or services against competition from private suppliers. Also, as technology changes, and as the perception of evils and hazards changes, regulations grow out of date: they must be constantly revised and made more appropriate to the needs of the age. Moreover, regulators tend to play safe and to demand standards which are beyond what is necessary and can be afforded by the customers. In the end it is the customers who have to pay for all industrial and commercial regulation, whether necessary or not.

The task before the Government in 1979 was thus not to abolish regulation of the supply side, but to bring it up-to-date. Much past legislation had to be discarded – as either inappropriate or unnecessary. But the Government made a mistake in talking about 'deregulation' as an end in itself. There was even a 'deregulation unit' established under the auspices of the Cabinet Office by Lord Young when he was Minister Without Portfolio. He published White Papers from 1987 to 1989 setting out progress in dismantling regulations and explaining the further heights to be scaled. During this period, I have to say, when I was Secretary of State for the Environment, I was busy working out new regulations to control water quality, waste disposal, and the discharge of toxic materials to land, sea and air. My colleagues were busy working out regulations for better animal health, food quality, safety on oil rigs and exposure to radiation, among many other things.

What we were doing was to make regulations appropriate to our own time. It was certainly a service to business to remove the unnecessary restrictions of the past – often designed to restrict competition rather than to protect consumers, or employees, or the environment. But perhaps we gave too strong an impression of a government that wanted to let industry free to do as it wanted, despite the reality that strict control was exercised over things that were relevant and that we rightly pursued.

David Young's 'deregulation' initiative – the unit and the white papers – despite the attendant press publicity, never really took off. The white papers got thinner and thinner, as avenue after avenue was explored, and few new opportunities for serious deregulation were found. Initially it achieved a good deal, but the barrel got scraped bare as time went by. In the end, ministers were obliged by the DTI to fill up questionnaires as to what they were 'reviewing' or what progress they could dream up to justify their departments' activities in relation to the 'initiative'.

There is still much to do to remove unnecessary restrictions on business – but it has to be directed to the realities of the problems on the ground, not just to compiling a score-sheet of abolitions. A modern industrial society has to have regulation: the real art is to keep the regulation strictly related to the needs of the present.

The privatization programme, however, was massively successful. Britain became internationally famous both for inventing privatization and for putting it into effect. Later we were asked to advise on and carry out privatization programmes in many countries of the world. In 1990 I even got a visit from two journalists from the Russian newspaper *Pravda* who asked me for an interview on how to privatize Russian businesses, 'on express orders from the Kremlin,' so they said. Who could have forecast in 1979 when we set out to implement my policy report on 'denationalization' that the Russians would have been following suit ten years later?

There were many advantages in privatization. They can be summed up as 'rolling back the frontiers of the State,' but in fact that encompasses many separate gains. Harold Macmillan believed that a token move was necessary. In the early 1950s he privatized 3,000 council houses. In the 1980s we privatized over a million. That was the difference between a gesture and a real transfer of resources back to the private sector.

There were many reasons why it worked so well in practice. One was that it saved the Exchequer a great deal of money. Harold Macmillan, later when he was the Earl of Stockton, described the process as 'selling the family silver'. What he should have added is that the 'family silver' was costing a great deal in anti-burglar precautions, insurance, cleaning and maintenance. The sale proceeds were not what counted – it was avoiding the running costs. Not only did the losses stop, but the burden of finding new capital for investment was transferred to the private capital market. The sale proceeds were only an added one-off bonus. The enemies of privatization came to concentrate their fire on this aspect: they accused the Government of being careless with public money by not getting higher prices. There was some truth in these charges on occasion, but mostly the criticisms were made with the advantage of hindsight after the market had taken up the price of the shares. It was difficult to get the City advisers to put high-enough flotation prices on new issues. Underwriters wanted to set the price cheap to avoid their being left with stock on their hands after a bad sale. I confronted a boardroom full of underwriters in order to set the flotation price for Amersham International in 1982. I was there as Financial Secretary, and Hamish Gray was there – he was Minister of State at the Energy Department, which was the sponsoring ministry. I couldn't get the assembled bankers and underwriters to accept a high-enough price for flotation. As a bargaining ploy I said I would pull the sale, and made as if to walk out of the meeting. My colleague remained seated and went on pleading. I had to return shamefacedly to the table! Amersham International went to a substantial premium when trading started in the shares.

The City took the view that these issues were known as 'successes'. When we sold Britoil, the shares actually went to a discount in first trading: that was known as a 'failure'. These were not my views. My conclusion is that it is impossible to get the sale price of a privatization right; it is far more important to get it off the public books. Sniping at the Government for selling it too cheap only proves that it is the only aspect of privatization which its opponents still felt strong enough to criticize.

I cannot take that view over the sale of the Rover Group to British Aerospace, which David Young carried out in 1988. On the first occasion that Rover was nearly sold, it was foreign-owned companies who were bidding for it. There was a storm of xenophobic protest in the House of Commons and the sale was frustrated. When BAe showed interest, David Young decided to negotiate with them exclusively. It was this failure to attract competition which led to the subsequent difficulties. I myself had later to handle as Secretary of State at the DTI, the storm over the revelation that extra sums had been paid to BAe at the time of the deal, which, it was alleged, had not been fully disclosed either to Parliament or to the European Commission. That was an extremely difficult issue to handle. Even then, the difficult part of the charge to answer was the one of concealment, rather than that of selling Rover too cheaply.

Another advantage of privatization was that it spread share ownership more widely, not only among the population, but more particularly among the employees of the company concerned. Special arrangements were made in all issues for employees to receive some free shares, some cheap ones, and an allocation at flotation price as well. Many of these shares were held onto, and the number of small shareholders grew enormously as the result of the privatization programme. The most successful example of all was the National Freight Corporation, which was the first company to be privatized, in 1982. The management and workforce together bought the shares, and the company went on to prosper mightily. The shares are now worth several times what was paid for them in 1982, and most of the employees have a substantial capital asset as a result.

The overriding advantage of privatization, however, was that it transferred the allegiance of the workforce and management to working for their customers rather than for themselves. It cut out the obstructive power of the trade unions, and enabled management to remove all restrictive practices. It was clear that better wages and improvement in the share price would come only from satisfying the customers: there was no longer a chance of getting money from the Government, which under state ownership had seemed (and, indeed, had been) a much easier way to prosper than earning a good living by providing a good service. Nationalized industries could easily run into loss, and the Exchequer had no option but to bail them out. There was no penalty for providing a bad service: in the private sector there was.

Moreover, gas, electricity, telecommunications, water, steel and transport are important elements for the rest of the economy. To have them provided efficiently benefited the nation as a whole. Since privatization, all these major suppliers have improved dramatically in their efficiency, their profitability and their standard of service to the customers. Management has been left free to manage, the motivation has been put right, and the rewards have followed.

It has often been asked why we privatized only smaller companies during the first of Margaret Thatcher's governments. The big ones all came later. I think the answer is that we learned how to do it with the smaller ones. The work on competitive regimes, the balance sheet, share structures, the pension fund and the form of the necessary legislation, taught us how to arrange things for the bigger industries. When the early sales proved an undoubted success, we not only felt emboldened enough to proceed with the bigger ones, but we knew how to do it.

In the Treasury between 1981 and 1983, as Financial Secretary, I handled the sale of Cable and Wireless, the Hydraulics Research

Establishment at Henley, Amersham International and Britoil. The main function of treasury ministers was to supervise the balance sheet, pricing and sale tactics. The bulk of the work which went into each privatization was preparing the company for sale, which was handled by the sponsoring department. Before offering an industry for sale, it was vital to create a competitive environment, to get the regulatory regime right, and to sort out a host of detail to do with things like the pension fund, redundancy entitlement and social obligations. It was necessary to legislate for each privatization separately. I once proposed to Margaret Thatcher that we should introduce a wider Bill to enable us to privatize three minor concerns in one. She refused; she didn't want to give a future Labour Government a precedent for nationalizing three or more concerns in one Bill. I thought the danger of that had receded, so successful had the policy been.

On my last day in the Treasury, in October 1983, we heard about proposals to privatize the National Bus Company (NBC) in one. Nigel Lawson, John Moore and I all reacted strongly against the plan; we believed it should be split into many parts in order to further competition in the provision of bus services. Next afternoon I found myself appointed Transport Secretary, and the task fell to me to do just that.

There was strong opposition from some within the Transport Department to doing anything about buses. They had been persuaded by my predecessor, Tom King, to accept privatization of the NBC in one lump, but they didn't want to go further. If the NBC were to be split into its component company parts – of which there were over sixty – then some measure of deregulation was also necessary. The bus industry had, in fact, been subjected to strict regulation in the early 1930s by the then Transport Minister, Euan Wallace, who happened to have been my uncle. I set about deregulating the buses, allowing competition on bus routes and creating a competitive service industry with many small firms operating. Uneconomic services could be subsidised by the county council when they believed it was necessary.

When I took my proposals to Cabinet, Margaret Thatcher was enthusiastic, and only one voice was raised against them – that was a colleague who feared the proposals would starve rural areas of bus services. The plan was quickly adopted. It caused a storm of protest, orchestrated by the staff of the National Bus Company, and backed by the Labour Party, the bus manufacturers and the unions. The Bill had a stormy passage through Parliament. Two successive chairmen of the NBC left in protest. It required great steadiness under fire to get the policy through; in this I had invaluable help and support from my Minister of State, David Mitchell, and from the civil servant in charge, Patrick Browne. In the event, the bus policy created 72 new small businesses, saved a lot of public money, netted £85 million after repayment of loans for the taxpayers, and greatly improved the service for customers – passenger numbers increased after years of decline. There are no thanks in politics. In this way, we were creating a property-owning democracy which was real, not token.

At the Transport Department I also prepared British Airways and the British Airports Authority for sale. Both sales actually took place after I left in 1985, but we did the preparatory work.

The BAA was the first statutory monopoly which came my way to privatize. The first monopoly that the Government privatized was BT, then came British Gas, BAA, the Water Authorities and, finally, electricity. I had not recommended privatizing natural monopolies in my original report. There was then an argument, which had convinced me at the time, that there would be no gain from putting a monopoly into private hands. Since there could not be competition, its prices would have to be controlled by the State if it were privatized, and no one would want to buy it with price control attached. So there would be no point in so doing. This conventional wisdom had prevailed for 50 years or more. With the advantage of hindsight, I now see why the conventional wisdom was wrong and I was wrong to accept it. The argument that price control would leave no scope for incentives to improve collapsed when the American system of price regulation was rejected. This consisted of stipulating a maximum rate of return on capital. It had the effect of stifling innovation and investment and research. The problem was solved by the introduction of Professor Littlechild's formula RPI − X. This was the method chosen for controlling prices: each year the monopoly was allowed to increase its prices by the amount of inflation less a factor of X per cent which represented the efficiency gain required. If the company could do better than X, it kept the proceeds. If it did worse, its shareholders took the loss. Thus, there was an incentive to become more efficient. The RPI − X formula of control allowed an incentive to invest, while still preventing exploitation of the monopoly. So this disadvantage was removed: an incentive to improve was provided.

The other reason why I became converted to privatizing monopolies concerned capital for investment. Treasury control of the borrowings of the nationalized industries had led to insufficient investment. Capital allocations in the private sector are rationed by price: in the public sector by arbitrary Treasury judgements. In fact, most of the nationalized monopolies were seriously underinvested. It was only when they were privatised that these deficiencies came to light and were remedied. The situation was extreme in the water industry. The Government had been responsible both for setting the standards for drinking-water quality and river quality, and also for providing the required capital to implement those standards. In order to avoid having to provide enough capital past governments had lowered standards or ignored them. Public investment in water had been halved by the Labour Government between 1974 and 1979, and although it had double again between 1979 and 1987, a large shortfall in investment had meanwhile occurred.

We had some amusing exchanges across the floor of the House on this. The Labour Party argued that on average water investment had been the same under the Labour Government as under the Conservative one. In fact, the figures were that they had cut it from £850 million in 1973–4 to £400 million in 1979–80 (constant 1985 prices).

Governments will always distort standards in order to economize if they can – whether they be standards of customer satisfaction, or quality control, or the provision of the necessary capacity. This had happened in telephones, water, airports, gas and electricity, under public ownership. It is now a thing of the past. There used to be up to two years' wait for a telephone not so very long ago! That was solely because insufficient investment capital had been made available to the nationalized BT.

Each natural monopoly that we privatized was established with its appropriate regulatory control. For gas, telecommunications, water and electricity, there was a Director-General in charge of price regulation who operated the RPI – X formula. For airports, the Civil Aviation Authority carried out the same function. It also regulated the BAA in relation to providing a fair deal for its customers – the airlines – and the environment, the people living near airports.

In addition, I came to the conclusion early in 1987 that environmental regulation was needed as well as price regulation in respect of the water industry. As Environment Secretary I had inherited plans for privatizing water which contained only price regulation. I couldn't see how the necessary improvement in water quality could be secured without it, or how disputes between water companies and polluters could be resolved, if both were private companies. The original plan left the water companies in the position of being both poachers and gamekeepers. I had to overcome strong resistance to my plan to set up a National Rivers Authority (NRA), both from some of my officials and later from the water company chairmen. But I insisted, Cabinet agreed unanimously, and I announced the establishment of the NRA as the 1987 election broke. This decision delayed privatization by nearly two years, but I am convinced it was an essential feature of running the water industry; it was another of the benefits of privatization. It could never have been done if water had remained publicly owned. The Government can't regulate itself.

At the end of Margaret Thatcher's premiership, only coal, atomic energy, the Post Office, railways and the London Underground remained publicly- owned out of all the main nationalized industries we inherited in 1979. It was a huge task to launch all these concerns successfully into the private sector. I believe it was wholly beneficial to the supply side of the economy: to the customers, the employees and the new shareholders, as well as to the taxpayers.

Would that the Eastern European countries and the Soviet Union could do the same. They see the advantages of privatization because of our pioneering work and they want to emulate it. But their task is vastly greater. We privatized about 7 per cent of UK productive capacity. They have over 90 per cent in public ownership. It took us 12 years to do it. How long must it take them? They will have to go much quicker than we did. Already in Eastern Europe they have met the same accusation as we met, of selling state assets too cheaply. In Poland and Czechoslovakia, and even more so in Hungary, they were alarmed at the prospect of privatized industries being acquired by foreigners or, worse still, ex-Communist bosses, on a bargain-basement basis.

While I see the political difficulties, even that is better than keeping them on the public payroll. It is also possible to exclude 'undesirable' purchasers. But this in turn allows the vendor to be accused potentially of selling the industries too cheaply. The last line of defence of the frustrated would-be nationalizer is to accuse the vendor of not achieving a fair price. But it is irrelevant if the prime objective is to get public assets into the hands of private citizens as quickly as possible in order to increase efficiency and satisfy the customers. It pays infinitely better to sell them cheap, or even give them away, rather than to get bogged down in time-wasting wrangles about the precise price of each asset.

Another major part of supply-side policy was reform of the trade unions. Jim Prior, the first Employment Secretary, was eventually pushed into reluctantly bringing forward the first Trade Union Bill in 1980. This was followed by three further Bills, which became the Acts of 1984, 1988 and 1990. I need not describe in detail their provisions, but the combined effect of the three Acts was greatly to restrict the immunities and privileges of trade unions under the law, and to give more control over elections, strike decisions, procedure and the use of union funds to the actual members of a union. Secondary picketing was prevented, and the closed shop in the end was outlawed, except in very tightly restricted circumstances.

How much these changes in the law contributed to the greatly improved climate of industrial relations which took place is hard to say. Making union leaders ballot their members before conducting strike action certainly averted some strikes and may have caused others not to be threatened when the union leaders knew a ballot would be lost. The measures probably saved a lot of individual union members from victimization and certainly cut back severely on intimidation by secondary picketing abuses.

On the other hand, industrial relations were bound to improve through better economic conditions. Inflation came down and remained low, so there was not the stridency of previous annual pay claims. There was no prices and incomes policy – the cause of so many strikes in the Winter of Discontent. Firms were prosperous and could afford to pay wage increases over the rate of inflation; and they did. More and more industries went into the private sector, where the pressure of the need to earn one's pay in a competitive environment had its effect: the Government was clearly not going to pay up to bail out bankrupt firms, or nationalize them, or give them grants, to tide them over. It was sink or swim – and nearly everyone swam in the 1980s. By contrast, in the public sector there was little, if any, improvement in industrial relations. In the National Health Service, the Civil Service and local government, none of the above factors applied. It is hard to know how much of the improvement in the private sector was due to industrial relations legislation as opposed to the improved economic climate.

Certainly the legislation did some good and very definitely it did no harm. The fear of general strikes and Britain becoming 'ungovernable', which Jim Prior had forecast if the unions were corralled by the law too tightly, proved to be a myth. Britain had taken a major step away from being the sick man of Europe.

All this seems minor set beside the trauma of the miners' strike. Indeed, it seemed as if the miners decided to cast themselves in the role of gladiators, to champion the cause of militant left-wing trade unionism against the hated Thatcher Government. While the private sector unions fell into line under the discipline of competition, and the public sector unions contented themselves with skirmishing and striking over the 'cuts', the miners' leaders took it upon themselves to try to overthrow the elected Government by frontal assault. Arthur Scargill, the miners' President, was no novice when it came to frontal assaults upon governments. He had been the inspiration behind the miners' strike of 1973, although he was then only President of the Yorkshire Miners' Union. The miners had twice routed Ted Heath, who imposed statutory control of prices and incomes in order to try to limit the inflation he had caused. On the first occasion, their pay claim was referred to the Wilberforce Committee, who unhelpfully found largely in favour of the miners' claim. The next year they tried to repeat the performance, but their pay demands this time were not met in full and the miners went on strike in the winter of 1973. The 1973 strike was pursued as a sort of military operation, seeking to close down the plants of the consumers of coal and the means of transporting the coal to those plants. The crucial battle of this violent campaign was the battle of Saltley Coke Works in the Midlands, where thousands of battling miners succeeded in defeating the police and causing the coke works to close. The general in command of the battle of Saltley Coke Works was Arthur Scargill.

I was not in office in 1973 and I viewed these events with scorn. I had opposed the prices and incomes controls which Ted Heath had brought in on the very grounds, among others, that they would lead to strikes for more pay than the controls allowed, and that such strikes would prevail. I was aghast when Ted Heath subsequently held the General Election of February 1974 on the grounds of 'Who ran the country?' – he or the miners' union, and at the same time offered to capitulate in public by establishing a body called the Relativities Board, which was virtually charged with buying off the miners. The electorate decided that Harold Wilson should run the country, and the miners were duly bought off.

It was the most difficult election I ever fought, because I was arguing both against the wage controls and against resisting the strike. These were the Tory party's main election platforms – although they destroyed even those platforms by offering to buy off the miners through the Relativities Board. Why I was elected at all when I didn't believe in my own Party's policy I know not. But my election result was no better or worse than the average.

All this history is relevant because the lessons of it were learnt by Arthur Scargill, and also by Keith Joseph. Arthur Scargill drew the conclusion that brute militant force would always secure him victory in a struggle against a Tory government. Keith Joseph learnt the lesson that such tactics must never again be allowed to prevail. In commissioning me to prepare the report on privatization policy in 1978, he asked me to include a confidential annexe to my report analysing how a future Tory government could defeat the NUM if it were ever again to try another frontal assault upon it.

I had been a junior minister in the DTI until my resignation in April 1972 dealing with, among other things, the coal industry. So I knew a little about the subject and I had been close to the events which led to the Wilberforce forced capitulation. I therefore found it quite easy to draw up a list of the precautions that should be taken. First, I said, sufficient amounts of coal should be stockpiled at the power stations, not at the pits, in order for them to survive a year's strike. Second, as many power stations as possible should be converted to dual coal/oil firing, so that the maximum possible amount of oil could be used to generate electricity in a coal famine. Special arrangements should be used to hire haulage firms who would not be intimidated in transporting coal by road in the event of a strike, and the police should be organized on a specially mobile basis so that they could concentrate wherever the strikers decided to concentrate for the purposes of closing down coal-using plants.

This document, along with the main report on privatization policy, appeared in *The Economist* in full in 1978. Who leaked it, or why, I never found out. It caused a furore and was seen, even by the Tory press, not as a list of sensible precautions which should be taken to avoid another Saltley Coke Works fiasco, but as a plan for a sort of direct attack upon harmless, downtrodden miners, who might one day seek to strike in pursuit of no more than a living wage. After the row had subsided a bit, I came out of hiding and went to see Margaret Thatcher to apologize – not because I had done anything wrong myself because the document had not been leaked by me, but because it had caused such a commotion. 'Never apologize, never explain,' she said. She wasn't in the least put out, and proceeded to file the necessary precautions in her mind against a confrontation which she seemed to know must inevitably come one day.

In my view, she always knew, even as far back as 1978, that she would face a pitched battle mounted by Arthur Scargill. She knew it would be ostensibly an industrial dispute, but in reality it would be a political assault designed to overthrow her Government. She never doubted that these were Arthur Scargill's ambitions.

Arthur Scargill was both a Marxist and a revolutionary. He was also careful not to appear as a revolutionary in the British media, cultivating a deceptive image of an old-style trade unionist. However, he did let the mask drop once in an interview with the intellectual bible of British Marxism, *New Left Review*, in 1975. 'Later in this interview,' Scargill tells the magazine, 'I will tell you of the most amazing picketing that ever took place (Saltley) during the 1973 strike, which was handled very similarly to a military operation. I believe in a class war you have to fight with the tools at your disposal . . . You see, we took the view that we were in a class war, not playing cricket on the village green like they did in 1926. We were out to defeat Heath and Heath's policies because we were fighting a government. We had to declare *war* on them and the only way you could declare war was to attack the vulnerable points . . . We were fighting a class war and you don't fight a class war with sticks and bladders. You fight a war with weapons that are going to win it.' It was to fight Scargill's 'war' that the Government carefully laid its plans.

Arthur Scargill was a traditional British revolutionary. He reminded me of those figures from British history – people like Wat Tyler – who decided to try to overthrow the establishment on the wave of support they enjoyed from their mates in the local community. Arthur Scargill had succeeded once before. He was now President of the NUM (National Union of Miners) and he was determined to have another go, now that there was again a Tory Government. In 1982 he put in a high pay claim, accompanied by demands that no more pits should close. It was beyond what any sensible Coal Board Chairman could accept. Margaret Thatcher asked to see the figures for coal stocks at the power stations, and to hear of the progress with installing dual firing. She realized that the electricity industry could not go on supplying electricity long enough for the miners to be able to be defeated. She decided to back down and allow the Coal Board to negotiate the best settlement with the miners they could get, but to make sure that coal stocks were adequate for the next round of the contest, which she knew would come. She also sacked David Howell and appointed Nigel Lawson, who was succeeded in 1983 by Peter Walker as Energy Secretary with strict instructions to prepare for the inevitable confrontation. Peter Walker was an odd choice, considering his non-belligerent character: but I suspect she thought his communication skills could be important.

The second assault came two years later, after the 1983 election. Arthur Scargill started by declaring an overtime ban, and then took the miners out on strike early in 1984. The *casus belli* this time was that there were to be no more pit closures, although many pit closures were necessary if the coal industry was ever to get close to a high standard of efficiency. As Margaret Thatcher had expected, it was not a normal industrial dispute between managers and men, but a political challenge to the elected Government by a Marxist revolutionary, riding on the back of the genuine fears of the coalminers about the future of their pits.

The situation got nastier through the summer of 1984, with scenes ever more violent, and deeds ever more barbaric, appearing nightly on the television screens. Margaret Thatcher judged that the public and the press would realize that this was no ordinary industrial dispute. In July, she felt strong enough in that judgement to make her famous allegation that the threat came from the 'enemies within'.

I was a member of the small group that Margaret Thatcher formed to fight the miners' strike, comprising those ministers who had a part to play in handling the situation. As Transport Secretary, I had to do my best to ensure that all coal possible was moved from pits to power stations, especially from the pits in the Nottinghamshire Coalfield where a breakaway union – the Union of Democratic Mineworkers – set up in defiance of Scargill and for the purpose of keeping the pits working. I had also to try to avert two attempts to get the docks out in sympathy with the miners. The group met frequently and regularly until the miners returned to work.

Throughout Margaret Thatcher showed a determination to win not just the strike, but the publicity battle surrounding it. Many media men were sympathetic to Scargill and they handled his publicity with considerable skill. The public approved of resisting the strike throughout – although at times it was a close-run thing. It was probably the violent and criminal acts to which some of the miners resorted, shown on television, which just kept public opinion on side.

I won't go through the detailed course of events of the miners' strike; they are well-chronicled elsewhere. But perhaps I might make a few personal comments.

The Government was throughout under the great difficulty that this was a strike ostensibly against the Coal Board, but in fact it was a strike against the Government. The Government couldn't leave it to the Chairman of the Coal Board – Ian MacGregor – not only because he was quite incapable of winning the propaganda battle, but also because far more forces had to be organized than the Coal Board alone could command: police, transport, electricity generators, docks, even the law courts. Equally, as it was a coal strike, the Government couldn't simply usurp the function of the Coal Board. This was a dilemma which Margaret Thatcher handled very skilfully, despite the attempts by the press to make attacks upon the apparent double standards involved in doing so.

It really was closer to a revolution than to a strike. The bitterness, the vindictiveness and the violence with which some behaved were ugly indeed – they were the acts of people with a deep political cause, not usually found in industrial disputes. It was very much in the nature of a Peasant's Revolt, or a Luddite assault upon new textile machinery, as well as a political attempt to humiliate and perhaps destroy the Government outside the parliamentary process. Scargill's choice of the Orgreave Coke Works as the scene of the biggest pitched battle with the police was very reminiscent of Saltley: coke works were his chosen battlegrounds. He won at Saltley; he lost at Orgreave.

He might have won at Orgreave if it hadn't been for the preparations which the Government had made. The coal stocks at the power stations held out. The maximum oil burn was achieved. Coal continued to be imported through the docks and coal moved on the roads and railways almost without interruption. The police were sufficiently well organized and equipped to prevail. Perhaps my 'confidential annexe' had been worthwhile after all. In the event, it turned out to be the exact blueprint that the Government followed.

Margaret Thatcher knew this challenge would come. Even after it was over she continued to fear it would be repeated. Indeed, there was a virtual re-run of the miners' strike outside the gates of Rupert Murdoch's Wapping newspaper plant during the winter of 1985–6. Once again powerful unions, this time the printers' unions, were locked in an often violent battle with a determined employer seeking to transform technologically the fortunes of an ailing industry. Once again, the hard left were on hand to exploit the situation and once again the Government, and the police, held firm. Margaret Thatcher somehow saw that she couldn't manoeuvre the unions into a responsible position through legislation, reactivate the supply side and create the enterprise culture without the hard left fighting back somewhere, sometime. With her knowledge of English history and the English people, she was expecting it from the beginning and she was prepared for it when it came. By winning it, she left the way clear for the enterprise culture to flourish and for the supply side to recover and prosper. It was a necessary event in the process of bringing Britain into the real post-war industrial world, and finally to lay the ghost of the sick man of Europe. But it required an iron nerve to see it through.

If she had failed, heaven knows what chaos would have ensued.

Those then were the supply-side measures which Margaret Thatcher's Government set in hand, and largely achieved. How successful were they in practice? How much did they contribute to the revival of Britain's industrial performance? There is no doubt that there was a revival – between the trough of 1981 and 1989, Britain's productivity, profitability, production, exports and investment were all transformed; alas, only to level off and decline from 1989 onwards.

These figures apply [see p. 168] to the performance of industry; the performance of the economy as a whole, including services and financial services, was good too – but it is the services sector which has been our saving grace for 50 years or more. The lament has been over the decline of industry. I do not think it is a disaster if we become an economy primarily based on the service sector. It isn't vital, as socialists seem to think, that we have a large manufacturing sector. They seem to think this mainly because Britain's old manufacturing industries used to be the basis of their political support.

Although it has declined, we do still have a large manufacturing sector in Britain. People are always making invidious comparisons between its performance and that of our competitors. How does our industrial performance compare with our chief competitors? What should be the correct industrial policy for Britain? What have we done wrong in the past? I believe there is a very simple answer to that question. We have constantly tried to achieve a fixed, and overvalued, exchange rate for our currency, while Japan and Germany have not. Whenever we have done this, our industry has begun to decline; whenever we have not done it, it has begun to prosper.

In order to demonstrate that this is so, it is necessary first to look at the industrial policy of Germany and Japan, and to see in what ways it differs from our own. Germany and Japan have certainly been more successful than we have. What is the secret of their success? Each of those two countries is, of course, very different, but both have had two favourable factors which have not applied in Britain. Both of them had much of their industry devastated during the last war, enabling them to start again with newer and better plant and equipment. Both of them have had their defence provided and paid for by the 'Allies'. This has not only saved them both the cash and the foreign exchange cost of stationing forces abroad, but they have had the benefit of the inflow of funds from the allied forces which were stationed in their countries. It has been estimated for Germany, even allowing for the offset agreement, that in the early years after the war, Britain's troops in

Germany alone turned a sizeable German payments deficit with Britain into a sizeable surplus. But that is about as far as their advantages go.

There is a belief that both countries subsidize industry from taxpayers' funds. Certainly in recent years that is not true, and in earlier years I suspect Britain paid higher industrial subsidies per capita than either of them. The Japanese MITI – the exact equivalent of the DTI – had in 1990 a budget smaller than the pro rata budget of DTI. In Germany industrial subsidies such as these would be in breach of the competition rules of the Community. Although there are areas of German industry which have been subsidized – aircraft production, for instance – the vast majority has not received any help for many years now. This cannot be the reason for the success of either country.

Some claim that these countries spend more on training skilled labour and on research than we do. They may do so – but it is industry which spends the money, not the Government. In this country there are large taxpayers' payments towards the cost of training – in Germany and Japan there are none. The Japanese do not use public money to pay for research unless it be basic research or research which the Government wants done for its own purposes, rather as we now do in Britain. Germany does pay more money to industry for research, although they claim its purpose is limited to basic research. If anything, British industry has the best overall deal in these areas, although the Government may be spending too little on basic research.

British industry has the best deal too over industrial taxation, which is much lower in the UK than in West Germany or Japan. This is also the case with labour costs: both wages and taxes on labour are much lower here. In Germany such taxes are in the region of 80–120 per cent. After the supply-side reforms, particularly the trade union reforms which Margaret Thatcher's Government put through, there is no disadvantage the British industrial climate suffers, as compared to these other countries. Indeed, it is clear that Britain has at least an equally favourable regime for industrial success. Evidence of this is the large number of foreign manufacturing firms which set up in Britain in the 1980s.

Some say the reason for the success of Germany and Japan is that they each have their own form of intimate financial relationship between banks, government and industry. In Japan there is certainly a network of cross-shareholdings both between industrial companies and between the banks and companies; but the Government does not appear to be involved. In Germany the Government is not involved either, but it is true that the banks hold very large amounts of the equity of German companies. This arrangement enables German companies to pay lower dividends than in Britain. That is certainly an advantage, but in no way does it outweigh the disadvantage of high German labour taxes. Many in Germany now want to restrict the banks to holding no more than 5 per cent of the equity of any one company, because they think it is an anti-competitive practice. All three systems are different, but I don't believe the differences give us a particular disadvantage.

There has recently been a spirited debate in Britain alleging that British industry suffers from 'short-termism', meaning that investors look only to high profits in the short term. There is some truth in this, although many would argue that it is merely the market working to allocate capital to the companies that can use it most profitably. The phenomenon shows itself too in a higher incidence of contested takeovers although, again, many would argue that this is just the market working effectively to allow good management to drive out bad. I myself, after much study, found it hard to decide whether this undoubted difference between Britain and Germany and Japan was beneficial or deleterious. The same phenomenon arises in America, and the debate there has also been inconclusive. I cannot bring myself to believe that it is an important element in our difficulties, especially when set against the much lower taxes and labour costs which pertain in Britain: indeed, many economists believe it is to our advantage.

Another charge, against Japan especially, is that they have a closed, or protected, domestic market. This can hardly be true of Germany since it is within the Single European Market, although there are still some restrictions. But it certainly isn't true for manufacturing industry in Japan either. When Margaret Thatcher visited Japan in September 1989 she had only three items on her shopping list of restrictions to ask the Japanese to remove: restrictions on imports of whisky and leather and the denial to us of two more seats for British firms on the Tokyo Stock Exchange. When I went in May 1990 there was only one of these left – the protection of the leather industry. It is true that selling into Japan requires a high initial investment in order to penetrate the distribution and retail chain. But many British companies have done so successfully. Japan, and Germany too, are indeed hard markets into which to sell. But this is not because of protection; it is because of a national prejudice to buy from home suppliers and the need for exporters to offer better value for money than can be obtained locally.

us, no one of the three countries – Britain, Japan or Germany – a totally open market, but the markets are so nearly open that the goods which represent the best value for money are almost always the ones that will sell. In addition, the tax regime, and the conditions under which industry operates generally, are very similar in all three countries. Each has its advantages, but the big advantage that Britain now has is relatively low wages compared to Japan and Germany, and low taxes on those wages.

In fact, we did better in overall terms than Germany – and, for that matter, France and Italy – over the decade of the 1980s. Our annual average real economic growth was 2.7 per cent, Germany's 2.0 per cent, France's 2.1 per cent, and Italy's 2.3 per cent. We actually came very close to the Japanese rate of growth over that period. But that was in the 1980s. From 1945 until 1981 the record was the other way round.

When I was Secretary of State for Trade and Industry from 1989 to 1990, I remember thinking how completely powerless I was to take any action to help industry as the 1990 squeeze began to bite. The policies which most affect industry – the interest rate and the exchange rate and taxation policy – were all decided by the Chancellor, and in secret. There was no collective decision-making: the needs of industry went unrepresented. True, I had access to the Chancellor, but it is an astonishing thing that the minister responsible for the health of industry is not privy to the making of the policy in the areas which most affect it. I argued against the 'shadowing the Deutschemark (DM)' policy on grounds that it would weaken industry's competitiveness – but I didn't believe that was remotely in Nigel Lawson's mind when he set out the policy. He was purely concerned with the macroeconomics.

I believe that this is a large part of the reason why Britain has fallen behind. This is demonstrated too if we analyse when we fell behind and when we have prospered. I do not believe one can simply explain it all away by saying we do not work as hard as the others, or that they have better management. The British people work as hard as anyone, and can manage as well.

It was the 19th century that was Britain's industrial heyday. We were the first industrial nation in the field as a result of the Industrial Revolution. We had a vast, protected market in the shape of the Empire. We had a laissez-faire industrial regime. The exchange rate was never a problem because Victorian Chancellors never printed money and never caused inflation. The money supply was kept continuously under strict control. We dominated the world until the end of the century.

If one goes back over the 20th century, when our industrial decline began to set in, one will find only two periods (apart from periods when we were at war) when British business recovered and began to prosper and grow. One was from 1933 to 1938 and the other was from 1981 to 1989. In both these periods the pound sterling was allowed to float freely. After about a two-year time lag, industry began to prosper. For all the other periods (leaving aside the wars) British industry suffered and declined: we lost world market share. During all these periods the pound was 'managed' in some way or another – the Gold Standard, the Bretton Woods Agreement, and later 'shadowing the DM' and finally the Exchange Rate Mechanism (ERM). All these artificial devices were designed to keep the pound higher than the markets would otherwise have it. As a result, our companies' ability to sell profitably was markedly reduced.

This is why the latest golden age of British industry was from the trough of 1981 until the peak of 1989. Not only did we put the right supply side policies in place, but the pound was allowed to float freely. The fact that it was high in the early years of the period did not mean that it was overvalued: indeed, as I shall show, we had a positive trade balance, even excluding oil and invisible exports, over the period. The trade balance only deteriorated rapidly when we started to shadow the DM in 1987, and it remained very poor indeed up to the time of writing owing to the policy of shadowing the DM being reinforced by our joining the ERM.

Germany and Japan have never allowed their currencies to be held at any artificial value, unless it be at a lower value than the markets would have it. Some may point out that Germany has been a member of the ERM since its inception. That is indeed true, but its effect has been to keep the DM if anything slightly below its true market value. Effectively the DM floats against the dollar and the yen and as the strongest currency in the ERM it tends to pull the other ERM currencies up and the DM perhaps marginally down. Membership of the ERM has never caused the DM to be overvalued against any currency in the world.

The inevitable consequence of seeking to peg the pound at a higher level than it would otherwise be is that the DM and the yen are at a lower level against the pound than they would otherwise be. This gives the opportunity for those two higher-cost economies to sell heavily into Britain and also to destabilize British industry by taking its markets or forcing it to sell at insufficient profit. The dilemma of industry when it is internationally uncompetitive is awful indeed. It either does not sell, in which case it declines, or it sells at insufficient profit, in which case it becomes starved of the necessary money for investment, training, research and development. The single most telling statistic is that over the period 1981 to 1990, British industrial profits quadrupled. Industry for once earned the money for the investment that is vital for success. Since that time, profits have fallen away rapidly because we have started again to manage the currency at too high an exchange rate.

Industry must have continuity in its ability to compete profitably in world markets. Investment needs to increase every year if we are to keep up with our competitors – modern production gets more and more capital intensive. The secret of success is very largely to be found in devoting huge sums to investing in training, research and modern plant. So the exchange rate, which determines whether or not industry can compete profitably, must always be allowed to float freely. It is no good having periods of floating, followed by periods of fixing it too high: during such periods the necessary profit to fund investment cannot be earned and we fall behind. Both Germany and Japan have either floated freely, or contrived to undervalue their currencies ever since the Second World War. That is the secret of their success.

The irony of it all is that when industry becomes uncompetitive owing to too high an exchange rate and it cannot make sufficient profit it turns to the Government for subsidy. It is impossible to blame industry for this. Government having denied it the means to prosper by overvaluing the currency, industry turns to the Government to make good the shortfall. Nationalization, investment grants, investment allowances, regional grants, selective employment grants and just straight grants have all been paid to British industry in vast quantities over the years. They have done nothing to make industry more competitive; they merely help industry to survive, not to prosper. It is significant that during the 1980s industry received no help and asked for none. Now that it has been brought to its knees by high interest rates and an overvalued pound again, the clamour from industry for subsidy is once more loud. But grants can never solve the problem: there is no substitute for being able to compete profitably. There is no comfort for the Labour Party in this analysis.

The answer is so simple; let the pound float. Indeed, the lesson of this book is that freely floating currency would be the best way to run our economy, as well as the best way to achieve a prosperous and successful manufacturing industry. Margaret Thatcher knew that; she did it from 1979 to 1987, and it worked. The tragedy was that she got pushed off course by Nigel Lawson in 1987, as I shall show. 'There is no way in which one can buck the market,' she said then. If only she'd stuck to it.

4

THE PUBLIC SERVICES

THE PHRASE 'THE social market economy' has lately become fashionable again. It is used by some current Tory ministers both as a way to emulate the policies of the German Christian Democrats, and as a way of bringing the two parties closer together. It seems to imply that the main point of the free market is to provide the resources for the social services and lavish provision of those services for all is the main purpose of political life. This is a very large change of emphasis from what Margaret Thatcher believed. But the phrase 'social market economy' was the one that Keith Joseph used in 1974 when he preached in the wilderness before the eventual emergence of Margaret Thatcher. It was the literal translation of *Soziale Marktwirtschaft*, the economic system that had worked so well in Germany during the post-war years of spectacular economic success. Keith Joseph was attracted to the *Soziale Marktwirtschaft* because, in economic terms, it was demonstrably successful, and it also provided for a sufficient level of social provision. Indeed, the phrase neatly conveyed the idea that social idealism was unrealistic *without* market economics. What Keith Joseph meant by a 'social market economy' was a market economy with social obligations. He campaigned for the Tory Party to accept the full implications of the market economy – free and fair competition, no subsidies, private ownership, control of the money supply, free trade, disciplined trade unions and an end to consensus. But he recognized that there had to be a public sector and that modern governments had obligations to maintain it efficiently: properly fund it, and keep it free to the customer. In the public sector were defence, police, fire services, public and local government administration, roads, the legal system and many other smaller public services. But it also included social security – the essential safety net for those who fell on hard times, a National Health Service free to the patient, the provision of free education for those who could not pay for it themselves, and subsidies for those who could not afford the market

78

price of a home. The emphasis was on provision for those who could not afford private health, education or housing.

This was only traditional Tory policy – the whole party accepted it; so did Margaret Thatcher – so did I. The argument had been about extending the list of public services and public spending into areas beyond these, like industry, investment on research, regional subsidies, employment creation, and a host of other grey areas. Keith Joseph wanted to define much more closely the criteria for paying for things with taxpayers' money – he didn't want to abolish the public sector. He wanted to target the welfare budget on those who really needed help, and in a way that didn't distort the working of the market. He wanted to spend taxpayers' money only on those things that the market wouldn't provide, and to do it much more effectively. That was what he meant by the 'social market economy.' He did not mean that it was preferable to provide the services collectively for all, which is apparently the latest interpretation.

Margaret Thatcher, when she came to power, embraced these ideals, but made some additions of her own. She disliked what she called 'the dependency culture.' By this she meant a society where people became dependent on the State for their education, or health care, or pensions, or housing, and in some cases their income. When this came about, people had no choice, and could not escape, or aspire to escape, from the monopoly provider of the service – the State. They were impoverished through extra taxation to pay for the services they received, making them more dependent still. Their dependency on the State made them owe political allegiance to their benevolent political masters who provided these services 'free.' Since there was no competition, the standards of the monopoly providers became slack, and the services more and more run for the benefit of the staff rather than the customer. The socialist aspires to such a society; to Margaret Thatcher it was anathema.

Moreover, she had observed that some people so ordered their lives as to maximize their drawings from State funds. If there is a grant to assist with the children of single-parent families, then some people will arrange to be in a situation where they qualify for it. If a benefit is available for those with children, then some people will have children simply to draw the benefit. If unemployment benefit makes some people better off than they were in work, then some will become unemployed deliberately.

There were more and worse examples of the dependency culture. Many left-wing councils decided to make a stand against the advancing tide of Thatcherism. They would keep council house rents at absurdly low levels and expect political loyalty to the council in return. They would pay grants out of ratepayers' money to lesbian and gay groups and to many other groups, such as ethnic minority groups, on the assumption that these too would become dependent and vote for the council that was the distributor to them of other people's money. One council even distributed a Christmas hamper free to all its tenants!

Dependency had become an industry by the end of the 1970s. Experts, including lawyers, were employed by the lobbies to interpret the law in order to obtain the maximum benefit for each group of beneficiaries. Careful and accurate guidance notes were issued through the Citizen's Advice Bureaux and elsewhere, setting out how to maximize individual entitlement; test cases were brought before the courts. The lobbies mounted campaigns in the press and in Parliament to have this or that benefit extended or increased. Margaret Thatcher feared that eventually too many of the population would be living off too few. She also disliked the whole concept. Welfare was for those who were in true need, not a way of redistributing income on egalitarian principles. She also wanted to weaken the power base of socialism by emancipating people like council house tenants on cheap rents, who became dependent upon socialists keeping them cheap.

Margaret Thatcher also included in her definition of the social market economy the need to keep public spending to a minimum. In 1979, public spending was high as a proportion of Gross National Product in Britain and was growing. She wanted to reverse the trend and to reduce taxes. She strongly believed that people knew better than the State how to spend their own money. The more of their own money they could keep, the more freedom and the more choice they would have, and the more they would be responsible citizens. She wanted to give people the maximum possible choice in the important areas of life – like schooling, health care, housing, and provision for retirement. She particularly strongly defended the right of people to opt out of State provision in health and education and to pay for a better service in the private sector. Indeed, she saw State provision in these areas as a free service necessary for those who could not afford higher standards, but she hoped that their numbers would dwindle as more and more families became able to afford to choose those higher standards in the private sector for themselves. She never believed it was either possible or desirable to bring standards in the public service up to the highest levels in the private sector: to do so would be enormously expensive. It would also destroy an area of choice, an ambition for which to strive, and restore an element of the dependency culture. She would prefer to see more and more people opting for private provision, leaving the State services as the safety net for those who couldn't afford to opt out. This is very different from the current search for public services which are so good that no one will want to use the private sector.

Thus, the two policies were totally interdependent. If people were to have their own money to pay for the service they chose, taxes must be reduced. If taxes were to be reduced, so must public spending. That could only be done by weeding out the dependency culture and concentrating public spending on those in real need.

She also believed strongly in the concept of the 'property-owning democracy' – a concept first articulated by Anthony Eden, but a course advanced hardly at all by successive Tory governments hitherto. To own one's own house, or business, or the capital which produced one's retirement income extended freedom of choice, gave people a stake in the nation's wealth, and required less taxpayers' money to be spent on them. It produced a large and growing number of people who were not 'dependent.'

All this seems very reasonable set out in terms of principles. But to achieve these principles involved taking on huge lobbies and interest groups, articulate representatives of those who benefited from the dependency culture. It also struck at three of the central articles of faith of socialism, the need for the State to redistribute income within society; egalitarianism; and the necessity for the State to provide essential services for all. The trade unions in the public services were particularly powerful – Confederation of Health Service Employees (COHSE), National Union of Public Employees (NUPE), the National Union of Teachers (NUT), National Association of Local Government Officers (NALGO) and the British Medical Association (BMA) etc. They saw their role as to maximize the number of their members in each service and to maximize the pay and condition of their members as well. They could never be subjected to the market disciplines which eventually overcame the power of trade unions in the private sector – there were no markets. All these – the lobbies, the beneficiaries, the left in politics and the trade unions – combined to defend the social public services, more or less as they were, against the expected onslaughts of the new Government in 1979.

Margaret Thatcher knew what she was up against. Any move to rationalize policy in this area would be, and was, greeted with cries of shame and outrage. The customers were immediately stimulated to protest. If better management was pursued, better use of manpower or higher productivity suggested, the same campaign of opposition was mounted. The strike weapon was often threatened and often used – both to preserve outdated working practices and to extract high pay increases. Always these campaigns were fought on behalf of the customers – the patients of the National Health Service (NHS), pupils at school, or drawers of benefit. Often the real purpose of the strikes was the welfare of the providers of the service – their numbers, their pay, conditions and working practices. The irony was that the public services demonstrated time and time again that they were producer-orientated, not consumer-orientated. I suspected they always would be. That is what happens with monopoly provision, be it in industry or in the public services.

I myself believed we would never overcome these difficulties while the public services were organized as monopoly state providers. I never questioned that these services should continue to be free to the consumer. But that didn't make it impossible to organize them in more efficient ways. One such way was to have at least 'comparable competition' so that the performance of one unit could be compared with the performance of another – a solution we later moved towards in health. It also seemed possible to provide some of the services under the control of the customers – a solution we later came to adopt to some extent in education and in housing. It seemed to me vital to bypass as far as possible the power of the monopoly unions, and another way forward was to have small, self-governing units which would go some way in that direction; that too we later tried in schools.

I also wanted to see proper costing and cost-control techniques introduced into the management of the services. Knowing what everything costs is a vital tool of management. It was virtually non-existent in the Health Service and in local authorities. With proper costing it is possible not only to improve value for money, but also to get at least some of the benefits that come from comparative competition. In turn, it leads to being able to charge for extra non-essential services which should not be free – like privacy in a hospital or lessons in playing the tuba in schools.

The Bow Group had published a pamphlet which I wrote in 1977, putting forward some of these ideas. It received little or no attention, as is often the way with political pamphlets. It seemed way out in the balmy days of socialist dominance. Beyond arguing for a modest 'hotel charge' for those in hospital, I accepted that the provision of these services should remain free; but I argued that much could be done to improve their performance and reduce the power of the unions to have them run for the benefit of their members rather than the benefit of the customers. The standards could be improved and the cost cut, I argued.

I had a talk with Margaret Thatcher about all these ideas soon after she became Prime Minister. She was adamant that she would not start down this sort of road at the beginning. There was enough to do sorting out industry, the economy, taxation and the trade unions. 'The supply side must come first,' she said. She didn't want to stir up the lobbies in the public services as well. She felt that we could come to that in a few years' time. The area where she could see an easy way to start was the sale of council housing, but the rest must wait. I understood her caution, and the reasons for it, but I was not entirely convinced that it was wise.

In the event, the lobbies in the public services were far from quiescent. They stirred themselves up – partly, I think, because, since no onslaught came from the Government, they believed their position was secure, and they could afford to turn the onslaught onto the Government instead. Vital reforms which could have saved money were delayed. The quality of service and the efficiency of provision remained woefully inadequate throughout the decade, a just complaint which was to haunt her later. Educational standards and health service quality were the subject of much justified criticism throughout her time in office.

Her critics always said that, far from the services needing reforming, the reason for these deficiencies was the 'cuts'. It became a constant refrain to blame the 'cuts'. The 1987 election was very much about the Health Service 'cuts'. Unscrupulous tactics were used by the media to ram the campaign home. A television crew visited a Gloucester hospital and interviewed the outpatients to get complaints about the waiting lists and the 'cuts'. There was quite a local storm because they refused to accept the views of the many who were satisfied customers and only recorded the views of the two who could be persuaded to complain.

Every deficiency identified in the field of education or health provision was blamed on the alleged 'cuts'. The 'cuts' in the social security budget had even driven those on benefits close to starvation. The adverse publicity and the oft-repeated use of the word 'cuts' more or less convinced the public that these had indeed taken place.

The actual figures for public spending on these three areas of policy are interesting. They show that the real increase on each programme (that is, over and above allowing for inflation) between 1979–80 and 1990–1 was:

Health	+37%
Social Security	+35%
Education and Science	+16%

During the same period, the Gross Domestic Product grew by about 25 per cent. So not only had the health and social security programmes secured huge increases, but those increases were far bigger than the increase in the national income. Only for education was it less, but this was because the numbers of pupils had fallen. Spending per pupil grew by 42 per cent.

These figures make one marvel at the ability of critics and the media to make the word 'cuts' stick. Even to suggest that these were cuts was brazen. Eventually I discovered the meaning of the word 'cuts' in a conversation with some left-wing teachers from my constituency who used the phrase as a sort of war-cry. What they meant went like this: 'This year my budget is £100 million; next year I want £150 million. You have offered me £120 million. Therefore I have had a cut of £30 million.' A purist would call this an increase of £20 million, but so passionate were the spenders, so deeply did they hate Margaret Thatcher, that their sheer zeal persuaded them, and much of the media, that there really were savage cuts in all the social programmes.

The Cabinet was rather nonplussed by these assaults. Treasury ministers knew they had allowed large increases in the social programmes, and spending ministers knew they were getting most of what they asked for. We jointly decided on a series of speeches to try to get the figures across to prove there were no cuts: but such speeches got no coverage. The media had decided there were 'savage cuts' and they couldn't allow themselves to be shown to be wrong.

I draw two rather melancholy conclusions from all this. The first is that would-be public spenders are blind to where the money comes from. They see the Government as a rich and stingy old Scrooge, who has plenty of money but, out of spite alone, prefers to hoard it rather than see it spent on good causes. To them it is legitimate to see the Government in terms of a rich Victorian mill owner who piled up his profits by sweating the labour that earned those profits for him; the old mainspring of socialism which arose out of the Industrial Revolution and the class war. The adjective employed is still 'mean', implying that money which could have been spent on welfare has been squandered on champagne, and money which could have been used to pay higher wages has been spent on yachts in the Mediterranean. They cannot see, or prefer not to see, that any money the Government spends has to come from the taxpayers (or worse, from abusing the taxpayers by debasing the currency). Taxpayers too have problems; the majority of them, in fact, are among the poorer sections of society. The idea of a Government wanting to be frugal in relation to the amount it took from poorer people by way of taxation simply did not enter their heads. This open and loudmouthed use of the word 'meanness' to criticize the Government because it felt it also had a duty to minimize the demands it made upon the citizens, in fact showed how little such people cared for the working people of Britain.

Often at my surgeries people would tell me they would willingly pay a little more tax towards higher public spending on this or that programme. No doubt they felt secure that they would not be taken at their word, so that they could enjoy the luxury of a self-sacrifice which they were unlikely to have to make. The same people sang a very different tune when their Community Charge came in – and the vast bulk of the Community Charge goes on education, personal social services and housing.

The other conclusion I draw from all this is equally uncomfortable. Margaret Thatcher's Government did not, in fact, succeed in controlling, let alone cutting, expenditure on the public services. The spending grew strongly in real terms. She got the worst of all worlds. She got the obloquy of the 'cuts' and she had to spend much more on the services as well. She had only achieved, at the end of eleven-and-a-half years, limited progress towards breaking down the dependency culture. The exception to this is housing, where much was achieved, as I shall show; but equally there was much more to do. In health and education and pensions, however, her reforms came too late, and in some cases were too timid, to bring results either on a sufficient level or in a sufficient timescale. She had to finance the ever-increasing costs of the same poorly organized monopoly public services, dominated by the trade unions. While she was being blamed for the 'cuts', the socialists somehow managed to manoeuvre the public discontent with service standards away from the socialist system by which they were provided and onto the Government, which was known to be hostile towards the system. The 'cuts' war-cry was the vehicle, however dishonest it may seem, by which this sleight of hand was achieved.

In retrospect, I believe she should have started on reform much sooner. The 1983 to 1987 Parliament has often been described as a wasted opportunity: that was the time when a serious effort to effect reform should have been made. There would have been time to see the results come through. I wish I had gone to reason with her before the 1983 election, as I had done in 1979, that her second term should have been devoted to the demand side: the supply side still dominated the programme in those years, although the programme, in fact, became rather thin. I felt I hadn't the influence to change her priorities. In any case, it wasn't easy for anyone to change Margaret Thatcher's priorities.

She did come to realize that she needed to give priority to reform of the demand side of the economy in early 1987. Owing to the success of the economy and the general feeling of prosperity, the Government suddenly became popular in the winter of 1986-7. In the public opinion poll ratings, the Tory lead over Labour rose from nothing at the beginning of 1986 to 12 per cent by the early spring of 1987. By that time it looked very likely that an election could be won. June was Margaret Thatcher's favourite month – twice already she had won elections in early summer, before the July blues set in. If she could win a June election – after a respectable four years of governing – then June was when she felt the election should be.

She resolved in early 1987 that she must embark upon a reform of the public services. There followed a remarkable series of meetings of groups of cabinet ministers concerned with subjects in which she was taking a 'special interest'. These subjects were housing and education. The Health Service reforms came later – after the election. She still feared that the reform of the NHS was too sensitive a topic to expose to the electorate, although, indeed, the poor quality of the NHS was a major issue in the 1987 election. Pensions and social security fall into a different time pattern. I will describe events as they unfolded in relation to all four of these important policy areas: housing, education, health and social security. Each was different – the problems, the solutions, the politics, the timing, all varied. The important point is that this sudden commendable burst of activity probably came too late: 1983-7 was a window of opportunity which, alas, she missed.

Housing

Housing was the area where Margaret Thatcher thought it was easiest to start to dismantle the dependency culture. It was not just poor people who were living in subsidized houses in 1979 – be they council or housing association houses. Many families had started in subsidized accommodation – the shortage of housing after the war had given them no opportunity to start anywhere else. The Macmillan Government had greatly increased the stock of council houses – by 1979 there were 5.4 million families living in publicly-owned houses, and 9.1 million in their own homes. Many council tenants were quite well off, and so an obvious way of making them into home owners was to allow them to buy their council houses. In addition, it was made attractive by allowing large discounts to compensate tenants for rent already paid. These discounts went up to 55 per cent, according to how long the tenancy had been held.

By the end of 1990, over one million houses were sold. This probably is close to the maximum number that are likely to be sold – those who will never want to buy will remain. Many live in properties that they do not want to buy because they are so unattractive – flats in tower blocks, for example. Many are too poor to be able to afford the mortgage necessary to purchase and the cost of keeping them in good order. Many just prefer to rent rather than to buy. So the question arose as to how best to provide for those who will remain tenants.

This was the problem that I came up against in 1986 when I became Secretary of State for the Environment. I came to the conclusion that we should seek to provide for these from the three main suppliers of housing to rent – councils, housing associations and private landlords. This way we could get the maximum number of houses available for renting, and hopefully at least some competition. I was determined to weaken the almost incestuous relationship between some councils and their tenants. Absurdly low rents, and a monopoly position in providing rented housing, allowed some councils to make their tenants entirely dependent upon them. They received a rotten service – repairs and maintenance and improvements were minimal – yet the tenants were trapped in their houses by the lack of availability of alternative accommodation to rent, and by such cheap rents that no other landlord could match them, even if he had a house to offer them. The tenants felt beholden to the Council, and most paid the price expected of them by giving their political support to them.

One Tory chairman of a council housing committee even told me that there was an agreement between the three political parties that the Council's rents would not be raised in an election year. As a third of the Council had to be re-elected every year, the rents had hardly been raised for years! The problem was not confined to Labour councils: the ratepayers in many areas were being milked to subsidize the council tenants, rich and poor alike, for political reasons, even though housing benefit was available for poor tenants.

I saw the solution as being to provide housing benefit on a sufficiently generous scale to enable all tenants to be in a position to pay their rents, and at the same time to bring rents up towards market levels. This would put all three classes of landlord – councils, housing associations and private landlords – into the same competitive position, giving tenants a choice, and putting the councils into a position where they had to improve their standard of service if they were to retain their tenants. In addition, I suggested giving tenants the right to form a cooperative to manage their own properties – in other words, to opt out of council management with the same level of subsidies as they received from the council. In this way, I hoped through time to provide a diversity of provision for rented accommodation, a large reduction in the costs to the State of providing public housing, and a choice of landlords for tenants, while ensuring that everyone could afford a decent home.

Ian Gow, when Housing Minister under Patrick Jenkin from 1983 to 1985, had put a not dissimilar plan to the Cabinet – a plan to free private sector rents for new lettings, and to make housing benefit available to help less well-off tenants pay the market rents that resulted. But Margaret Thatcher, with the Cabinet's agreement, had turned it down. There was no limit to the level to which rents could have been increased, and consequently no limit to the cost of housing benefit. So the Rent Acts had remained. By 1987, however, Margaret Thatcher had come to the conclusion that she must begin to attack the dependency culture, and she was at last prepared to tackle the Rent Acts. They had been in existence since 1919, and had had the dubiously successful result of reducing private rented properties from 7 million to 2.3 million. I myself was determined to end such stupid and spiteful legislation, which had caused so much hardship to many poor landlords, and yet reduced the stock of homes to rent so drastically.

So she was receptive to the housing reforms I proposed. These were considered in the usual small ad hoc group of about six ministers who were the ones concerned, in the few weeks before the 1987 election. The pressure of time was such that we met almost daily, and the policies which resulted in the Housing Act 1989 were agreed and put into the Manifesto. One further provision was added: the proposal to

(*Top*) Sir Keith Joseph speaks at the 1977 Party Conference, with Margaret Thatcher attentive alongside him. 'We greatly admired Keith Joseph. He had a fine intellect and was exceedingly brave in stating his opinions. I think that he was right not to offer himself for the leadership ... even he would admit that he was less incisive in taking action than Mrs Thatcher turned out to be.'

(*above*) The Shadow Cabinet (left to right): Teddy Taylor, Lord Carrington, William Whitelaw, Margaret Thatcher, Sir Keith Joseph, Angus Maude, Francis Pym, Patrick Jenkin, Tom King, Humphrey Atkins, Norman St John Stevas, John Nott, James Prior, Lord Thorneycroft, Sir Geoffrey Howe, Sir Michael Havers, John Davies.

(Right) Triumph at
the Party
Conference, 1979.
(Left to right.)
Norman St John
Stevas, Francis
Pym and Lord
Carrington applaud
Margaret Thatcher.

Mrs Thatcher's first Government, June 1979. The formal photograph in the pillared room at No. 10 Downing Street shows, standing, left to right; Michael Jopling, Norman Fowler, John Biffen, David Howell, Norman St John Stevas, Humphrey Atkins, George Younger, Michael Heseltine, Nicholas Edwards, Patrick Jenkin, John Nott, Mark Carlisle, Angus Maude, Sir John Hunt. Seated, from left, Sir Ian Gilmour, Lord Soames, Sir Keith Joseph, Lord Carrington, William Whitelaw, Margaret Thatcher, Lord Hailsham, Sir Geoffrey Howe, Francis Pym, James Prior, Peter Walker.

Mrs Thatcher with Airey Neave, who was killed by a bomb at the Houses of Parliament in 1979. 'She grieved greatly at his loss: perhaps she never quite got over it.'

Lord Hailsham poses outside No. 10 in 1983.

Lord Whitelaw speaks confidentially to Margaret Thatcher at the Party conference in 1985. 'I suggest that William Whitelaw's support in the early part of her partnership was vital to her survival.'

RESO

Margaret Thatcher at the Party Conference in 1982. 'Above all, she wanted to give leadership.... She was determined to change what was wrong and to lead Britain back to prosperity, success and enhanced prestige in the world. She had the iron will to do it.... It was this unshakeable resolve which made her unique among post-war politicians.'

N.U.M. President Arthur Scargill, flanked by Mick McGahey, during the Miners' Strike. 'In my view, Margaret Thatcher always knew, even as far back as 1978, that she would face a pitched battle mounted by Arthur Scargill. It would be ostensibly an industrial dispute, but in reality a political assault designed to overthrow her Government.'

The strike at Easington, Co. Durham, in September 1984.

Demonstrators against 'the Cuts' outside the Tory Party Conference, 1983. 'The adverse publicity and oft-repeated use of the word 'cuts' more or less convinced the public that these had indeed taken place.... In fact the health and social security programmes had secured huge increases, far bigger than the increase in the national income.'

Poll tax protesters in Parliament Square, March 1990. 'The principle of ability to pay had been swamped by the unexpectedly high levels of the Charge in the first year.'

Geoffrey Howe presents his budget, March 1982. 'Despite the pressure from all the critics, Margaret Thatcher and Geoffrey Howe held firm to the strategy and by 1982 the beneficial results began to be discernible and the wets became more muted.'

Geoffrey Howe's Treasury team on Budget Day, 1983. Left to right: Nicholas Ridley, Sir Barney Hayhoe, John Wakeham, Geoffrey Howe, Jock Bruce Gardyne, Leon Brittan. 'Geoffrey Howe was not an easy man to work for. Delegation was not a word he understood. . . . he was careful, thorough and lugubrious.'

(*Below*) Nicholas Ridley, Margaret Thatcher and Lord Caithness at the opening of the Ozone Conference in London, 1989. 'It is technically easy and not too expensive to save the ozone layer; all that is needed is . . . international agreement.'

The famous litter-collecting stunt. 'All went well until the press found out from the park attendants that they had been mysteriously told to distribute litter there earlier that morning.'

(*Below*) Nicholas Ridley.

create Housing Action Trusts in order to concentrate public money on repairing the very worst council slums in the country. In the event it proved most unpopular and didn't achieve its objective.

The housing reforms could only achieve their full objective slowly. The private sector has to be confident that there will not be a Labour Government which might reimpose something like the Rent Acts. Council rents must be allowed to rise closer to market rents before there can be fair competition between the private and the public sector: and the gap remains a large one. The Treasury will have to allow enough money for housing benefit as that happens. There is a much bigger saving to public funds if the public sector does not have to provide new houses and goes on selling existing ones, than the extra needed for housing benefit. It is too early to judge whether we will ever get back to a proper rented housing market. All we did was to set the policy in motion. Even then, the cost to public funds of housing fell by 54 per cent in real terms during Margaret Thatcher's prime minister-ship. This was achieved by weaning people out of council housing, through the Right-to-Buy, through reinvigorating the private sector, and through concentrating the subsidy on people rather than on bricks and mortar. In terms of the dependency culture, by 1989 3.4 million more families became home owners, and the total number of council tenants had fallen by 1.2 million since 1979.

My period at the Department of the Environment – from 1986 to 1989 – was an exceptionally difficult one for housing, because a large shortage of homes developed in the southern half of the country. This was due to the unparalleled prosperity of the time. One of the first things people seek when they become more prosperous is better living conditions. They want to escape from overcrowding. Young people want to leave their parents' home and establish their own. Unhappy couples divorce and separate. Families want grandparents to move out into their own homes. All these social changes accelerated as people could afford the extra houses needed. In addition, the population were living much longer. It was for all these reasons that the extra demand for houses mushroomed at the time. Moreover, most of the extra demand was for single person accommodation – divorced people, widows and widowers, spinsters and bachelors; many had had to live with relatives before. For so many people to be freed from over-crowded conditions and from living with others on less than happy terms was a considerable social advance and one that I welcomed. But my problem was how to see that the houses were provided.

Prosperity both created the demand and created the resistance to the demand being met. The established householders in the south of England were even more prosperous – they did not want their 'secluded residences' to become less secluded. They hated the thought of new houses, new estates, or even new towns. They objected violently to every application for planning permission – they fought all new development as if it were a sort of deadly pollution. They interpreted Margaret Thatcher's declaration of war against the 'greenhouse effect' and her espousal of the cause of protecting the environment as meaning that their environment should be protected from new housing. In fact, Margaret Thatcher was as concerned as I was at the difficulty we had in getting enough land upon which to build houses, factories and other premises. I had to take the brunt of what I can only describe as fury as I tried to get enough building land through the system to secure roofs over the heads of the population. In this I regard myself as having been very much more caring than my critics. To the extent that I didn't succeed, there developed a problem with homelessness and I was castigated for that too. Once in the House of Commons I had to answer for both 'failures' of my policy on the same day: the shortage of homes for homeless people and the excessive number of homes which had been given planning permission. Nobody wanted to see the connection – it was inconvenient to them and smoked out their prejudices: prejudices which came from the political right and left.

The word 'homelessness', in fact, is a misnomer. In law it means those who are in priority housing need, who have to be housed by the councils. More than half go into council houses straightaway; the rest into bed and breakfast accommodation. These are families and children and all those who are infirm. It is certainly true that more homes are needed, which is why I tried to revive the private rented sector, as well as increasing new building by the housing associations. The shortage of land with planning permission accentuated the problem. Much bed and breakfast accommodation was indeed dreadful. But the 'homeless' do, in fact, sleep under roofs. People thought the 'homeless' were those who slept on the Embankment in cardboard boxes. These are single people who do not qualify for priority housing need. Hostels are where they should sleep; the number of beds in hostels was continually increased to meet the need but some even seem to prefer the streets and refuse to go to empty beds in hostels. These are the drop-outs, people making a protest against society, the victims of the age we live in. There are empty houses all over the north of England, whence many of them came. One of the difficulties with housing is having to provide for people wherever they want to live. The drift from the north over the past ten years has made the problem much harder to solve.

There was one other category of people with which I had less than total sympathy – they called themselves 'one-parent families'. Margaret Thatcher was less charitable than I about these ladies. Dr John Habgood, the Archbishop of York, was even less charitable about them. Early in 1991 he said: 'Single parents who are single by choice play truant from the school of charity. A child . . . wanted as an act of defiance, wanted in extreme cases as a kind of accessory, has to carry too much of the emotional burden of its parent's needs.' Single parents were also free-riders on the system, directly exploiting the dependency culture. A young lady with a child is in 'priority housing need' – one without is not. It became a way of living for some to have one or more children by unknown men, in order to qualify for a council house. The rent and rates were paid by benefit. In addition, the lady was eligible for income support and child benefit. So, without husband, without job, and without effort, young girls could house, clothe and feed themselves at the taxpayers' expense, provided they had children. One has every sympathy for the lady with a young baby whose husband dies, or leaves her, or the girl who becomes pregnant by mistake, they deserve every help. But putting oneself in that position as a way of living, deliberately eschewing the husband's role in the family by not having one, is clearly socially undesirable. It is living off the taxpayer deliberately. It also greatly added to the housing shortage. The number of single mothers who had never been married grew from 130,000 in 1976 to 230,000 in 1986, according to the Office of Population, Census and Survey. This is apart from widowed, divorced and separated mothers, whose numbers were also growing. This was an aspect of the dependency culture to which it proved impossible to find an answer.

I remember one day canvassing in the 1987 election. I knocked on a door and a young woman opened it. I explained my business and asked her 'What do you do?' 'I'm a one parent family,' she said, 'and I want an increase in the money I get from the security.' She had three young children and they were living in appalling squalor. The idea of bearing children as a way of life still rather shocks me.

For Chris Patten, my successor at the Department of the Environment, all these problems eased as Nigel Lawson cut back prosperity through high interest rates from 1988 onwards. People could no longer afford to improve their living conditions. The pressure for more housing eased. I would rather have the prosperity and the problems notwithstanding.

Education

At the same time as Margaret Thatcher resolved to embark upon the housing reforms, she decided to reform aspects of the system of education. The results State education was producing were very poor. The number of children leaving education who could neither read nor write was a disgrace. There was no doubt that on international comparisons, Britain was performing badly. Except for those with large incomes, there was no choice of school for parents, nor did they have any say over the standards and quality of the education their children received. The quality of teaching left much to be desired. All these deficiencies were as usual blamed on the 'cuts' – which really meant that they wanted more money available for teachers' pay. Relations were bad, and there was a series of teachers' strikes throughout 1984 and 1985.

Margaret Thatcher took a very great interest in education, not only because she had been Secretary of State for Education in Ted Heath's Government, but also because she believed it was vitally important in creating the sort of society she wanted to see. She thought that it should be encouraging the enterprise culture, and not the dependency culture. A good educational system was essential for the future success of the nation.

She started first to establish a national curriculum. Kenneth Baker was then Education Secretary and together they hammered out the details. She wanted to get back to the 'three Rs', a factual teaching of history (mainly British history), and a strong emphasis on science and technology. The national curriculum is largely in place now, and it can be judged a great improvement. It took a great deal of her energies to get it the way she wanted it.

Far more difficult was the question of how to get more choice, more parental control, and higher standards into schools. There was a strong body of opinion in favour of some form of voucher scheme. The basic idea was that a voucher could be issued for each child of primary or secondary school age, and parents could encash it at the school of their choice. On the surface, it seemed an ideal solution and Margaret Thatcher was instinctively in favour of it. But it had difficulties. One problem was how far away from their home parents might choose to send their children, and who would pay for the travel costs. Another, more serious one, was what would happen if a certain school became fashionable, and another one unfashionable: would the first school be allowed to expand, and the second one to contract or even close? Wouldn't this result in a very wasteful use of school buildings? Or would a school close its doors once it was fully enrolled, in which case there was little difference between the voucher system and the existing system. Both of these difficulties could have been overcome, I believe. Choice and competition always produce some waste. The place in the school that is not taken up may well be wasted.

These, and other, difficulties had persuaded the education establishment and the Education Department, to oppose the voucher system. Successive education secretaries were asked by Margaret Thatcher to study it again; they all came to the conclusion that it was undesirable. She remained convinced of the need to find some variant of the scheme which produced parental choice; indeed, just before she fell from office, she talked of finding a way of making 'the money follow the pupil' after she had won her fourth election. But she never persuaded any of her secretaries of state to produce a workable scheme. Kenneth Baker was no exception.

Thus the difficulty in 1987 was that there were no plans for change in education before her and yet she was determined to achieve more choice for parents and higher standards for pupils. The decision to set up the City Technology Colleges had been taken some time before. These were secondary schools of some size, one each in centres of population. They were set up to give better-quality education with a strong emphasis on technology and science in order to produce the skilled workers of the future. They were paid for directly by the Exchequer.

Despite its success, this initiative was not designed to achieve Margaret Thatcher's ambitions of wider choice and higher standards for all. She decided to 'take a special interest' in the problem.

I was a member of the small group that was set up to consider the problem since I was Environment Secretary. I put forward the plan that was eventually adopted, which was to allow all schools eventually to opt out of local authority control and be run by their governors. Since the governors were largely parents, it did give parents a much greater control over their children's education. To some extent it gave more choice too – the parents could at least choose how to improve their school and change its culture. It was, in effect, a plan to give vouchers to the school as opposed to the parents. Margaret Thatcher liked the plan and eventually it was adopted, despite the unhappiness of Kenneth Baker's officials; he himself accepted it. It went into the 1987 Election Manifesto and was eventually enacted in the Education Reform Act.

It is too soon to assess how much difference 'opting out' will make to the quality of education in Britain. It has done nothing but good so far in making parents and governors more involved in the management of their schools. It is certainly removing the monolithic nature of local authority provision. It makes for diversity. I believe it will prove to have been a reform that was well worthwhile, and one upon which it will be possible to build. First, it gives a way of funding schools directly from the Exchequer, which could be used to reduce the amount of money passing through local authorities; this could be of great help in improving the Community Charge or whatever system of local taxation may be employed. Second, it makes it easier eventually to introduce some form of education voucher. The voucher system is one of the bits of unfinished business that Margaret Thatcher had still to tackle; I suspect we will continue to need more choice and more competition in schools if we are to get that really high quality which is necessary.

Both the housing and the education reforms were hammered out in a remarkably short period of time – no more than a month. By Easter 1987 I think Margaret Thatcher had decided to hold the election in June. The polls were favourable – we were 13 per cent ahead of Labour. She did not want to get too near the five-year limit of a Parliament. There was just a short period in which to work out the programme for her third Parliament after she had won again. So she drove the Education and Housing groups to complete the outlines of both policies in time for the Manifesto. We sat on into May, beyond the Dissolution of Parliament. Kenneth Baker took a lot of 'driving' – he was hesitant about the plan throughout. There were some magnificent scenes as she dragged him inch-by-inch in the direction we all wanted to go. He was pulled back by the officials in the Department of Education and Science (DES) when he got back there; many times his papers were rejected. The meetings were all conducted in good humour. I think even Kenneth Baker enjoyed them, although it was he who received the rough edge of her tongue.

These reforms should have been embarked upon years earlier, when we would have had more time to think them through. In the event, she made up for lost time in a pretty effective way.

Health

The cost of the National Health Service grew inexorably over the whole of the 1980s. Many factors came together to produce this result. More and more people lived for longer and longer, requiring more medical care towards the end of their lives. The number of people employed in the NHS grew strongly as the service struggled to keep up with this extra demand. More and more expensive drugs and medicines were invented, each better able to contribute to saving more lives, and each costing more than its predecessor. On the other hand, there was little, if any, increase in efficiency to offset these extra costs. So the cost went on rising steeply, and the patients got no improvement in the standard of service.

Margaret Thatcher resolved only to try to introduce a measure of managerial reform after the 1987 election. The Royal Commission on the National Health Service, the Chairman of which was Sir Alec Merrison, and which reported in July 1979, actually contained these words by the Commissioners: 'We had no difficulty in believing the proposition put to us by one medical witness that "we can easily spend the whole of the gross national product."' Margaret Thatcher was inclined to quote this passage quite frequently. Not only did this prediction seem to be being borne out, but standards were deteriorating. If she had started on this enterprise much earlier, there would have been time for the dividends to come through earlier. It takes at least three years to work out proposals of this nature, put them into legislative form, and get them through Parliament. Then it takes perhaps another year or two before the benefits are felt. During all this time a reforming government is vulnerable. The reactionaries, the critics, and the customers have the chance to complain bitterly about a reform, and the Government can only promise its advantages; it cannot demonstrate them. We saw this happen over the sale of council housing, trade union reform, the reform of the bus industry, education reform and a host of others. It was to be the same with the NHS reform.

The 1987 election was a bruising experience so far as the NHS was concerned. The media and the Opposition stirred up and tried to make capital out of the discontent with long waiting lists, poor standards and poor service. It was all the fault of the 'cuts'. The Cabinet that reassembled after that election were determined not to have to go through that experience again. If we were not to embark upon reform, the only solution would have been to throw unlimited extra money at the problem. We didn't want that either.

Margaret Thatcher took a 'special interest' in the Health Service reform. Soon after the 1987 election, she set up a small group consisting of herself and the relevant Ministers. They first considered the case for one of the 'refinancing' solutions to be adopted. This term covered a number of possible systems. In France, the patient is charged for medical care but 'refinanced' by the State, depending on the circumstances. In other countries various systems are used based on insurance – either private insurance or some form of compulsory State insurance. There are other systems as well. These ideas were all rejected, since the service would no longer have been free at the point of delivery and anything other than that would have aroused maximum political opposition. I nevertheless believe myself that one of these routes is the right way to go to get real managerial efficiency in the provision of health care in Britain.

Instead, a useful package of reforms was worked out which put more responsibility onto hospitals to manage their affairs and enabled the resources of the service to be more fully utilized. A measure of costing and budgetary control was introduced. An attempt was made to employ all available hospital facilities more efficiently by ending restrictions on patients being able to go to any hospital where there was a bed available.

In July 1988, Margaret Thatcher split the Department of Health and Social Security into its two constituent parts, leaving John Moore as Social Security Secretary. She appointed Kenneth Clarke Secretary of State for Health, with responsibility for the Health Service reforms. Kenneth Clarke early on resolved to extend reform to the General Practitioners as well as the hospitals. He rewrote their contract with the NHS, and introduced a number of other changes; larger practices could operate independently with their own budget, and each doctor was given his own drug budget in order to assess the cost of his prescriptions.

These proposals were met with a storm of protest from the doctors. They resolved not only to campaign against the reforms that affected them directly, but also against the proposals for hospitals.

Doctors had largely taken the place of vicars in the local community as the respected and responsible persons to whom people can turn for advice, even confession. They are believed to be non-political, honest and impartial. They set up a chorus of complaint about these relatively minor changes in the NHS, which Kenneth Clarke was trying to put through Parliament. Many people automatically believed them and took up their cause with their MP. The doctors handed out protest letters or put up notices in their surgeries asking their patients to write and complain.

My own view about the reforms was that we were being 'hung for stealing a lamb'. I am sure they are worthwhile and will lead to some improvements and better use of the resources for the further development of the Service. They are at least a first step in the direction of trying to get some management into the NHS, and to use proper budgeting, costing and monitoring techniques. Much more will need to be done before both hospitals and medical practices function at maximum efficiency. But the fuss the doctors kicked up was out of all proportion to the changes they were being asked to make. Many of them who wrote to me totally misunderstood what was proposed. Concerning the drug budgets, some actually thought they would have to stop prescribing if they reached their ceiling. Some also thought they were not going to be free to send patients for operations to the hospital of their choice, whereas it was part of the reforms to make it easier for them to do so.

Underlying their protests was, of course, the new General Practitioner contract, which made a move in the direction of rewarding doctors who worked hardest more, and those who worked least less. When I heard from a chairman of a neighbouring health authority that his GPs worked an average 34 hours a week, and knowing that many do work long hours, one wonders how many there must be who work very few hours indeed. I can see no reason why this disparity in their work effort should not be reflected in their pay. They protested that it was quite wrong to make them take on too many patients in order to earn a living – turning the argument on its head. The new contract was probably the main reason for their desire to stir up the public and campaign against the reforms. They countered any argument in favour of value for money and better management by complaining about the 'cuts' and demanding unlimited extra money for the NHS. 'Underfunded' and 'under-resourced' became the fashionable words.

The public got the impression from all this that there were indeed 'cuts' in the NHS budget and that some awful tourniquet was being applied to doctors and hospitals alike as a result of the 'cuts'. They were more ready to believe their doctor, whom they saw as 'impartial' rather than their MP, who was 'political'. It was a major source of political trouble during 1989. It is a perfect example of the difficulty of reforming anything in Britain, and the political opposition was as fierce as ever. It was all going to be forgotten by the next General

Election, but it was a factor still unsettling Tory MPs in the autumn of 1990.

Social Security

Margaret Thatcher never weakened in her determination to concentrate social security benefits upon those in need, rather than allow benefit to become an alternative way of living, albeit a frugal one. Social security was the main source of the dependency culture, and she was adamant in her desire to cut back dependency. Contrary to popular myth, she was in no way harsh in her attitude to those who genuinely fell on hard times. But it was inevitable, if the level of any benefit was sufficiently attractive to support a reasonable living standard, that others would stop trying to earn their living, and live on benefits instead. Trying to frustrate such 'free riders' meant that benefit levels had to be no higher than adequate, and that rigorous efforts were needed to restrict them to those who needed them.

But what standard is 'adequate' in this context? The left wing and the sociologists began to mount the argument that there was still much 'poverty' in Britain. Indeed, they claimed that one third of the population was 'living in poverty or on the margins of it.' John Moore, while Secretary of State for Social Services in 1989, published a pamphlet debunking the use of the word 'poverty' at all. He quoted Professor Kenneth Galbraith's redefinition of the word 'poverty': 'People are poverty-stricken,' he said, 'when their income, even if adequate for survival, falls markedly behind that of the community.' John Moore pointed out that this was not an absolute definition: it was a relative measure of the lack of equality in incomes. He showed that even those on benefit had had a large increase of 28 per cent in their standard of living between 1970 and 1985, as against the average of 26 per cent for the population as a whole. He went on to analyse the standard of living of those on income support. Most had a telephone, a television set, a washing machine, a refrigerator, and half even had a car and central heating. They spent 55 per cent of their income on the necessities – fuel, food and housing – as opposed to the national average of 44 per cent which still left 45 per cent for non-essentials. It is impossible to describe this as poverty and very possible to describe it as adequate. Needless to say, John Moore's pamphlet came under violent attack from the left wing and the lobbies.

This adequacy was underlined by the existence of what was called 'the poverty trap' and the 'unemployment trap'. These 'traps' have now been successfully banished from the scene. The 'poverty trap' arose where someone on benefit became worse off if he or she obtained part-time earnings. The thresholds for benefits were so abrupt that a few extra pounds a week could disqualify someone from benefit worth far more than the extra earnings – so he or she had a positive incentive not to earn. The problem was eventually solved by providing more generous tapers, so that benefits always diminished more slowly than the extra earnings which caused them to diminish. The similar problem with retirement pensioners, who unlike old-age pensioners did not draw their pension as of right – was the Earnings Rule, whereby their retirement pensions were abated as they continued to earn money. This problem, different in nature but not in effect from the poverty trap, was eventually solved by abolishing the Earnings Rule altogether.

Both solutions – more generous tapers and abolishing the Earnings Rule – were expensive. But it was a far better way to spend extra money than by simply uprating benefits, leaving the 'traps' and their disincentive effect in place.

The 'unemployment trap' described the situation, quite common in the early 1980s, whereby it paid people on low wages to give up their jobs and live on Unemployment Benefit instead. Unemployment Benefit was higher than what was then called Supplementary Benefit.

I remember a number of my constituents showing me the figures which proved conclusively what a disincentive the 'unemployment trap' was. One was the man who used to clean my windows. I couldn't justify, on his figures, putting pressure on him to continue, and for a long time my windows went dirty.

Moreover, benefit was not taxable, while wages, even low wages, certainly were. In 1980 Unemployment Benefit was uprated by 5 per cent less than the rate of inflation, until arrangements could be made to make it taxable. This was achieved by April 1983. This change, together with the replacement of child dependency additions to Unemployment Benefit by normal long-term child dependency grants in 1984, effectively removed the disincentive to getting a job, and ended the unemployment trap.

These three phenomena are not evidence that benefit levels were close to 'poverty': they are evidence that they were more adequate than many people's earnings.

The argument in relation to pensions was a different one. Margaret Thatcher believed that the State Pension should be kept at a level which would support an adequate standard of living, with extra payments for those in special need. But she also believed that extra retirement income over and above the basic minimum pension should be earned and saved during people's working lifetimes. Clearly it would be several decades before all pensioners would be in this situation – many who were already retired had little or no income other than the State Pension. She saw that if the State Pension continued to be indexed to average earnings, as it was in 1979, as opposed to being linked to prices – in the shape of the Retail Price Index – we would indeed have a situation eventually where the pension was sufficiently generous for some people to decide that saving for old age was no longer necessary. This in turn would bring increased pressure to increase State Pensions more. It would be immensely costly in public expenditure terms – another expensive public monopoly form of provision, this time for 8 million people. It would also result in far less saving nationally.

She decided to break the link between the pension and average earnings, and instead link it to the Retail Price Index. At the same time, everything possible was done to help and encourage people to subscribe to extra forms of pension provision, encouraged by tax reliefs. Occupational pension schemes were grafted onto the back of the state scheme – both employer and employee had to contribute to this form of second pension. Share Options, employee share ownership schemes, Personal Equity Plans (PEP) and a Tax Exempt Savings Account (TESSA) were introduced as vehicles to help people save for their old age. The Earnings Rule for retirement pensions was abolished. All of these schemes were tax free – they all involved removing all taxation charges from saving. Together they represented a formidable array of easy ways to save for retirement.

Although these major reforms were clearly right, breaking the link between pensions and earnings was both awkward and contentious. In the fullness of time – when practically everyone has sizeable extra pensions – she will be praised for it. But the fullness of time was no good for those approaching retirement, or already retired. There was much resentment at the breaking of the link with earnings, and the Labour Party in its furious fulminations vowed to restore it. Yet already some 84 per cent of pensioners have additional income. Over her period in office, the average income of pensioners rose by a surprising 37 per cent by 1990 in real terms. That average indeed conceals many who had only their State Pension to live on – but it shows how successful the policy was beginning to be even after only a decade or so.

My last example of Margaret Thatcher's assault on the dependency culture must be Child Benefit. For decades there had been an income tax allowance for those with dependent children. This was of most benefit to the rich, of some benefit to the average, and no benefit to the least well off who were not income taxpayers. It was crazy. It was rightly replaced by Child Benefit in 1977 when a weekly sum was paid to the mother on behalf of every child instead. This was better, but it had the effect of giving equal help to rich and poor alike. Margaret Thatcher believed social benefits should be concentrated on those who needed them – a view with which I cannot disagree. The better off certainly did not need a weekly grant for each child. She wanted to concentrate the money on those who needed it.

She ran into stiff opposition over this, opposition which I could never understand. For the socialists and a number of 'wet' Tories, to argue for benefits for the better off always seemed to me to be turning 'social justice' on its head. For Ian Gilmour and Tony Benn to find themselves in the same lobby voting for benefits for the better off was certainly bizarre. But that is indeed what they were doing. So strong was the opposition that she decided she could go no further than a policy of letting Child Benefit 'wither on the vine' – that is, never to uprate it for inflation. The less well off were protected because they received higher benefits for children than Child Benefit itself, through the Income Support supplements for children, and these were improved and continued to be uprated. It became an annual political battle, as each uprating came up, with the Government proposing not to increase Child Benefit, and the Opposition, backed by some Tory rebels, forcing it to a close division. It was an unwelcome signal when Norman Lamont reversed this policy in the 1991 Budget, by promising continually to uprate Child Benefit for all.

There were no 'cuts' in social security spending, although that allegation was constantly made. It rose by 35 per cent in real terms during Margaret Thatcher's prime ministership. She certainly succeeded in reorientating this huge sum of money more towards those in most need. She succeeded in raising the standard of living of the poorest in the land. She also helped people to provide much more for their own retirement.

It is probably true, however, that the dependency culture lives on, albeit at a reduced level. The higher the standard of living of those who have no other means but benefits, the more will some people be tempted to join them. It cannot be possible, therefore, to concentrate social security policy on those who really need it, and to increase their living standards without others seeking to join in. But Margaret Thatcher got as close to targeting the needy as is probably possible. The difference between Margaret Thatcher and her critics was that she wanted to, and they did not.

In conclusion, it would perhaps be right to contrast Margaret Thatcher's objectives in relation to the social programmes – more choice, more private provision, less dependency and better targeting –with the German concept of the *Soziale Marktwirtschaft*, and the new concept of the social market, making the public services so good that no one will want to go to private provision. They are, in fact, diametrically opposite policies. The latter policy would cost untold billions. The 'market' would have to be bled white to pay for the 'social'. It's strange how the same word can have two such very different meanings!

5

THE ENVIRONMENT

'ENVIRONMENT' IS A dreadful word. It comes from the French word *environs* meaning the surrounding area of a city. In English it has come to mean the surroundings in which we live, but it covers a wide variety of meanings. It was also the name given by Ted Heath to the department that used to be called the Ministry of Housing and Local Government and other Departments. It was there that I found myself in May 1986 as Secretary of State until the reshuffle of July 1989.

Much of my task concerned local government reform, the introduction of the Community Charge, the housing reforms and water privatization, which I discuss elsewhere. But there were two subjects which definitely were 'environmental' in character – pollution control and planning. The best collective adjective for these topics is 'green' – and that is the subject matter of this chapter.

The word 'green' was the name given to various environmental and ecology movements, particularly in Germany, but there were plenty of them too in England – like Friends of the Earth, Greenpeace, the Council for the Protection of Rural England, and the Ecology Party. There were many more. They are militant campaigners for their causes.

For many years they seemed a bit cranky – a bit extreme – to the general public. A candidate from the Ecology Party stood against me at one election in the 1970s and received only a handful of votes. Then suddenly in the mid-80s the Green movement became fashionable, even orthodox. Indeed, in the 1989 European Parliamentary Elections the Green Party became the main repository of protest votes against the Government at a time when we were not riding high in popular esteem. They overtook the Liberals, who are usually the main beneficiaries of Tory unpopularity. By the end of the decade, their electoral appeal seemed again to have largely evaporated. After their period of being fashionable, some of them became more extreme again, as hopes of being taken seriously receded. Mr David Icke, who for some time was the national spokesman for the Green Party, announced in 1991 that he was 'a channel for the Christ Spirit. The title was given to me very recently by the Godhead.' He went on to predict global disasters on an unprecedented scale, thereby linking his new-found ability to prophesy with his old convictions as an environmentalist. The Green movement was never far from the cult movement. As Dryden said, 'Thin partitions do their bounds divide.' Even in Germany, where the Green movement is stronger and more powerful than in Britain, there was a surge in the strength of the Greens during the middle of the decade.

Why this was so is not quite clear. Certainly it was a period of prosperity and personal affluence. Greenery is *expensive*. It is not just a question of willpower, but of building extremely expensive sewage works, incinerators, treatment plants and fitting coal-fired power stations with sulphuric acid scrubbers. People appear not to be nearly so concerned about greenery when they are feeling broke. The poorer nations of the world seldom want to know about it at all. When I visited China in 1988 to discuss pollution with them, they told me that 97 per cent of their sewage went untreated into the rivers and the sea. They said that to do otherwise was a luxury they could not possibly afford. Nor did they think it mattered – life went on just the same, and it had always been thus. They were very ready to cooperate over combating the threat to the upper atmosphere – they saw the point of that – but sewerage was very low on the list of priorities of a very poor country. When Britain was in recession both in 1979–81 and in 1989–91, interest in green issues was markedly less. The mid-decade boom was certainly part of the reason for the mid-decade upsurge in environmental concern.

There was another reason. Margaret Thatcher always kept in touch with senior and sensible scientists. She had been trained as a chemist and had even practised her skills in a humble fashion in the first jobs she secured after leaving Oxford. She understood about chemical elements and reactions. She became persuaded by some senior members of the Royal Society and by the writings of James Lovelock that the atmosphere really was in danger from two potential threats – the depletion of the ozone layer and the concentration of 'greenhouse' gases in the upper atmosphere. She was never remotely influenced by the emotional appeal – one might say the shock tactics – of the Greens. But when scientists who knew what they were talking about voiced their concern to her that the modern world was upsetting the carbon cycle, she understood the seriousness of the point immediately and decided to use her position to do something about it. She told me at the time that she remembered the importance of the carbon cycle from her school chemistry lessons. I had to confess that I did not. She prepared a speech on these dangers, with assistance from them and the Department of the Environment (DoE) scientists, who entirely shared her concerns. It was delivered on 27 September 1988, shortly before the Party Conference.

What Margaret Thatcher actually argued in that famous speech on 27 September was that the amount of carbon dioxide now in the upper atmosphere was forming a sort of protective blanket round the world. This would prevent the heat of our planet escaping into space and cause our climate to get warmer. If the temperature rose by a few degrees centigrade, it would have the result of melting the polar ice, causing sea levels to rise and flooding much low land. She was much impressed by the President of the Maldives, who told her that no point on that island was more than seven feet above sea level. His whole island might disappear if there were global warming due to the 'greenhouse' effect.

The ozone layer problem was different. Chemicals used primarily in aerosols, but with other uses as well, were destroying the ozone layer high up in the atmosphere. The ozone layer protects human beings from harmful radiation. It was therefore essential to phase out the use of these chemicals as quickly as possible.

Margaret Thatcher's speech certainly had its desired effect, and rather more as well. She was hailed as having been converted on the road to Damascus to the 'environmental cause' and of 'going green'. Requests poured in for action on a hundred other fronts immediately – water quality, sewage at sea, litter, chemical wastes, toxic fumes, lead in petrol, waste disposal, car fumes, lorry and aircraft noise, transistor radios, the rooting out of hedges and shelter belts, intensive farming and the protection of badgers, and much else: surely all these menaces were now to be banished? Worse still, so wide was the meaning of the word 'environment' that it encompassed the view from one's house and the seclusion and privacy of every country residence, which were now presumably going to be protected under the planning laws? Surely no more housing estates would be allowed, no more roads would be built, and no more factories, offices and out-of-town shopping centres, let alone nuclear power stations allowed? It gave a huge boost to the green movement. Paradoxically they recruited many new members!

I was entirely in support of Margaret Thatcher's initiative on the upper atmosphere. But I was apprehensive at the way it triggered off a whole new wave of political concerns about a range of subjects so disparate and diverse that it was impossible to deal with them all in a rational way. Some of it made good sense, but some of it was nonsense, and some allegations were untrue. Much of the lobbying was conflicting. Little of it was based on scientific evidence. It was highly emotional and its implications were highly expensive. It took a couple of years to work through the consequences of Margaret Thatcher's 'conversion to greenery' speech, which she had meant to refer to the need to safeguard the ozone layer and to reduce the 'greenhouse gases' alone. But it also allowed us to deal effectively with many of the real problems.

I hastened immediately to set out principles upon which each green issue should be judged, in the vain hope of getting the debate onto a basis of logic rather than emotion. In a speech at the Party Conference shortly afterwards, I set out the principles upon which I suggested we should base our policy.

The first principle was that we should convince ourselves of the validity and soundness of the science underlying any environmental policy, although it is sometimes necessary to adopt the 'precautionary' approach. The second principle was that 'the polluter must pay' – which actually meant the customers of the polluter. The third principle was that we should not do things which were not necessary or desirable, particularly since it was always in the end the customers who had to pay, and many of them were not well off. The fourth principle I set out was that pollution does not acknowledge physical boundaries. Although some problems are local, or confined to the UK – like litter, or river pollution – many are regional, like acid rain, the pollution of the North Sea from filth coming down the Rhine, and nitrous oxide damage to European forests – and some are global, like the destruction of the ozone layer and the greenhouse effect. It was possible only to deal with national problems at the national level. Regional problems had to be solved by cooperation at the regional level – which seldom bore any geographical relation to the European Community (which left out many countries with major interests). World problems could only be dealt with through global organizations – particularly the United Nations.

Looking back, I believe these principles are still the right ones, still relevant, still true. That they have not always been followed in recent times has to be acknowledged, but they still remain the yardstick by which to measure the extent of aberration for 'political' reasons. We have gone far to meet them domestically, far too far in Europe, and not far enough globally. Perhaps this is simply a reflection of the relative prosperity of Britain, the Community, and the world as a whole. I still believe that the truth is that environmental purity is the prerogative of the prosperous. There is a fundamental absurdity in the position of the extremists in the green movement. Their solution to some of the problems of the environment is to go back to the sort of life of two hundred years ago – no cars, minimal use of electricity, no fertilizers, no pesticides, most chemicals banned. Such a life style would impoverish us – indeed, they themselves call for 'negative growth'. It is not clear how the expensive plants for reducing pollution could be paid for in that sort of economy. It is only through economic growth that the poorer nations of the world will ever be able to clean up their environments. The doctrine of 'sustainable development', adumbrated in the Brundtland Report, called after the Norwegian Prime Minister who was Chairman of the Commission, sets out the best way forward. All nations should be helped to achieve as much economic growth as is consistent with improving their environments, thereby enabling them to afford to do better to protect them.

I for one do not want to resort to travelling on horseback and cooking and heating with peat or wood fires. I do not want to wear a hair shirt, but I do want to safeguard the planet.

The difficulty was that individuals saw their own problems about 'the environment', quite naturally, in terms of their own experiences. A dirty street, covered in litter, smoke from a nearby factory, or new housing going up where previously there had been green fields: these were the 'pollutions' that concerned ordinary people. The problems which were of real concern to the welfare of mankind – like the upper atmosphere – were not what they were worrying about. Indeed, solving some of the less important problems merely made the more important ones worse. The green pressure groups were highly prejudiced and did not have to have a comprehensive policy which was free from anomalies, as the Government did. We were forced by public opinion to make a number of mistakes; that perhaps a less resolute Government would have made more is my only defence. To crown it all, the European Council of Environment Ministers was continually trying to take quick political tricks in this field, usually at our expense and the expense of the European people. It had been a vain hope of mine indeed that I could keep the debate on a logical, scientific and value-for-money basis. Politics took over.

I refused to be emotional about all this. That in itself was a red rag to

THE GUARDIAN: 20 DECEMBER, 1989

the green bulls, who saw it all as a religion – a question of faith, and passion and commitment. Like Mr Icke, they were always close to seeing it as a cult. My insistence on getting at the scientific truths irritated people who had adopted a cause, whether valid or not. My mentioning value-for-money seemed profane. My taking people through the consequences of what they were demanding seemed mean. I will exemplify each of these inadequacies of my approach. I couldn't win because there was a national mood comprising a mixture of guilt for the filthy state of our planet and a self-righteous, crusading zeal to do something about it. It is just the mixture that appeals most to the British character. The press sensed it and ran with the mood as a good way to increase their circulations.

I became the culprit for the state of the earth and the target at which to direct this self-righteous zeal. I was said not to 'care' about the environment. The press got quite unpleasant. I rest content that I prevented many silly mistakes being made, although not all. The paradox is that I also succeeded in doing more of the essential things than any environment secretary before or after me.

It is technically easy, and not too expensive, to save the ozone layer; all that is needed is for all nations to replace the dangerous chemicals with safer ones. That requires international agreement. I suggested to Margaret Thatcher that we should hold a conference in London to further both publicity for the cause and the solution of getting that international agreement. She was content with this idea, and we held the London conference in February 1988. It was a great success, in which she played a full part.

The greenhouse gases present a far greater problem. The vital need is to put less carbon dioxide into the air; and to do all possible to reduce what is already there. The latter can only be done through the passage of time and by planting more trees. The former can mainly be done by burning less coal, wood, oil and gas. Thus to take the greenhouse effect seriously requires making the top priority to reduce the burning of fossil fuels. There are many minor ways by which this can be done, but the best way to do it is to generate more electricity from nuclear energy, in order to reduce the burning of fossil fuels. Such a policy was, however, opposed violently by the Greens themselves because they had a huge prejudice against nuclear anything, and by the Labour Party because it means far fewer jobs in coal mining. For economic reasons, both got their way. In the process of privatizing the electricity industry, for the first time the true costs of producing electricity from nuclear energy in Britain became known. They were far higher than the cost of generation from gas, oil or even coal. Since we were embarking on privatizing electricity, there was no way that a large increase in nuclear capacity could be justified. In fact, nuclear electricity priced itself out of the market. It would need a large public subsidy if we were to do the right thing and provide more. This is another example of how very expensive greenery really is.

Other green policies also cause more carbon dioxide to be emitted. Taking the sulphur out of coal-fired power station emissions in order to reduce acid rain causes much more coal to be burned. Again, the best environmental answer to acid rain is more nuclear power capacity.

The French have been very wise in this respect. They generate over 70 per cent of their electricity from nuclear energy. They therefore cause by far the least pollution of any nation in Europe. Heaven knows, however, what it has cost them in subsidies – they keep the true cost very much to themselves.

The European Community forced upon us, with strong support from the Greens, measures to reduce emissions of nitrous oxide from motor car exhausts. This too results in much more carbon going up to heaven.

There is a real choice between the catalytic converter which reduces nitrous oxide but increases carbon, and the 'lean burn' engine which reduces fuel consumption and therefore carbon emissions, but cannot reduce nitrous oxide emissions by as much as the catalytic converter. Nitrous oxide is probably part of the cause of German forest damage, so naturally it was the German priority to reduce it. We saw the 'greenhouse' threat as the higher priority. Margaret Thatcher was particularly vehement on this point, and rightly so, but once again we were outvoted in the European Council and had to accept what I still believe was the wrong decision. The German argument dominated the Council, although we had the best scientific argument.

My last example concerns the North Sea states who pressed for us to incinerate harmless treated sewage sludge, rather than dumping it at sea. This too will increase carbon emissions. It was another wrong decision, which will increase carbon dioxide by another half million tons a year.

In such ways did we actually increase our emissions of carbon dioxide. (So did the Europeans.) Much of this was a result of Margaret Thatcher's speech calling for a serious attempt to arrest the 'greenhouse' threat and reduce them. The Greens, and the Europeans and the press, spatchcocked their own pet prejudices onto her alleged conversion to greenery in general, with the result that they slightly increased the dangers to which she had drawn attention. Avoiding global warming is far more important than the susceptibilities of the Greens about nuclear power, or the damage from sulphuric acid or nitrous oxide, important though they are; disposing of treated sewage sludge to sea is certainly the best way of dealing with it environmentally.

In fact, the areas where we succeeded in reducing pollution and cleaning up the British environment in the 1980s were many and important. As I have said, huge investment is now going into coal-fired power stations to remove sulphur emissions to reduce acid rain, although it increases carbon emissions. We greatly reduced the amount of lead going into the atmosphere by our campaign to get people to use lead-free petrol. I designed the comprehensive legislation to make local authorities and others remove litter. It is novel and exciting nowadays actually to see people on motorways, stations and streets removing this most offensive nuisance.

It all started when Margaret Thatcher drove back from Heathrow one day along the M4. That road was strewn with litter on either side and on the central reservation. I remember getting a considerable battering for not having prevented it from happening. I agreed with her about litter and I took my battering seriously. I set about the complicated task, with the aid of the 'Keep Britain Tidy Group,' of how to make it actually happen. It was a complicated problem because so many different types of landowners were involved and each had to be put into a position where they did something. In due course I suggested a stunt to Margaret Thatcher to get press coverage of our determination to reduce litter. I asked her to appear before the cameras with me in some litter-strewn part of London, while we both set about physically clearing it. She readily agreed and asked me to make the arrangements. Unfortunately, security considerations ruled out her appearing in all the nearby areas where litter was an endemic occurrence, so instead we had to mount the stunt in St James's Park. All went well until the press found out from the park attendants that they had been mysteriously told to distribute copious amounts of litter there earlier that morning.

The setting up of the National Rivers Authority (NRA), for the reasons I have already described, was probably my biggest single contribution to dealing with what was certainly Britain's worst problem of pollution – dirty rivers and estuaries; our drinking water was never as bad as the critics made out, and a lot of money is going to be wasted in the future on complying with the European Directives, which go far further than is needed. But we shall soon reach a state when our rivers and estuaries are virtually free from sewage and chemical pollutants, which will probably be a unique position among industrialized countries, and well ahead of any other Community country.

'By 2010 we will almost certainly have the best water quality in Europe as a direct result of recent legislation. Getting on for £30 billion will be spent over the next ten years on as ambitious a water clean-up programme as there is anywhere in Europe. We'll have far cleaner rivers, a virtual end to pollution from sewage and much higher quality drinking water.' That was confirmed in a speech made in February 1991 by Chris Patten.

Fish and plant life soon return to rivers once pollutants are no longer entering them. I believe fishermen will be able to catch fish in every river of Britain by the end of the decade. I would like to take credit for that, when the time comes, for insisting on setting up the NRA with the necessary powers.

The measures we set in train to remove pollution of the sea were the phasing out of the burning of toxic materials at sea, of discharges to sea of poisonous effluents, and of dumping of toxic solid wastes at sea. We also set up Her Majesty's Inspectorate of Pollution, as the overall regulatory body for the control of all emissions to air, land and water, with a remit to operate a system called 'integrated pollution control' based on applying the 'Best Practical Environmental Option', as it was called. We designed a full new system for the regulation of waste disposal, both household waste and toxic waste. This, together with litter legislation, was enacted by my successor, Chris Patten, in the Control of Pollution Act 1990, along with a number of other minor measures. The filthy and dangerous rubbish dumps we are used to should soon be a thing of the past. Even if we made little progress with reducing the greenhouse gases, Margaret Thatcher's speech of 1987 resulted in a full harvest of useful gains in a host of other areas – far more progress was made than in any other period of our history. Yet I was constantly accused of not 'caring' about the environment!

One thing that annoyed me while I was dealing with pollution at the DoE was the way some played politics with environmental issues. It fell to me to chair the Conference on the North Sea, attended by all the governments of the states bordering the North Sea, which was held in 1987 in London. The Conference went well enough; there was not very much pollution entering the North Sea from Britain, but there was a great deal which came down the Rhine, the Elbe and the Meuse. You wouldn't have thought so; the Germans sought to draw attention away from this by trying to dub us in the role of the 'Dirty Man of Europe', with the full support of our Greens and our press. We all agreed to tighten up on various minor blemishes and to accelerate a few programmes to phase out various pollutions which were not of great substance to start with. Not enough pressure was put on the Germans to clean up their industrial rivers.

Other natural phenomena which were taking place at that time were also the subject of much political mischief making. One was an outbreak of poisonous algae in the sea off the Dutch coast, which spread up to Norway. Such outbreaks of toxic algae have taken place naturally for centuries. They poison the shellfish and do certainly damage fish stocks. Of course, this outbreak was alleged to be the result of pollution, which it wasn't. I had a hard time with an angry Swedish lady Minister who tried to blame us for it. Outbreaks of poisonous algae have occurred as far back as there are records.

The other was a virus epidemic which struck the common seals in the North Sea about the same time. Again, such epidemics are natural and endemic. The grey seals in the North Sea had suffered one such attack in the 1930s; there was also an outbreak in the Falkland Islands, and another one in Lake Baikal during the 1980s. These viruses are nature's way of controlling seal populations which outgrow the food resources available to them, similar to myxomatosis with rabbits, or UDN with salmon. Of course, the epidemic was blamed on some unspecified 'pollution' caused by Britain, by the Greens and more stridently by the *Daily Mail*. Sentimentality about attractive animals dying combined with the fashion to blame British pollution for everything unpleasant was a best seller for that newspaper. As a result, the public may have been left thinking pollution from Britain was the cause of the seals dying.

Another controversy at the time concerned the disappearance of a huge colony of nesting sea gulls and terns on the west coast of Cumbria. This was alleged by the Greens to be due to nuclear radiation from leaks from nearby Sellafield. It so happened that the Nature Conservancy Council (the NCC) conducted an enquiry into the reason for the birds moving elsewhere. They found that the reason was foxes harassing the birds and eating their eggs and newly-hatched chicks. Foxes had not been controlled in that area; a plague of myxomatosis had wiped out the rabbits upon which they normally fed, so the hungry foxes had taken to eating the eggs and chicks instead. All these three examples of wrong diagnosis, wrong response and wrong solutions are typical of the Greens.

The Greens were able to play on the British love of animals to spread such misconceptions. Perhaps some of the blame must be laid at the door of the delightful books of Beatrix Potter for the British attitude to animals. She not only portrayed animals as humans, but categorized them into good and bad humans. Rabbits, mice, squirrels and hedgehogs were good – foxes and rats were downright bad. No one has ever wanted to preserve the habitat of rats and most people agree with the control of the fox population. Everyone thinks pit bull terriers should become extinct including the RSPCA. But the good ones must be preserved at all costs. In logic, those who are against controlling animal populations should be just as concerned about rats and foxes.

Most of the population of Britain, and most Greens too, are urban dwellers who see the countryside as idyllic, a beautiful place in which birds and animals and butterflies should be allowed uninterruptedly blissful lives. What they do not understand is that it is beautiful because the countryman has made it so, and there are birds and animals and butterflies because the countryman has enabled them to continue to thrive. They see him as the enemy, whereas in truth he is the best conservationist of them all.

In fact, many wildlife populations are best controlled by man, both for his own sake and for the sake of the wildlife itself. Most wildlife feeds on other wildlife, and to keep our rich variety and healthy numbers of each species, it is better to limit the numbers of those predators which become dominant and which do most damage to others: crows, magpies, herons, great black backed gulls, cormorants, mergansers, goosanders and some hawks, foxes, grey squirrels, stoats and, dare I say it, seals, are examples. In Britain the countryman has always done this for us. Although at times he has been excessive in his zeal to deal with predators, over the centuries he has done it very well. Yet now many of these species are on the protected list; and the European Commission in its blundering ignorance has tried to add more to it. The Nature Conservancy Council has never understood this vital point either.

I was born and brought up in a rural part of Northumberland. I spent all the daylight hours outside, getting to know the birds and their nests, trying to catch fish in the river, and learning the wild plants, insects and animals. I had to spend half of each school holiday working with the farm workers, or the woodmen, the masons, the joiners or the gardeners, learning their trades. I thus knew exactly how both the balance of nature and the rural economy worked. Ever since my boyhood, I had understood just how interdependent they were. As a countryman myself, I found it most frustrating to see the way the pressure groups, the Europeans and our own NCC, understood so little, and sought to preserve everything, even though to do so threatened much that was precious. The countryman in Britain knows more about preserving wildlife than the lot of them put together.

What is a countryman? A countryman is someone who, like me, was brought up in the countryside, experiencing the cycle of the seasons and the activities of the farming community. He is someone who has seen a stoat kill a rabbit and a sparrow hawk kill a songthrush. He knows how to catch the trout in the brook and flight a wild duck in the evening. He knows the wild flowers and the butterflies. He does not need to be told about conservation by the town dweller. I was fortunate to have had such an upbringing myself.

The conservation of habitats is another matter, and it is on this that the campaigning bodies should concentrate. Thankfully, during my time at the DoE it was possible to do something about it. The pressure for more and more agricultural production had eased by then and this

114

meant less land was needed for agricultural production. This in turn enabled John MacGregor (who was then Agriculture Minister) and myself to make some useful changes, which are now contributing a lot to bringing back more of the traditional English wildlife habitats. We set up the set-aside scheme, whereby owners who had land not needed for farming left it untilled and ungrazed and were recompensed. We added 'top-up' grants for creating specialized habitats on such set-aside land. We moved subsidies to forestry from tax reliefs to grants, and encouraged farmers to plant on the low ground and to plant more deciduous trees. I even succeeded in denying grants for forestry planting above the 800 ft contour – the heather line – in England to keep the tops of the Pennine Hills clear of ugly spruce trees, which hardly grew there properly anyway. But the best initiative was the heather initiative. I asked the NCC to organize a programme to try to restore the 40 per cent of English heather moors which had been lost since the last war. The cause of this loss was running too many sheep on the hills. The idea was to restore the heather through grants, and give advice and help to the sheep farmers. However, we failed to remove the most damaging factor at work – the European Community couldn't be persuaded to change the method of paying the subsidy for sheep: the existing one had the effect of actually encouraging farmers to run too many sheep. Thus again did the EC succeed in frustrating a valuable environmental improvement. Nonetheless, I hope some heather may still be restored in the beloved Pennine Hills as a result of the heather initiative.

Margaret Thatcher was a good chemist, but she has never been a country person, who understood and felt deeply about these things as I did. For me it was a wonderful opportunity to have been given a pretty free hand at the DoE to deal with some of the real menaces – the threat to the hills, the rivers and the estuaries; and unsightly litter strewn across roads and streets. I thought it was a more worthwhile thing to do than to pander to some of the wrong-headed campaigns of the Greens.

No doubt they will prevail more now that I have gone. I fear for the English countryside, the English countryman and much more our wildlife if that happens. I fear that Britain will be turned into one great designated national park, staffed by wardens, with the public ordered out, or at least ordered about. The countryman will be prevented from following the traditional practices and trades and skills which have made Britain such a green and pleasant land. It will be a paradise for scientists, wardens and predators, but it will no longer be the true countryside which I was brought up to love and to revere and to preserve. The countryman could become an endangered species.

Despite all that was said and alleged when I was at the Environment Department, the English countryside has in fact been largely preserved from development. If you fly around southern England in a helicopter, it is astonishing how small the built-up areas are, compared to the open country, and how well preserved the villages and the hamlets are. In 1979, 87.5 per cent of southeast England (excluding Greater London) was undeveloped; by the end of this century the figure is expected still to be 86.5 per cent. For the rest of England the figure is nearer 90 per cent. It is an astonishing success story, despite what people think. The pressures for more development land, resulting from a large population living in a pretty small country, could in fact be met without significantly more land being lost. For Scotland and Wales the problem was never acute.

I resolved at the DoE to continue my predecessor's policy of maintaining and even extending the Green Belts round the cities, which were designed to stop the cities sprawling outwards. There were only one or two very minor breaches of Green Belt policy during my three-and-a-half years there, again contrary to popular myth. But some smaller towns, not protected by Green Belts, had sprawled further and further outwards, making for bad planning and unsightly development. The beauty of many villages had been compromised by a slab of ugly 1960s-type new housing being added to them. I judged that simply concentrating new housing development in additions to existing towns and villages would both be unpopular and would, indeed, be bad planning. I therefore tried to launch a new policy of creating a few new small towns and villages. This would both have taken the pressure off expanding existing settlements, and avoided the familiar clash between traditional architecture and modern brick 'boxes', which had put so many people against new housing. The idea was generally welcomed in principle, but predictably every new settlement was bitterly opposed. One new town had to be turned down because it was in the Green Belt: two others were refused after my time, although they appeared to me to be of high quality. One it fell to me to determine. This was at Foxley Wood in Hampshire. It went to an Appeal and the Inspector who took the Appeal recommended in its favour. The land comprised a series of gravel pits worked out before the war; it had been used as an army camp during the war. This unsightly mess had then been disguised by planting conifers all over it. It was hardly a jewel of the English countryside; moreover, Hampshire had a large need for extra housing. I granted permission. There was the usual storm of protest – I was even burnt in effigy. My successor, fearful of a similar fate no doubt, overturned my decision. The policy of new settlements was dead. As a result of reversing my decision, there were four thousand fewer homes. The desire to be popular had triumphed over both common sense and the interests of people seeking only a house to live in.

It was strange to me why it was so unpopular to seek enough land on which to build the houses that people wanted. I came to be deeply disliked by many people for that very reason. When you put the argument to friends and acquaintances that some permissions must be granted, or some people would go without homes, they always replied, 'Yes, but put them somewhere else.' Since everyone had the same reaction, there appeared to be nowhere for them to go. This reaction came to be known as the NIMBY attitude: 'Not in my back yard.' The press had a field day when they discovered that back in 1980 I myself had objected to a planning application near my home. I was accused of being NIMBY myself – despite the fact that many houses had been built nearby to which I hadn't objected. The site in question was the flood plain of the river, as well as the nearest thing to a village green.

It was a thankless task to run the planning system in the mid-80s. One was blamed personally for every consent granted, although 98 per cent of them were given by local authorities. I remember an angry group that was incensed by a permission granted 30 miles from where I lived. They resolved to walk to my house and demonstrate before the house and before the television cameras. After spending a night in pouring rain, only three bedraggled protesters eventually arrived. The police, who were there to see that all was peaceful, took pity on them and drove them straight back to their homes. But why should they want to take it out on me?

To some extent the problem was caused by those moving into new houses, who were the strongest objectors to any more being built. The last one in was the most vehement. The local villagers tended to be more philosophical – particularly as so many of them wanted houses, which became beyond their reach financially.

I will not go over all the difficulties we experienced at this time in providing the houses that were needed. The best guess at a forecast was that about 570,000 more houses would be needed by the end of the century in the south of England. I doubt if we will see that number built. The consequences of this continuing shortage of homes is not just that those who are at the margin cannot get a house, leading to more homelessness or overcrowding. The consequence of the shortage of the supply in relation to the demand for houses was that the price of building land, and therefore of homes too, soared. House prices rose to absurd levels in the late 1980s, fuelled by the ready availability of cheap credit, and with the assistance of mortgage-interest relief. This became a factor of considerable political importance. Shortage of sites for offices and industrial buildings, and of homes in which to house the employees, virtually brought economic growth in the south to a halt. Many people were priced out of becoming home owners or suffered repossession when their mortgage interest payments later became more than they could afford. Increased house prices made it more expensive for the Government to provide subsidized houses for the less well off to rent through the housing associations and the councils.

It was perhaps no accident that the credit boom both sent demand for houses spiralling upwards, and also the supply of sites downwards, as the new affluence made people keener still to protect their 'environment' and frustrate development in their back yards. Some colleagues at the time asked me to try to find a way of getting more planning consents through in order to increase the supply. In order to demonstrate the strength of opposition to more planning consents, I replied to them that I doubted if I could hold my seat in Parliament if there were an election at that time – and certainly I would not be able to do so if I forced more permissions through. The solution was to reduce the demand and to cool the credit boom, I suggested. I discuss all that elsewhere, but the protection of the environment as it was interpreted in relation to planning had some extremely damaging consequences. Nor was it remotely connected with pollution, let alone the pollution of the upper atmosphere, which was Margaret Thatcher's concern when she made that famous speech. Letting ordinary people have a house of their own, by whatever means, cannot be called pollution.

6

THE POLL TAX SAGA

IT COULD BE said that the origins of the Poll Tax affair were in 1974. Margaret Thatcher had a brief spell as Shadow Secretary of State for the Environment between February and October 1974. She pledged the Tory Party in the October election to abolish domestic rates if the Tories were re-elected. History alleges that Ted Heath was the originator of this pledge: but having been the mouthpiece through which it was made, Margaret Thatcher felt she owed it a stout defence at the hustings. The Tories were not elected, so technically the pledge fell. Some say that she felt the pledge lived on for her, since it was she who had made it.

I think it would be more accurate to say that the rates were an extremely unpopular form of taxation, even in 1974, and for very good reasons too. Over the years, until she became Prime Minister, rates became even more unpopular; and the injustices inherent in domestic rating became even more glaring as council spending climbed. She disliked the rates in 1974, she disliked them more in 1979, and even more again in 1984. It wasn't the 1974 pledge that made her continue to want to end the rates, but the manifest unfairness in this particular form of taxation. Rates became even more unpopular when properties were revalued, as they were in Scotland in 1986.

The rates are an old institution. Perhaps they are first recognizable, as a tax similar to the one that was abolished for domestic homes in 1990, in the 19th century. People of property in the towns and the cities and the suburbs began to prosper and to want to improve the services and amenities of their neighbourhood. They wanted better roads upon which to drive their carriages. They wanted the neighbourhood kept clean and tidy, and public parks to be provided and well maintained. They wanted a piped water supply, and suitable arrangements for taking away the water they had dirtied – in other words, sewage – though they would not have called it that. Then came gas, and later electricity, supply. All these things were better done communally and paid for communally. They pressed for, and got, local government boards to provide these services for their properties. How better to pay for them than by a property rate, based on the rental value of the property, since renting was common and a good surrogate for capital value in those days? Only property owners had the vote: only property owners benefited and only property owners paid. Services to property for property owners were paid for by rates levied on the rental value of each property. It was a typically sensible and practical Victorian arrangement.

Ever since that time the system has been hijacked by central government. They took away most of the property-related elements of the local government boards' functions. The provision of water, sewerage, gas and electricity were all nationalized.

Services to people were spatchcocked onto the responsibilities of the local boards. Education was the first, but later personal social services were added and also the duty to house people who could not afford to pay for their own housing. Numerous other minor services to people were added: often to serve the convenience of central government. Local government ceased to be a provider of property services for the few who were property owners, and became a provider of personal services to all the people. It ceased to provide what its original contributors wanted it to provide and instead it was made to provide what central government wanted it to provide. During these fundamental transformations, the nature of the financial regime to pay for local government changed not at all. The rates on property were made to pay for it all, and the right to vote was extended to all.

As a result, the rates became intolerable because they were too high. A contribution towards property-related services became a swingeing impost to pay for free education and for various elements of the social security budget. Instead of realizing that the wrong tax base – the property base – was being used to pay for social policies in relation to people – not property – successive governments decided to abate the impact of the high level of rates by paying ever-increasing grants to local councils in order to enable them to keep the rates down.

By 1979 the grants paid by central government to English local authorities had reached 61 per cent of their expenditure – only 39 per cent came from local tax revenues, the business and the domestic rate. Yet those local revenues were still based on the hundred-year-old concept of the local property rate. Even paying only 39 per cent of the costs, groups of activists 'against the rates' sprang up. In my constituency there was a group called 'People Against Bureaucracy', or PABs, whose main object was to keep the rates down. They took a number of council seats in the 1970s. The rates were neither able to provide the revenue that was needed by local government, even in 1979, nor were they seen as fair.

There were many anomalies that were often quoted, like the poor widow paying the same as four earners in the identical house next door and people who improved their houses being asked to pay more in rates. But there were two worse defects that were much more substantial and were not generally known. The first was Resources Equalization, whereby £1.2 billion was taken from local authorities in the south of England and distributed to the authorities in the areas of historically low rateable values in the north. Resources Equalization had just grown up over the decades. The origin of it was that rental values were very low historically in the north, and much higher in the south. Thus, if all councils were to set the same rate of a certain number of pence in the pound far less money was raised in a northern authority than in a southern one. The practice had been to redress this imbalance by giving a large proportion of the government's grant to authorities with low rateable values at the expense of the grant to those with high rateable values, with the result that for any given rate in the pound, every authority would receive the same amount of money per head. It was illogical, and it was not fair because it resulted in the ratepayers in the south heavily subsidizing the ratepayers in the north. We ended Resources Equalization when the Community Charge came in in 1990. This was the reason for the large increase that people had to pay in the north, and in Ribble Valley in particular. The trouble at the Ribble Valley by-election in 1991 was not really the Poll Tax, but the ending of Resources Equalization: the average family had to pay about three times more as a result. The strange thing about Resources Equalization was that no one seemed to know that it existed: neither those who paid too much, nor those who benefited from it. It wouldn't have lasted as long as it did if they had! If there had been a revaluation in England in the mid 1980s, the historically very low rateable values of the north might have been increased to more realistic levels. There would have been the same sort of increases in the amount people had to pay, including in Ribble Valley!

The second defect was the effect of rates rebates for the less well-off, which Ted Heath had introduced in 1974 – not unreasonably, since by then the burden of the rates was becoming intolerable for some lower-income groups. By the 1980s these rebates had had the effect on average of leaving less than half the population paying full rates. But that average concealed the fact that in some areas in the cities as few as 18 per cent or 20 per cent of the residents paid full rates. This had enabled high-spending Labour councils, like Liverpool, Lambeth and Newcastle, to levy a very high rate, knowing that most of their political supporters would not have to pay, although they benefited from the spending. The result of all these anomalies is that under the old rating system half the population paid nothing at all, the south subsidized the north, people in large houses subsidized people in small ones, and single people subsidized families. There was no logic in it at all, let alone any relationship with ability to pay. The councils went on increasing their spending with impunity.

People in better houses and businesses who had to pay were faced with enormous bills, with the result that over time they tended to move out to cheaper areas, further exacerbating the problem of too little commercial activity in the cities, and causing higher rates still to be needed. This aspect of local property taxation should not be ignored. High differences in a local tax between one area and another do affect where people decide to live, causing movements of population away from areas of high property taxes and upsetting the social balance in these areas.

Rate bills in England for similar people and businesses could vary by a factor of three or four times owing to the way the system had developed. At the same time many paid nothing at all. No wonder people complained about the unfairness of the rates.

In 1979 Margaret Thatcher was quick to set about reform. She asked Michael Heseltine, her then Environment Secretary, to draw up options for an alternative local tax to rates. His report when it came out put three options as alternatives : it trotted out the three well-known and often-examined options of a local income tax, a local sales tax and a poll tax. Margaret Thatcher could find no way forward. The reform was shelved. I was not a member of the Cabinet myself, so I cannot describe the arguments.

Meanwhile, Geoffrey Howe at the Treasury had determined on a policy of cutting the grant paid to local authorities as a percentage of their spending progressively year by year. Nigel Lawson continued the policy. It fell from 61 per cent of total expenditure in 1979 to 43 per cent in 1989. The result of this was inevitably to increase the rates. Local authority spending continued to rise, and as less came from the centre, more had to come from local ratepayers. As a discipline to make councils curtail their expenditure it didn't work, because the most extravagant councils were those where ratepayers were in a minority in the electorate. But it did have the effect of making the rates higher, and therefore more intolerable still; and also, later, when the grant was further cut to 39 per cent of expenditure in 1990, to make the Community Charge far too high to be tolerable when it came in. In retrospect it was a mistake, because it put too great a burden onto the local taxation system – neither rates nor Community Charge was designed to take such a heavy burden.

I mentioned in Chapter 2 how, at a lunch at Chequers on 23 June 1985, a few of us persuaded Margaret Thatcher to try once more to find a way of reforming the rates. The task eventually fell to Kenneth Baker, who became Environment Secretary a few months later. He was assisted by William Waldegrave, who was the Minister of State. At that time Margaret Thatcher was not aware of the results of the Scottish revaluations which became public knowledge early in 1986. New rental values were published in Scotland for rating purposes following a revaluation. Rateable values in Scotland had not been reviewed since 1978. There were large changes in the valuations put on many houses – some even doubling and trebling relative to others. There was a major political protest. The variation between what different people had to pay, although their circumstances were similar, was indefensible; and many didn't have to pay anything at all. There was much justified indignation at the result of the revaluation. The inherent unfairnesses and anomalies in the system of rating were sharpened and brought into focus by the large and arbitrary changes that were suddenly proposed. The Scots thought they were being victimized by having their revaluation before the English one. They demanded remedial action. The government had to legislate to cushion the impact of the increases.

So great was the protest, and so arbitrary were the results of the revaluation, that it led the Scottish Secretary, George Younger, to say in a radio broadcast: 'We have had one go at trying to reform rates and everyone was against the alternatives. This time we have to deliver. Not acting at all means there will be severe political consequences. No one is prepared to put up with the system as it is, and I agree with them.'

It is worth remembering those words when considering a return to a property tax for local taxation. Most of us were convinced there had to be a change even before the Scottish revaluation. After it, there could be no doubt.

The last revaluation in England was in 1973 – and it was clear that if a revaluation had been carried out in England in the mid-80s there would have been an even greater storm of protest, with the new values bringing forth even greater changes, unfairnesses and political anger. On the other hand, to continue on the old 1973 valuations negated the principle of rating – that it should be based on the rental value. After twelve years, values were completely different. The passage of time continually changes such values, as had been demonstrated in Scotland.

Kenneth Baker and William Waldegrave busied themselves in the search for an alternative. Precisely when the choice of the Poll Tax came to be made, or how it was selected, I do not know, since I was not a member of the small group that handled it. I was then Transport Secretary. All cabinet ministers were canvassed early in the process; I remember William Waldegrave canvassing me. My reaction was to be strongly in favour of getting rid of the rates, and also in favour of a flat-rate charge, provided the level of the tax was not too high. I never saw it as a large revenue raiser; indeed, I believe I suggested at that time that another source of revenue might be necessary in addition to the Poll Tax. I found the arguments about accountability very powerful. Under a Poll Tax, everyone would have to pay something, even if it was very little. Thus everyone would have a financial interest in keeping their council's expenditure to reasonable levels. Everyone would wish to hold them to account at the next elections if they failed. Everyone had the vote. It was the same symmetrical arrangement of voting, paying and benefiting from services that had made the original concept of rates acceptable in Victorian times.

Kenneth Baker took the proposal to Cabinet at the end of 1985. There was a general acceptance of the proposals, although Nigel Lawson, as he has since made clear, was firmly opposed. I am not clear whether he wanted to face up to, or once more postpone, the revaluation. Discussion mainly centred on the arrangements Kenneth Baker proposed for 'dual running'. The plan was to keep the rating system going and bring in the Poll Tax alongside it, and gradually transfer the burden from the old to the new system. At one time it was even proposed that the rates should simply be frozen and allowed to 'wither on the vine' as inflation eroded their value. I disliked this plan very much. It never seemed to me right to have two taxes in operation at once, and the accountability advantages of the Community Charge would be completely obscured. It meant keeping the rates for countless years to come, when we were setting out to abolish them. The plan was later amended to one of phasing out 'dual running' over a five-year period. In the end, I managed to get rid of 'dual running' altogether and we were at last able to abolish the rates. 'Dual-running' had no friends when the proposals were debated publicly. It was the Party Conference of 1987 that finally killed it, when speaker after speaker denounced the plan. Margaret Thatcher was sitting next to me on the platform. She whispered in my ear, 'We shall have to look at this again, Nick.' The television cameras picked up the incident, and lip readers were employed to decipher what she had said. I claimed later that she had said, 'Do you want another glass of water, Nick?' I don't think I was believed. It shows how all-pervasive is the television camera.

The famous Green Paper, 'Paying for Local Government', introducing the Community Charge – the new name given to the Poll Tax – was published in January 1986.

Its reception was less hostile than might have been expected. The prospect of the rates coming to an end was welcomed by many, and the flat-rate head charge had many adherents. Much of the argument concerned the plans for phasing out the rates over a long period and the plan to introduce the Community Charge at £50 per adult. It did not appear likely to rise much above £150 per adult on average, even when rates had been abolished finally. The Green Paper demonstrated how rebated Community Charges were much fairer than the old rating system had been, and much more closely related to ability to pay. The rebate system proposed in the Green Paper was that the proportion of a full charge which the less well-off should pay varied from 20 per cent to 100 per cent as incomes increased – reflecting ability to pay.

The Scottish Secretary was by then Malcolm Rifkind, who had replaced George Younger when he became Defence Secretary following Michael Heseltine's resignation in January 1986. He resolved to get the new system installed in Scotland as quickly as possible. Resentment at the rating revaluation was still running high in Scotland and it was judged expedient to get the new system in place before a general election, which had to be within a year or two. The Cabinet agreed to bringing the Scottish Bill forward, and it was introduced into Parliament in October 1986, becoming law before the June 1987 General Election. The English and Welsh Bill could not possibly have been got ready and passed through Parliament in time, so it was agreed to defer it until after the election. Although designed to help Scotland in response to their indignation at being the first to have a revaluation, this decision came to be strongly criticized on the grounds that we were making Scotland a 'guinea pig' for the new system. It is hard to be right with the Scots! They duly took it out on the Conservatives in the 1987 election, reducing our representation in that country to ten seats. I am no expert on Scottish politics, but I suspect this was more due to a long-term political swing against the Tories for reasons other than the Community Charge.

In May 1986 Keith Joseph finally retired from office as Education Secretary. He felt he had reached the age when he needed a less hectic life. He remained active in politics and strong in his support for Margaret Thatcher from the Conservative benches in the House of Lords, always putting his great intellect at her service. Margaret Thatcher moved Kenneth Baker from the Environment Department to take his place and she moved me from Transport to Environment. I was telephoned late at night by her Private Secretary and asked to appear at Number 10 at 9.30 the next morning. I left my office on the pretext of wanting to buy something in the shops and returned there only to say farewell to my excellent staff. I remember having mixed feelings as Margaret Thatcher asked me to take on the task of implementing the Community Charge proposals. The task was daunting, particularly as there were so many other irons in the fire at DoE – but I gladly accepted the challenge. I was also thankful that she hadn't sent me to Education, a Department I never wanted to be in; nor did I feel capable of doing the job there.

I was fortunate in my Local Government junior ministers. Until the 1987 election I had Rhodes Boyson as my Minister of State. After the election, I had Michael Howard. I was also fortunate in the fact that the civil servants in charge of local government finance were of the very highest calibre. They knew the subject backwards. They had carried out two full reviews in five years: they little thought they would have to do a third review in only four years' time.

I wanted to make sure for myself that the Community Charge, being a flat-rate tax per head, could be made fair. I was particularly concerned that, in requiring everybody to pay something, it should not have the effect of making anybody pay too much. I even examined again all the alternatives myself before I was satisfied that it was the right solution. As many have done before and since, I found none of the alternatives was really satisfactory. Given that the premise is that a proportion of local spending should be financed by a tax raised locally, there are only four real options: a local sales tax, a local income tax, a local property tax, or a flat-rate charge. No one believes a sales tax would work, or be sensible. Our local government areas are so small that most people would be happy to go a few miles to shop in the next council's area if the sales tax were less there. Also, major retail sales tend to take place in some councils' areas and few in others'. The receipt of revenue would be most irregular and unfair. Not many realize that a local income tax is not practical, although in my view it is also undesirable. It is simply not possible to identify the income of each person who lives in a local authority's area. It proved hard enough to identify the names of the people who live in each area; the Community Charge Register sets out to do that, and is only succeeding in doing so with difficulty. If it were necessary to find out their income as well, the task would prove impossible. Nor could the Inland Revenue help. It is not only banned by statute from releasing details of taxpayers' incomes, but it does not know where the majority of people live. Most people pay their income tax through PAYE (Pay As You Earn). The Revenue rely on the employer to deduct tax, and have no direct contact with individual employees. Thus they know the addresses of only a minority of taxpayers. Nor is it desirable for them to know, because I do not think local authorities should have a weapon for the redistribution of income.

There is a key here to what is really the best solution. The criticism made most frequently of the Community Charge, and of the rates before it, was that they were not related to ability to pay. If that criticism is accepted, it means those with higher incomes paying more than those with lower incomes. It is not possible to make sure those with higher incomes pay more than the standard tax or charge, because they can't be identified, and they certainly would not volunteer to identify themselves and their income if the result was that they had to pay more. If the standard tax or charge is set at quite a high level, and generous rebates are provided for those with lower incomes, the desired result can be achieved. Those entitled to rebates will be quick to claim them, and it is easy to verify their claims. Few, if any, will miss out on an opportunity to claim a reduction to which they are entitled. There is little likelihood of low take-up. This is why rebated poll taxes are the only form of local tax that can be related to ability to pay.

As to property taxes, the whole purpose of the operation in 1985 was to end an unpopular and unfair property tax – the rates. It is easy now to forget the antagonism to rates which grew throughout the 1960s and 1970s; and also to forget the experience of the Scottish revaluation. The need to have an English revaluation was the clinching argument. The reason for this antagonism was that rates were not closely related to ability to pay, as I have described earlier. No other form of property tax can avoid the anomalies and unfairnesses of rates – they are endemic in the form of a tax which is based not on ability to pay, but on the value put upon the property in which one lives. People gloss over this point by saying that 'broadly, the more valuable someone's house is, the better off they must be.' But for something to be 'broadly' true is not enough as there are many poor people living in expensive properties, and wealthier people in modest homes. Moreover, if the tax is to be based on the value of a property, that value should be established accurately and kept up to date. Income tax is based on the value of one's income which is quite rightly valued to the nearest pound each year. To operate an accurate annual property tax, the authorities should really obtain an accurate annual valuation of every property in the land – an impossible proposition. If revaluations are held only at long intervals, all hell breaks out when they do take place, as Scotland showed. Annual valuation of every property every year would be a mammoth task, which would turn us into a nation of valuers. And it would result in immediate penalization of those who improved their homes.

So I came to the conclusion in 1986 that the Community Charge was the right way forward. But I believed it would be right only if it were not at a level too high for anyone to pay. The principle that everyone should pay something seemed paramount at that time, after our experience of only 20 per cent of the electorate paying rates in some local authority areas. Equally, I was sure it should be properly rebated for those on low incomes, to make sure it was within their ability to pay at all levels of income.

Margaret Thatcher, I suspect, saw all this more in terms of the primacy of the need to get rid of the rates. The worst feature of the rates, she thought, was that they were a tax on those who improved their homes. Home ownership and home improvement and the building up of the family round a home were at the heart of the society she wanted to see. She herself will probably regard as one of her greatest achievements the increase in home ownership of 3.4 million families which took place during her Prime Ministership. She was determined to keep mortgage-interest relief, which assisted this desirable process, and she was determined to get rid of the rates, which she believed hindered it. She wanted to give the middle classes a fairer deal than hitherto and penalizing them for improving their homes was the opposite of that.

So we set about designing all the details of what became the Local Government Finance Act 1988.

The Scottish Bill received Royal Assent before the 1987 election, and the English and Welsh one started its progress soon after it. It had a turbulent passage through Parliament. The Labour Opposition were not the problem. They were always on the defensive because they agreed with abolishing the rates, but could not say what they would put in their place. They put up option after option, which we succeeded in ridiculing. In the end, after they had supported abolishing rates, they came back to advocating them. It was the Tories who were critical of the Bill who were the problem. A major revolt was led by Michael Mates, Tory MP for Petersfield, who advocated a system of 'banding' whereby those on higher incomes would pay one and a half Community Charges. This was, in fact, impractical, for the reason I have given: that it is impossible to find out who the better off are in a local council area. We had a major debate on the 'Mates amendment' in an atmosphere of crisis, and won the Division by only 25 votes. Margaret Thatcher was extremely concerned: I remember her relief sitting next to me on the bench when the teller announced the result of the Division.

There was one other aspect of the 'Mates amendment', however, which was much more attractive. At the time of the passage of the Bill, we thought the Community Charge would work out on average at

"ONE MORE STEP - AND I'LL BLOW YOUR BRAINS OUT!"

about £200 per head. We designed the system of rebates for the less well off, reducing the proportion of the Charge to be paid progressively from 100 per cent to 20 per cent at the income level of those on benefit or pension alone. Thus, a single person with no other income would pay about £40 a year, and a couple £80. We also increased the level of benefits over and above inflation by similar amounts in April 1989, so that those who lived in an area where the Charge was indeed £200 would be neither better nor worse off. Nevertheless, all would have an incentive to see lower council spending, since all would gain from it, including those on benefit.

The original plan for the rebate was that those on income support levels would get an 80 per cent rebate; for every extra £5 of income, £1 extra Community Charge would be payable. Thus, at a certain level of income, the full 100 per cent would be payable, depending, of course, on the level of the Charge in the particular area concerned. The crucial point lay in fixing the level of income at which entitlement to a rebate ran out. It was at the income level where it ran out that the burden was likely to become onerous. The 'Mates amendment' sought to extend a 50 per cent discount to all who did not pay income tax. This would have assisted those at this crucial level of incomes. I thought he was right; but the better way to meet his point was by improving the rebate system still more by flattening the taper from £1 more Charge for every £5 more income to £1 more Charge for every £6 more income – or from 20 per cent to 15 per cent. This we agreed to do. It more than met Michael Mate's point, in an administratively practical way.

This improved system of rebates would indeed have been adequate if the average Community Charge had worked out about £200. But it didn't; it worked out at nearer £400. Two authorities, Wandsworth and Westminster, did indeed manage to live with Community Charges below £200. I have never quite understood why the first year's Community Charge came out in practice quite so much higher than we expected when we fixed the grant level in July 1989. I left the DoE thereafter, but I think the reasons for this surprising result were many. First, in part it was because many local authorities resolved to increase their spending by even more than usual, often deliberately in order to discredit the new system. Second, most budgeted for much lower rates of collection than we had allowed, often not trying very hard afterwards to collect the Community Charge from those who did not pay. Third, many authorities incurred higher costs in setting up their Register than we provided for. The Community Charge cost about twice as much to collect as the rates, because twice as many people had to pay it, but the councils budgeted higher than we expected for the cost of collection. Finally, the Revenue Support Grant turned out to be inadequate. Inflation was gathering pace at the time, and the grant contained insufficient allowance for that. The policy was still to squeeze the grant down, as it had been since 1979, and it just turned out to be too small. I had tried to secure more from John Major, the Chief Secretary to the Treasury, but I had not succeeded. Neither of us realized at the time, however, by how much it was going to prove inadequate. There was something we both knew: that the greater the grant the more the local authorities spent, rather than passing it on to their electors in lower taxes. In fact, the proportion of spending covered by the grant was cut again, in 1989, from 43 per cent of local authority expenditure to 39 per cent for the first year of the Community Charge.

Those were the reasons, but the consequence of community charges coming out in the region of £400 was that the rebate system was inadequate. Some people whose incomes were just above the level where the rebate ran out were expected to pay 10 per cent or more of their net income. This was the aspect which was hardest to defend; the principle of ability to pay had got swamped by the unexpectedly high levels of the Charge in the first year.

There was considerable political protest, which came to be exploited by the extreme left. There were a number of riots, the worst one taking place in Trafalgar Square, with dozens of casualties as well as arrests resulting. The riots didn't persist, in my view because the protesters realized they were being exploited by the violent element in society.

There was also a movement, particularly in Scotland, to refuse to pay the Charge. Many councils did not try very hard to collect what their electors owed them. It became a political cause to encourage non-payment. The Scottish Nationalist MPs and some Labour MPs actually advocated breaking the law in their determination to oppose.

During the winter of 1989 the first councils that had done their sums began suggesting that Community Charge levels would be as high as twice what we had expected. On learning this, Chris Patten, my successor, went back to the Treasury and managed to get another £300 million in extra grant. He spent it mainly on transitional schemes, designed to ease the burden of those who had benefited from low rates and would now have to pay a higher Charge. In my judgement, this was an error: the money should have been used to improve the rebate scheme. It wouldn't have mattered if the Charge was high, so long as it was properly rebated down the income scale, according to ability to pay.

Later, after John Major became Prime Minister, Michael Heseltine returned to the DoE and obtained a further 1.25 billion from the Treasury, which he put into a new device called the Community Charge Reduction Scheme. Finally, in the 1991 Budget, a further £4.25 billion was thrown at the problem by increasing VAT from 15 per cent to 17.5 per cent. This was used to bring all Community Charges down by £140 across the country for 1991–2.

Including the annual grant uprating, and, after I left DoE, £8.5 billion was found to moderate the Community Charge, and not one penny of that went directly into Community Charge rebates. With hindsight, for less than half that sum of money, the problem could have been solved and the charge tailored to ability to pay through the rebate system.

We should have seen the key point in 1988 when there was a notorious leak of a Government paper. When I persuaded my colleagues to extend the rebate scheme by flattening the taper from 20 per cent to 15 per cent, in response to the Michael Mates's amendment, they had insisted that the £360 million which that cost should be 'clawed back'. This meant that the total of the Revenue Support Grant from the Government to the councils should be cut by £360 million to pay for the rebates. The minute of the meeting at Number 10 when this decision was taken was leaked to the press. The words 'clawed back' were greeted with shock, horror and alarm by the press. By reducing the grant, the Community Charge would be that much higher – 'how dreadful' screamed the press.

In fact, it was pretty meaningless, because the grant had not been fixed at the time. The principle, however, was obviously right – to allow the Charge to rise for those on reasonable or good incomes, in order to finance a generous rebate for those less fortunate. The press were wrong to criticize the 'claw back' decision, and the Government should have taken the lesson on board. The Community Charge should have been high – even as high as £600 or £800. But it should also have been reduced all the way down the income scale – from 100 per cent at an income of, say £20,000, down perhaps to 5 per cent at incomes of benefit or pension levels alone. In that way everyone would have had to contribute something, it would have been truly related to ability to pay, and it would have been acceptable to the British people who feel very strongly about 'fairness'.

One of the difficulties was that the rebates were called 'Community

Charge Benefits', and administered by the Department of Social Security. They thus seemed like welfare payments and the argument was used that you couldn't pay welfare payments to those on average income or above. In fact, they were no more a welfare payment than a lower rate of income tax is a welfare payment to abate the higher rate of income tax.

The British take the concept of 'fairness' a little further, however, and include the requirement that the 'rich' should pay much more. The press (wrongly) attributed a remark to me at one time. 'Why shouldn't the duke and the dustman pay the same?' I was alleged to have said. What I had said was that the duke and the dustman did pay the same for many things – but redistribution of income was properly the function of national taxation, not local taxation. In fact, dukes did pay far more than dustmen towards local government because they contribute heavily through income tax to the half of its revenue which comes from the Exchequer in grant. A higher-rate taxpayer paid about 15 times more than someone on benefit towards local government in total, even with the Community Charge at quite high levels.

The only way that 'rich' people can be made to pay more towards local government is to have a higher top rate of national income tax. As I have said, it is not possible to find out what is the income of everyone who lives in a particular council area. In 1988 the government foreclosed this option for itself. Nigel Lawson, in that year's Budget, reduced the top rate of income tax from 60 per cent to 40 per cent. So not only did we bring in a system of local taxation which didn't require the 'rich' to make a large direct local contribution, but we actually reduced what they had to contribute centrally by a large amount. The combination of the two was unfortunate, to say the least. With a level of grants which had the result of causing the Community Charge to come out at nearly double what we had expected, this was not an auspicious start for the new system. Indeed, my successors found it necessary to increase the grant by £8.5 billion within the next 18 months. That was far more than was needed, and it was applied in the wrong way. It was used to bring down the Charge for both dukes and dustmen, instead of giving the dustman a rebate and letting the duke pay a high Charge. A duke and duchess with three houses benefited by £840 from the 1991 Budget and by very much more if they paid their employees' Community Charges too, as many did.

In the end, the Community Charge was to play a role in Margaret Thatcher's fall from power. Michael Heseltine's challenge to her was based on exploiting its unpopularity by promising yet another 'fundamental review' of the system. The other two contenders – John Major and Douglas Hurd – could hardly do otherwise than offer the same. I believe Michael Heseltine had not the faintest idea of what he wanted the result of the fundamental review to be. The Labour Party had been wrestling with the problems for the five years over which this saga developed. They had failed to find a better solution. Both John Major and Douglas Hurd had been members of the Government from 1986 to 1990 which had also failed to find a better alternative. It would have been surprising if anyone had suddenly found the crock of gold in November 1990. The three months of confusion that followed the setting up of the Government's Official Review was evidence of this: leak followed leak, each option to be withdrawn quickly as soon as its reception was seen to be unfriendly. It seemed as if every possibility was being floated in public, only to be immediately rejected. The reason for the confusion, as I kept pointing out at the time, was that there really was no obviously better alternative. The confusion surrounding the Government's Review in early 1991 showed how difficult they found it to come up with a replacement. I doubt very much whether it will prove to be a better system than the one it is designed to replace. By then, however, the Government had itself discredited the Community Charge, causing it death by a thousand cuts. It seemed as if the purpose of the operation was to exorcize its ghost, rather than to find a better system. Michael Heseltine was clearly trying to cash in on its unpopularity without any constructive alternative in his mind when he offered the Fundamental Review to the Tory MPs whose votes he sought; he was determined to see it die.

Be that as it may, Margaret Thatcher was vulnerable on this issue in November 1990. She hadn't taken the action necessary to ensure the new system's acceptability by relating it more closely to ability to pay. It was perceived as 'unfair'; indeed, it was unfair without an adequate system of rebates. Two years hence, and after much debate and legislation, we will know the full details of the new system of local taxation to replace the Community Charge. No system of property tax can ever be 'fair', or related to ability to pay. Memories seem surprisingly short. There will be many who will lose as a result of the change, and they will protest just as loudly as those who lost from the Community Charge.

In the middle of all this turmoil, the Government suddenly decided to reduce every Charge by £140 in the 1991 Budget. They had, as it were, cured the problem at a stroke, despite the fact that they were striving to find an alternative system. Michael Heseltine wrote in

March 1991, 'The average Community Charge actually to be paid in England in 1991–2 will be about £170, while the amount paid in rates per adult in 1989–90 was about £230.' It's hard to see what all the fuss is about if that is so. In a sense, they had even vindicated the rioters and those who had refused to pay. Lawlessness seemed to have paid off. It wouldn't surprise me if, when we get there, there will be an overwhelming clamour to leave the present system in place. Now that the average Charge 'actually to be paid' is about £170, instead of £400, it may well prove acceptable, and the existing rebate arrangements will work at this level to protect poorer families from being asked to pay too much. It may even be that after all the fuss, the Community Charge will seem not to be so bad as to justify bringing down Margaret Thatcher. When all is said and done, most people spend more on the milk bill than they now spend on the Community Charge.

7

EUROPE

THERE HAD BEEN no policy group on European policy before 1979. None had seemed necessary. Margaret Thatcher knew what she thought about Europe. It was not an issue of contention in the Shadow Cabinet, nor much of an issue elsewhere. There was a small, diehard minority of dedicated anti-common marketeers still active in the Tory Party. There was a larger one in the Labour Party. But the topic presented few problems to the Government elected in 1979.

British thinking about Europe has, in fact, remained very much the same since the end of the Second World War. Britain wants to see a Europe that cooperates, works together, and grows close. We want a Europe that practises genuine free trade, both within its boundaries and in relation to the rest of the world. We do not want to submerge our identity, nor our freedom to manage our own affairs in some European federal structure which has ultimate control over our destiny. All that has happened over the decades in Europe, and Britain's contribution to it, can be explained by those three consistent and continuous strands of policy, from Winston Churchill to Margaret Thatcher. Throughout, this policy has been close to the views of the mass of the British people. They are not inward-looking or xeno-phobic. They look to Europe for free trade: it is the way they have always earned their livings. They want friendly and cooperative relations with all the nations of Europe. But they have a rugged confidence in their own political institutions and they are determined to maintain their independence. In my view, the British people would reject any government that sought to cede control of the country to a federal Europe.

By contrast, the continental nations of Europe have different preoccupations. By far the most important is the overriding desire for Franco-German rapprochement in order to prevent a possible third European war. All Germany's neighbours share the same ideal; memories of the last war run deep across the whole continent. But the

Franco-German relationship is both the kernel and the symbol of this desire. Germans, more than anyone else, want to be integrated into something bigger and more powerful than themselves in order to frustrate forever that aggressive element that they fear still lurks in their character. As one prominent German put it to me recently, 'We want to be tied down, tied in and tied up.' Most of Germany's neighbours see their priority as to oblige them.

The continental nations tend to be half-hearted, too, in their approach to free trade. Their history is riddled with cartels, monopolies, protective barriers and tariffs. Most of them traditionally have traded internally, or within the continent, rather than being major world-trading nations. Although they pay lip service to open markets and the Single European Act, it is surprising how many exceptions and derogations they cling to, or reinvent, each in their own different ways. There are large public sectors, particularly in France, Italy, Spain and Greece, which are used quite shamelessly, but legally, to distort fair competition. The Common Agricultural Policy (CAP) is their pride and joy – it is about as far from free trade as it is possible to get. Even the German market is closed in a number of important respects.

With such different objectives and attitudes, it is not surprising that Britain has never been a full-hearted member of the Community, and that the others describe us as intransigent and laggard. This difference of objectives explains all the major events from our decision not to sign the Treaty of Rome in 1957 to our current refusal to have the Single European Currency imposed upon us in 1991. It is worth pointing out, however, that we have attained a far higher proportion of our objectives than our continental friends have of theirs. Europe nearly is a single market now; it is a market fairly open to the outside world, although with too many notable exceptions; and fair competition is being enforced by the Commission with welcome vigour. The areas of substance where decisions are imposed on member states by majority voting are, in the main, those where it is necessary for the financing of the Community and for the enforcement of fair trading in all its manifestations. Thus, British policy has been pretty successful, despite the endless criticisms of 'too little, too late' and 'Britain is isolated' and 'Britain does not share the European ideal.' Britain indeed does not share the 'European ideal', and probably never will, if that means a federal Europe.

Certainly Margaret Thatcher did not share the 'European ideal' in 1979. She was in favour of our membership of the Community, and had voted for it when we joined in 1973, and in the Referendum. But she always wanted Britain to retain the maximum amount of control, and to yield as little power as possible to the centre. She expressed this view often using the word 'Sovereignty'. Although critics would point out how complex a concept 'sovereignty' is, to her it was a simple concept of 'who decides?' Perhaps for her it has a useful connotation too with the 'sovereign'. The two images together are understood and shared by the British people. In her attitude to Europe, Margaret Thatcher spoke for the vast majority of the people. As so often, she embodied their prejudices and instincts very closely. She was at the centre of the political spectrum in her views on Europe.

In 1979 the new Government was more or less of the same mind in its attitude to Europe; moreover, there was no great issue of principle confronting it. The only cloud on the horizon was still no bigger than a man's hand. The Exchange Rate Mechanism had come into operation a year before, but we were not members of it, and there was no pressure for us to be. The only issue which was of current concern, and had been for some time, was the excessive size of our contribution to the Community Budget. In terms of our gross contribution, we were certainly paying more than our fair share; and less than our fair share came back to Britain through Community spending. This was because, as the member state with the greatest proportion of our production traded, we paid more than the others in the levies and duties which were collected on imports and paid over to the Community. On the other side of the account, our relatively small agricultural industry received less of the huge European subsidies than our nominal share. So our net contribution was certainly excessive.

Margaret Thatcher seized on this issue as an example of discrimination against Britain, which indeed it was. It gave her a chance to be seen to be fighting publicly for British interests and to do battle with the Community on an issue unlikely to split the Party because it was not in any way concerned with sovereignty or the 'European ideal'. The Treasury prepared a paper setting out exactly how our contribution was calculated and precisely how much we were being exploited. With this evidence, she went to work. It was in fact a highly complex subject, but as was her wont, she mastered the detail completely. She fought a long battle over this – throughout which she had the advantage of knowing exactly what she was talking about, which her opponents often didn't. Our net contribution was so palpably unfair that it was foolish of the others to refuse to recognize it as such, let alone do anything about it. The French were particularly irritating over the issue. They lectured us haughtily about the sanctity of the Treaty of Rome and the inevitability of Britain subsidizing small continental farmers, because it was so ordained in the Common Agricultural Policy. No wonder; they were net beneficiaries of the system.

Margaret Thatcher achieved a temporary success in May 1980, when she persuaded her colleagues that for two years a sum of £1,400 million was to be repaid. The formula agreed also produced a lesser amount for 1982. But there was no provision for any rebates thereafter. She began the battle to secure a satisfactory, and permanent, solution early in 1983. It was not until 25 June 1984 at the Fontainebleau Summit, that the matter was finally resolved. She achieved a solution very close to her original objective, with 66 per cent of our excess contribution agreed to be repaid. The matter was discussed at no less than twelve European summits.

The leaders of the other European states had been determined to frustrate her. They all benefited from Britain's forced largesse and they didn't want to pay any more money themselves. They thought a mixture of obduracy and haughtiness would win the day. They scorned her, and we know what happens when a woman is scorned. She did behave with that reputed fury at times – but she also displayed immense tenacity at meeting after meeting. At times she blocked progress on all other issues; she turned down compromise offer after compromise offer, until she at last achieved her objective. Her insistence – many called it intransigence – saved the British taxpayers very large sums of money over the years. It required great determination to stick to her guns. The others seemed determined to extract as much money from Britain as they could.

At one time I was a great enthusiast for the European cause. I had been from 1962 to 1966 a delegate to the Council of Europe, where I had 'gone native' and become converted to a much more federalist point of view, shielded, I suppose, from reality by the fact that we were not then even members of the Community. I remember John Foster, an eminent and rumbustious Tory lawyer, once accusing me in the House, in jest, of being a 'federast'. Anyone who has had ten years of experience of the working of the Council of Ministers and the Commission is likely to be converted back again from being a 'federast', and I certainly was, as I will explain.

I came across this same mean attitude towards Britain. As Financial Secretary, from 1981 to 1983, it was my job to attend the Budget

Councils, where the Community's budget was agreed for the year. In 1983 there were two extra sums of money due to us under the 1980 agreement – one of about £36 million and one of about £42 million. The Council tried to ensure that neither sum should be paid, thus breaking the agreement which they had signed with us some two years before. I attended a Council meeting of two days and nights in order to try to secure our just dues. On the first occasion, we argued all through the night, and I managed to persuade them to agree to the £36 million item. In the middle of the night I was called back to London in order to vote in the House of Commons at some ghastly hour like 6.00 am: the Whips were expecting a close result in some important Division. I remember arriving at Luton Airport in a small plane specially hired for the trip, and being driven to London at great speed.

After I had voted, Margaret Thatcher called me into her room. I described the success we had achieved so far and added that I had had to leave before it had been finally tied up; but I was sure that the officials who had remained behind, could do this. 'No, Nick,' she said. 'You had better go back now and make sure it's all right.' I don't think I could have done so, I was so tired by then. I am afraid I refused – but we did get the agreement.

Despite another all-night sitting soon after, we never secured the other sum of £42 million. The French minister took particular pleasure in organizing a majority to block it. They had few arguments – they were just determined to do us down, and were not in the least concerned by the clear breach of the earlier undertaking. I had no doubt about the soundness of our case. It didn't make me a devotee of European union.

Franco-German rapprochement may indeed be the mainspring of the Community, and very welcome it is. But in practice it was distorted into a Franco-German axis, operated to secure the objectives of those two countries. In return for French forgiveness and friendship, the Germans were prepared to pay the bill and to support the French, unless this clashed with one of their vital interests. The French returned the compliment. Thus they became a powerful combination in the Community, usually able to outvote us.

This same divergence of objectives between Britain and most of her Continental neighbours leads to another complex problem – what should be the future nature of the Community's political institutions and how to secure greater democratic accountability within them? It is admitted on all sides that there is a 'democratic deficit'. But the solutions are clearly very different depending on whether one sees the future of Europe as a federal one, or as one of a 'Europe of member states'. One can understand how the present arrangements grew up. It was necessary in 1957 to have a driving force to push the original six into cooperating and creating a Common Market. The Commission was given this task, and it was expressly set up as both unelected and unaccountable, the better to be able to perform it. It probably was necessary then. But 30 years on it is not, and it is no longer acceptable for member states to be told what to do by an unelected and unaccountable executive. The Commission alone can propose legislation – neither the member states nor the Parliament can. The Commission also enforces directives. It is both lawmaker, policeman and prosecutor.

Margaret Thatcher saw the future of the Commission as eventually becoming the Civil Service to the Council of Ministers – a major change, but one consistent with developing a Europe of sovereign states. The Commission saw themselves as the embryonic government of a European federation, and were prepared to concede only that one day they would have to submit themselves to direct election and to increase their democratic accountability to the European Parliament.

Margaret Thatcher saw the European Parliament as an irrelevant talking shop, and was determined to prevent it gaining more powers. I remember sitting next to her on one of the rare occasions when she addressed the Strasbourg Parliament. You could feel the waves of hostility emanating from her. An Irish MEP started shouting at her offensively about H-Blocks from the back of the hall during her speech. Afterwards someone made an interminable speech in Italian about 'building Europe'. There was no love lost either way.

The Commission want to see the powers of the Parliament increased in order to detract from the role of national parliaments and to build up the central democratic institutions of the Community. They want to see national parliaments dwindle to the role of regional or local government.

There can be no resolution of these different views of how to bring more democracy into the Community until it is resolved whether we have a federal Europe or a Europe of nation states.

There are other aspects of the democratic deficit in Europe. One is the control of Community expenditure. As I have said, it was part of my job as Financial Secretary to attend the Budget Council. This Council was supposed to scrutinize and limit the Community's spending. It was ineffective in doing so. It often ended up increasing spending; and the Parliament had power to increase it still more. The system of majority voting with twelve nations present is not a good way of performing this rather detailed task. The Council was also capable of descending to farce. One night, when Britain had the Presidency and I was chairman of a meeting, we sat through the night until 3.00 am. We were deadlocked on some minor issue: no solution could be found. Finally, after ten minutes of silence, the Irish Minister said, 'Mr President, I have a compromise to propose.' He duly elaborated it. I put it to the Council in the customary form of a *'tour de table'*. 'Oui,' said the French Minister, 'Ja,' said the German, 'Si,' said the Italian, and so on round the table, until I came to the twelfth minister, who was the Irishman – 'No,' he cried in a loud voice! We were back in deadlock.

This Budget, when it finally went to the European Parliament, was hijacked by it and vast extra sums were added to it, which the Commission had not even asked to spend. The experience shocked me deeply. A 'parliament' which simply wants to spend as much as it can extract is not a parliament to represent the taxpayers. Indeed, it is a good example of the evils of taxation without representation. Instead of seeking to rectify this, our Community partners go on insisting that the Parliament should be given more powers.

Another area of concern is what is known as the doctrine of 'subsidiarity'. This alien word means that that which is 'subsidiary' – i.e. not important – should be decided by national parliaments and not the Commission acting through the Council. It involves drawing up a list of topics – either a list which it will be for the centre to decide upon, or a list which will be the exclusive preserve of national parliaments. In some ways such a policy is much needed. We really do not need to be told what health warnings to put on cigarette packets, nor whether we can shoot crows, wood pigeons and magpies in the breeding season, let alone that carrots are fruit. In such stupid and unnecessary ways has the Commission succeeded in alienating vast sections of the British electorate. These and many other petty regulations have done more to put the British against Europe than anything; they are in no way relevant to free trade, or the Single Market, or any other essential ingredient of a Common European Policy.

The second event to concern Margaret Thatcher's Government was the Single European Act. The Single European Act was negotiated in 1985 and was brought into force in Britain by the European Communities (Amendment) Act of 1986. This amended the Treaty of Rome in several ways. Its main purpose was to hasten the creation of the Single Market and to set the date of the end of 1992 for its completion. It also contained two other important provisions (as well as one or two minor ones). One of these placed increased emphasis on more political cooperation in determining European foreign policy. The other placed renewed emphasis on European 'union' and mentioned once more the ultimate goal of economic and monetary union – although it defined it as economic and monetary cooperation.

Margaret Thatcher and her government were wholeheartedly in favour of the provisions relating to the Single Market. Apart from setting a tight timetable, they introduced majority voting, as opposed to unanimity, into a range of subjects necessary to complete the Single Market. An open market in Europe was what we had always wanted, and although the Government did not think it was actually necessary to amend the Treaty to attain it, they were content to go along with it.

More political cooperation was also acceptable – there was no coercion involved. But the restatement of Economic and Monetary Union (EMU) as an eventual goal worried Margaret Thatcher. It was declaratory, rather than binding; indeed, in Europe all Treaty obligations can only be made effective if enacted by legal directives, which would come later. Nevertheless, to agree to the Single European Act seemed to imply accepting at least the principle of EMU.

Indeed, it was held against her later that we had accepted the principle by agreeing to the Single European Act; an argument which I believe to be fallacious, since it would be true only if Britain had agreed to a directive bringing about EMU, which we would never have done. After all, there had been many earlier declaratory commitments to EMU by the EC. Margaret Thatcher hesitated over this dilemma, but eventually the Government agreed because of the advantages of the Single Market, and the Single European Act was approved by Parliament.

I am sure we were right to do this. It has resulted in very great progress being made towards freeing the market of the Community. Indeed, it was a British Commissioner, Lord Cockfield, who produced the list of scores of directives arising out of the Act that were needed to achieve the Single Market. The Single Market Council has been working through these directives ever since, and some 80 per cent of them have now been passed. We have a free internal market in the Community now for the vast majority of goods and services, apart from some notable exceptions. The main ones are, of course, agriculture (which is outside the provisions of the Single European Act); Japanese cars; steel and some areas of information technology which are still covered by Voluntary Restraint Agreements; insurance; company takeovers; air services and some other aspects of transport. I believe this is relatively satisfactory progress so far from the British point of view, though there is still much more to do. It has been a hard task to make as much progress as we have against the instinctive resistance of the protectionist elements in the Community.

'Political cooperation', as it is called, really means consulting about, and hopefully agreeing upon, a common foreign policy for the member states. Peter Carrington, when he was Foreign Secretary, made great efforts to advance this concept, as did Geoffrey Howe and Douglas Hurd when they had responsibility. The Single European Act added little to the process other than repeating its importance. It is the reality which has been the failure, although on some issues Europe did manage to speak with one voice.

The most notorious failure was over the Iraqi invasion of Kuwait. In the first phase, before war began, the Community stuck reasonably well together in supporting the United Nations Resolutions. But at the same time there were unilateral and disparate moves to negotiate with Saddam Hussein – particularly at the eleventh hour by the French. Nor could they agree when to conclude that sanctions against Iraq had failed – many wanted to wait for an unspecified period of time – in other words, put off the evil day. In the second phase, after war had started, our partners could hardly be said to have a common policy. The Belgians refused to supply Britain with ammunition. Only the French sent a force of any significance to fight alongside the Allies. The others did little or nothing.

Particularly irritating was the German attitude. The German Government was caught between its desire for 'political cooperation', indeed for political union, and the objections of a large section of German public opinion who were virtually pacifist. It shielded behind a provision in the German Constitution which, they claimed, prevented German forces being deployed outside the geographical area of NATO. This prohibition seemed to disappear when later German troops were used to good effect in the relief operation in the Kurdish crisis. After some delay, the Germans did come up with financial help towards the enormous costs that the Allies were incurring in prosecuting the war.

The Commission and its supporters had to admit the failure of Europe to pull together over the Iraqi war, but ascribed these failures to the absence of binding decision-taking institutions. It so happened that at that time there was much talk of the need for a common foreign policy and a common defence policy binding on member states. The truth is that if there had been such institutions, and if they had reached common foreign and defence policy positions, the Community would probably have played no part in supporting the Americans in the Gulf, certainly in kind, and perhaps even in cash too. There would have been a large majority against involvement – we would have been 'isolated' again.

These events mostly took place after Margaret Thatcher had ceased to be Prime Minister. But they completely vindicated her position over Europe.

A more significant development began in 1988. In June, the President of the Commission, Jacques Delors, was charged by the Hanover Summit with setting up a working party to study and propose steps which would lead to Economic and Monetary Union. The Group consisted of Delors himself, one other member of the Commission, the twelve central bank governors sitting in a personal capacity, and three so-called 'experts'. Their report was submitted to Heads of Governments on 14 April 1989.

Jacques Delors had been the French Finance Minister. In 1985 he was appointed one of the French Commissioners at Brussels. He was elected Chairman of the Commission and re-elected four years later. He was pleasant enough to meet. He is a small thin man, with a quizzical expression. He was also a typical French socialist. He was pragmatic in the extreme, believing more in the importance of power than of socialism, and he was intensely ambitious. As President of the Commission he resolved to use his position to press ahead with building the sort of dirigiste, centralized Europe which a French socialist would like to see. He had the opportunity to combine his country's desire for Franco-German rapprochement with his party's desire to see a centralized federal, slightly socialist Europe.

Margaret Thatcher was naturally apprehensive about this working party. She had observed Jacques Delors at many Council meetings, and he was a regular caller at Downing Street. He was much given to lecturing Britain about not being a good enough European, and made no secret of his wish to see Britain firmly under the control of central Community institutions, which would in fact give a dominant role to the Commission. He never would accept that she meant what she said about sovereignty and a Europe of independent nations.

Margaret Thatcher's relationships with the chief leaders of Europe were cordial enough individually. I attended a few of the bilateral summits which happen with remorseless regularity – I can remember very jovial meetings with both Chancellor Kohl and President Mitterrand. It was when they got together behind her back to try to get their own way that things got more difficult. I doubt if her relations with Jacques Delors were so cordial: she spotted in him a very ambitious politician, when she thought he should behave like a civil servant. Nor did she like his politics, which were socialist, dirigiste, and centralist. So the prospect of the Delors Report seemed menacing, and she resolved to stake out her ground first, in the hope of heading off the working party. She made a carefully prepared and powerful speech at Bruges in Belgium on 20 September 1988.

First she translated her own political philosophy for Britain onto a European scale. 'From classical and medieval thought we have borrowed that concept of the rule of law which marks out a civilized society from barbarism,' she said. Second, she emphasized Britain's historical involvement in Europe, while stressing the separateness of the great European nations. Third, she touched on a theme which was later to grow in importance. 'We must never forget that east of the Iron Curtain peoples who once enjoyed a full share of European culture, freedom and identity have been cut off from their roots.' Lastly, she set out at length her concept of a Europe of nation states, and explicitly rejected a federal future for Europe.

The speech got a lot of publicity and was heavily attacked by the Commission and eurofanatics the world over. The drift towards federalism got a severe jolt. It gave heart to many who were beginning to think it was inevitable. That was the argument which was hardest to answer: 'It is inevitable.' At least the inevitability had been challenged by one important European leader. The gloves were off from the Bruges speech on. Margaret Thatcher had made it clear that she would have nothing to do with Economic and Monetary Union.

This was the background to the publication of the Delors Report on 14 April 1989. The first stage was to achieve the completion of the internal market, free movement of capital within the Community and all currencies participating in the Exchange Rate Mechanism. During the second stage, the necessary institutions would be set up to run future European economic policy, including the 'Eurofed' – which was to be the central bank to manage the single currency. A proportion of national foreign exchange reserves would be transferred to the Eurofed for it to use in intervening to support the single European currency. The machinery would be developed to pay grants to the more backward economies (for competition-policy reasons these would be restricted to infrastructure, training and research). In the third stage, it was proposed to lock exchange rates irrevocably; by this act the single currency would be a fact and with us for the rest of time. It would be managed by Eurofed, free from 'political interference'.

There was one particularly arrogant suggestion in the Report. This said that the decision to enter upon the first stage would be a decision to embark on the entire process. This made us particularly angry – for we deeply disliked Stages II and III. Nigel Lawson never changed his attitude of hostility towards the single currency. Others among the Cabinet didn't even like Stage I – with its commitment to join the ERM. Stages II and III had few friends. Margaret Thatcher's worst fears about the Delors Report had been borne out. Some, like me, were against joining the ERM, but I was not aware of anyone who wanted to go into the single currency. The Delors Report seemed presumptuous to the whole Cabinet in 1988 when its contents were revealed to us.

I will describe later what happened in relation to Stage I and the pain and grief which the ERM issue caused Margaret Thatcher and her Government. I have written enough later about the dangers of fixed exchange rates not to need to repeat here the argument against both the ERM and EMU. There is, however, one consequence of the Delors Committee's ideas for a single currency which was covered fully in their report and which needs to be spelt out.

With a single currency and economic management confined to Brussels, there are no economic weapons left in the hands of national governments if their economies become uncompetitive. Devaluation is no longer possible and interest rates are decided centrally. Even budget policy would have to be controlled from the centre. The Delors Report proposed that the Eurofed should set for individual member states precise rules relating to the size of annual budget deficits and the method of their financing. Although this idea proved so unpopular that it was later partially withdrawn, it will be reinstated because it must be right in principle that individual member states cannot run up large budget deficits without the consent of the managers of the single currency. So national governments would not even be able to spend their way out of a depression. They would have no solution to offer the unemployed if their number grew alarmingly, and no powers to do anything to alleviate the distress.

The only means at the disposal of the Community to assist under such circumstances is to pay regional grants, such as we have paid for decades to assist the less prosperous regions of the United Kingdom. The Delors Report acknowledged this, and warned of the need for 'strengthening' community structural and regional policies, and of the increase in the Community's resources that that would imply. Such grants were to be restricted to 'research, training and infrastructure' investment, because more general forms of industrial subsidy are ruled out as 'anti-competitive' by the Treaty of Rome. It is obvious that research, training and infrastructure grants, however large, are unlikely on their own to cure a major problem of industrial uncompetitiveness, especially in 'regions', which could be as large as a whole nation. Our own experience over many years of regional grants has shown how little they achieve and how slow are their effects in Scotland, Wales, Northern Ireland and the north of England. The concept of a nation being limited to the Community's generosity – or lack of it – in the provision of research and infrastructure grants as the sole method of relieving massive and deep depression is surely alarming.

On the one hand we, along with the Germans, would be a major contributor towards paying such grants; on the other hand, we might also be a recipient, if we had the misfortune to lose competitiveness against the others. The Mediterranean countries and Ireland were expected to be the most likely recipients – which explains in part their willingness to go along with the single currency. It is likely that these grants would soon become a massive item of expenditure under a single currency.

Nor would they solve the problems of depressed regions – such problems are mainly caused by wages being higher than employers in the region can afford to pay if they are to maintain their competitive position. All experience shows that grants can't cure this: they just don't work. England has had a single currency with Scotland for some 300 years, yet the Scottish economy has never been quite able to keep up with the south, for reasons of geography and periphery. We currently pay grants of about £2.5 billion per annum to help the Scots. The Scots find these inadequate, the English find them excessive. This in turn leads to tension, animosity and, in the end, to resentment and separatist political movements, just as we have seen in Scotland. This sort of Community policy would actually have in it the seeds of the Community's own disintegration, because it wouldn't work. It would also be very, very expensive.

As I have shown, currency adjustments are the correct way to take account of such variations in industrial performance. But these are by definition ruled out with a single currency. It is not, in fact, possible to have a single currency except where the various economies within it are moving parallel in their pace of development. This manifestly does not apply in Europe, with countries whose economies are as far apart as Greece and Portugal and Ireland on the one hand, and Germany on the other. It is a basically flawed concept. As Margaret Thatcher and Nigel Lawson and John Major constantly pointed out, there has to be economic 'convergence' before there can be a single currency. That convergence must not only exist at the time of merging the currencies, but it must persist thereafter or strain will emerge.

There is one more consequence of a single currency of the sort proposed by Delors which is important. It effectively prevents any one member state from engaging in a large expenditure, certainly if it is not covered by a commensurate increase in tax yield. It is hard to see how Germany could have carried out unification – which, together with Eastern Europe, is costing it about £60 to £80 billion a year. The Chairman of the Bundesbank, Karl Otto Poehl, has described it as 'a disaster'. Since the tax increases imposed to pay for it yield no more than £20 billion, an uncovered deficit of £40 billion to £60 billion has arisen. The Eurofed would have had to intervene to prevent such a situation arising. Germany has incurred exactly that which is condemned in the Delors Report – a large uncovered budget deficit. The same could even have been true of Britain's heavy extra expenditure in the Gulf War to the extent that it had not been reimbursed by others. Otherwise it would have had the same effect – an increased budget deficit. In theory the Eurofed, managing a single currency, would have had to prevent that too. As John Maynard Keynes once said, 'Whoever controls the currency, controls the Government'.

These considerations set almost all the members of the Cabinet firmly against Stages II and III of the Delors Report. The press claimed that Geoffrey Howe and Douglas Hurd remained open to the concept, seeing it as they did through Foreign Office eyes. However, for some reason the idea took hold that it would be wrong to be entirely negative in our response to Delors and just say 'No.' We could perfectly easily have done that: to implement the Delors Report would require a new treaty, and that could only be done if the member states were unanimous. It also required legislation: the House of Commons had the power to reject it and would certainly have voted against it. That seemed to me, and probably to Margaret Thatcher, to be the right reaction. The Foreign Office influence, however, kept pressing for us to put forward an alternative suggestion, a counter-proposal, that would at least keep us present in the negotiations, and thus not jeopardize our good European 'credentials'.

To this end Nigel Lawson at the end of 1989 came up with the suggestion of 'freely competing currencies'. The idea was that all EC currencies would become legal tender in all member states. Those who wished to do so could trade, save and invest in any currency they preferred. This was the first British idea to head off the drive towards a single currency, and prevent the British being 'isolated'. It was a brave try but it was not taken seriously in Brussels. The concept of so many currencies in circulation in one country having to be exchanged into other currencies in a vast number of transactions, both great and small, wasn't really practical.

The second idea came from Sir Michael Butler. For many years he had been our Permanent Representative at the Community, and he knew the European scene intimately. He retired from the Foreign Service and took up a job in the City. In 1990 he and others put forward a plan to Margaret Thatcher which became known as the 'hard ECU'. It was improved and tested by the Treasury, and eventually put forward in the summer of 1990 under that name. Margaret Thatcher was receptive to the suggestion. It was a much better runner than 'freely competing currencies' had been, and in truth was a possible way of moving voluntarily towards a single currency.

The ECU – European Currency Unit – already existed, of course, but it was only a 'basket' of the national currencies, suitably weighted according to their current values. It was not widely used. The hard ECU plan was to set up a 'European monetary fund' to manage the hard ECU in such a way that it would be an extremely non-inflationary and stable currency. Like the Eurofed, the EMF would be given a proportion of national foreign exchange reserves with which to intervene in the currency markets. Each member state, and each bank or company, would be free to operate in hard ECUs if it found them preferable to its own currency. If 'convergence' was in fact achieved, over the years, it could well be that a number of member states would adopt the hard ECU, and the use of the currency might spread to the point where it was de facto the one single currency in use. The other currencies would fade away. It avoided coercing member states to accept something they didn't want to do; and it allowed enough time for convergence to become real before any parities were locked. Equally, if convergence did not take place, we could all go on trading in our own currencies.

Nevertheless, the majority of our partners at first rejected the idea. Although there was more merit in it than the 'freely competing currencies' plan, it had the same fatal defect in the eyes of the federalists. Neither scheme allowed power to be transferred to the centre. Neither provided for central economic management of the whole Community. Neither led to the centralized control which was their goal. Neither 'tied Germany in, tied it down and tied it up.' The Single Currency Plan, the Delors Report, was not really about Economic and Monetary Union: its purpose was to create a supra-national authority governing a political union, while sweeping under the carpet the undesirable economic consequences of the scheme. That the hard ECU plan did not do this was its defect in their eyes and its merit in ours.

The hard ECU did give Britain an alternative case to argue. The Spanish seemed to flirt with it in the autumn of 1990, and as time went by at the IGC [Inter-Governmental Conference] others began to see its advantages. It's hard to predict the final outcome of this saga: but the hard ECU plan did give the Conservative Party a middle position over which to unite, and it did give the Government a tenable negotiating hand in Europe.

Margaret Thatcher saw the hard ECU in those terms – a useful political initiative which took the heat off her both at Westminster and in Brussels. I doubt if she, like many, really believed it would be accepted or adopted by our partners, as she was to reveal at a vital moment later that year.

There was one other area of difficulty and dissent associated with the Delors Report. Delors, with strong support from the Germans, and Karl Otto Poehl in particular, as well as many others, believed strongly that the new Eurofed should be independent of political control. This was the position of the German Bundesbank and the American Fed. The Bank of England, on the other hand, was firmly under political control.

Nigel Lawson said in his resignation speech of 31 October 1989, '. . . a year ago, I proposed to the Prime Minister a fully worked-out scheme for the independence of the Bank of England.' The answer from Number 10 had clearly been a firm negative. This was the first time any of us had heard of this. Once again the Cabinet had been bypassed and this 'difference of view between Prime Minister and Chancellor' had not been 'resolved privately and, where appropriate, collectively' to quote from Nigel Lawson's resignation speech. Had it been resolved 'collectively', I would have joined in the fray against the idea with enthusiasm. I strongly disagreed with the vague concept of independence for central banks which had become the fashionable idea of the time.

Central banks traditionally have done three things. First, they borrow on behalf of governments from the public in order to fund their debt, and they manage that debt for them. Second, they put interest rates up or down. Third, they manage the exchange rate, and intervene in the foreign exchange markets.

Incidentally, the Delors Plan for the Eurofed gets into a real muddle over the question of what the Eurofed is to do. Member states will still be free to borrow and manage their own debt. The Eurofed will manage the interest rate. The finance ministers will apparently manage the exchange rate of the single European currency against other currencies outside Europe. So the Delors proposal is to split this function three ways – three different hands are to be on the economic tiller. This is not a very good way of achieving consistent economic management.

Each of these three functions of a central bank is different. I have no objection to 'independence' being given to a central bank in its role of managing the government's debt, although it is not proven that central bank governors would never resort to inflationary financing, which is the assumption behind their demands for independence. But the idea of giving a central bank independence over the management of the interest rate and the exchange rate is not one that I support. For what purpose would they use interest rate policy? In order to try to secure an artificial exchange rate, or to control the domestic money supply? The Bank of England is well known for its attachment to interfering with the exchange rate, and could never be trusted to operate interest rate policy for the sole purpose of domestic stability. Herr Karl Otto Poehl may be more trustworthy, for he is on record as saying, 'In my view it would therefore be desirable to embody in the statute of a European Central Bank a clause to the effect that domestic stability must have priority over exchange rate stability.' It must be wrong, in my judgement, to deny the chancellor of the day the power to make sure a central bank does just that. Independence for the Bank of England in interest-rate policy would remove one of the most vital weapons from a chancellor's armoury – just as joining the European Single Currency would do. There is no need for the British government to rush to jettison the essential powers it has with which to manage the British economy. This is the area where sovereignty matters, and where parting with it is the parting of the roads – one going towards a federal Europe and the other towards a Europe of member states.

By 1989 that new factor, to which Margaret Thatcher had drawn attention in her Bruges speech, entered into the European equation fully. The Soviet Union began to disintegrate. The European satellites were soon to regain their independence. Poland, Czechoslovakia and Hungary are certainly European; whether Romania and Bulgaria are is a matter of less certainty. These first three at least were soon to be democracies, all embracing the principles of the free market. On these grounds they became in theory eligible for membership of the Community. They all wanted to join.

This presented the federalists with an awkward dilemma. To facilitate their earliest possible membership would involve unlimited delay in the rush to union. Taking new members on board the Community in itself takes years; but for these potential new members, it would need longer still for them to achieve economic success sufficient for them to compete in a Community which had already achieved EMU and political union. Their accession to a Europe of member states would present fewer problems, but accession to a federal and united Europe would be virtually impossible for them.

The choice was between pressing ahead and leaving them out, or delaying European union until the new candidates could join, and this meant a long delay. When they had joined, they would probably become opponents of a federal Europe. Having just shaken off control by Moscow, they were unlikely to want control by Brussels.

There was another awkward dimension to their new freedom, a freedom which should have been received with unreserved joy by the Community. It was vital for the East European nations to export to the West in order to obtain hard currency. Many of their products were of poor quality and unsaleable. But they could produce foodstuffs, textiles, ceramics and steel, among other things, which were saleable in the Community. Yet those were just the kind of imports which the Community rigorously limited – or even prevented. Admitting Eastern European countries to the Community would have meant a flood of these products disrupting the cosy position of domestic suppliers. It would have appalling consequences for the CAP. It didn't suit those countries in the West who were trying to maintain as much protection for their industries as they could.

So the continental Europeans, after havering for a while, selfishly decided to ignore their claims. They decided to press on with European union, and salve their consciences by a goodly ration of charitable giving, rather than by opening their markets freely to exports from the East. Margaret Thatcher insisted on at least offering them 'Association Agreements' which gave them some assistance. It was Britain that suggested these limited forms of help – no one else did. They could hardly resist the idea. It was a small sop to them, when put alongside the great advantages that would have come to the Community by allowing these countries to enter fully into the Community market. Anyone who has travelled a little in Eastern Europe and met the new ministers cannot fail to be aware of their courage and determination, but also of the size of the problems that face them. There is also a certain emotional attachment – which both Margaret Thatcher and I felt – between them and Britain. It is easy to see why if one remembers the history of the last hundred years. Their relationship with Germany is a very different one indeed.

I brought the issue more clearly out into the open in a speech I made to the Bruges Group. The Bruges Group had been formed to promote the principles enshrined in Margaret Thatcher's Bruges speech. Speaking to them on 5 June 1990, I said: 'As Europeans we cannot fail to be deeply interested in the stability and prosperity of Eastern Europe, not just for emotional reasons, but because we cannot sleep securely with turmoil on the eastern borders of Europe. The more European countries which are democratic and have free market economies, the more secure we will be. It was natural for the EC to end at the Iron Curtain so long as the USSR controlled all the states beyond it, and the USSR was both militarily hostile, and with an alien centrally-planned economic system. But all that is changing. We cannot proceed as if the Iron Curtain was still there, and leave a number of nation-states beyond it sandwiched between the walls of the Community and Russia.'

I went on to suggest that the claims of the Eastern Europeans upon the EC did not allow the Community to justify moving forward to EMU if that meant excluding them.

I had some difficulty clearing this speech through the Foreign Office. I suspect it took a firm word from No. 10 before they reluctantly cleared the text. Margaret Thatcher had already made the point and she continued to stress it. The consciences of some in Europe were smitten by the Community's reaction to the liberation of Eastern Europe. The issue certainly received serious consideration; but the Commission, and particularly Jacques Delors, decided to motor on regardless. He had little difficulty in getting the Franco-German axis to come in behind him in turning a blind eye on Eastern Europe. It was interesting that Michael Heseltine shared their view in a speech he made at the 1990 Party Conference.

The Germans saw the answer as 'investment' by Germany in these countries: public sector 'investment' in grants and export credits, and private sector 'investment' in buying up existing assets cheap or creating new ones. By these two methods, they bought market share, they bought exports and they bought off their consciences. But it did not give Eastern Europe the trading opportunities it needed. German longing for European unity does not seem to extend to Eastern Europe. Chancellor Kohl was initially reluctant to recognise the Oder-Neisse Line as the permanent border between Germany and Poland at the time of reunification. Happily Margaret Thatcher encouraged the Poles to resist strongly. He backed off – but the memory lingers on.

If the Germans were not keen on the acceptance of Eastern Europe into the European family, they were desperately keen to reunite with East Germany themselves, automatically bringing that territory into the Community. Many people had doubts about German reunification: not so much doubts about whether it should be allowed to happen, but doubts about how. There were enormous implications for trade between the Community and the Eastern Bloc; there was concern about the effect upon, and the cost to, the CAP; and about the consequences of immigration controls and population movements. There were constitutional problems arising from the Treaty of Yalta, and there were defence problems under the NATO Treaty. Germany's partners – including the US – wanted to analyse and take stock of all these problems, and to find solutions before giving their blessing to reunification. But the Germans would have none of it. They rushed ahead at breakneck speed. The legal and constitutional problems were eventually sorted out by the so-called Two plus Four talks – the two Germanies and the four wartime allies.

But the matters causing concern in the Community were never really properly addressed, and to the extent that they were, it was after the main decision had been taken. They thought they had satisfied the need for bringing their partners along with them by providing for a German minister to deliver a situation report at every meeting of the Council of Ministers: effectively, we were kept continually informed, but not consulted.

Not even lip service was paid to Germany being 'tied down, tied in and tied up' in those hectic days. They had set their minds on early reunification, whatever the consequences, and whatever anyone else thought. The Community had to be humoured, but it had no more influence over the Germans than the League of Nations had in 1936. A vital interest of theirs was at stake, nothing was going to stop them achieving reunification. To my mind it bodes ill for the concept that the Community can bind Germany into the unity of European nations. If the Germans have a mind to do something, they take little notice of others' point of view. The consequences of German unification were not happy ones either for Germany, or for the rest of the Community. By offering the East Germans 1 DM for 1 Ostmark, instead of 1 DM for 5 or 6 Ostmarks, which was more like their worth, Germany incurred a massive surge in public expenditure. This in turn destabilized the DM, which fell 15 per cent against the dollar in early 1991. The Bundesbank had to increase interest rates, to the detriment of the rest. As a result, the DM ceased to be the stable currency in the ERM, removing all of its alleged advantages for the other members. As a result, the other members of the ERM may have to engage in inflationary policies, if they are to maintain their parities within the ERM. This demonstrates what a fundamentally flawed concept the ERM is.

Even the French became restive. They openly talked of a closer relationship with Britain. French ministers even appealed to us at this time to set up a closer relationship by our joining EMU as a way of establishing a counterweight to Germany. They saw this as a way of constraining Germany by the French and the British dominating the course of events in Europe. I saw it as a way of giving Germany the hegemony over the whole of Europe. We agreed to differ.

There is no doubt that the determination with which the Germans carried out reunification shows how real is the strength of Germany in Europe. Although few objected to reunification, it was done in such a way as to reawaken old memories. It reinforces the case for helping the Eastern Europe countries. While East Germany was soon a full member of the Community, the Eastern Europeans had to remain outside, having to sort out their economic problems without even full access to the Community's market. Yet it was they who most feared German domination, and had suffered most from it. These countries saw Margaret Thatcher as their champion. She had encouraged the resistance movements when they were struggling to be free. She had pleaded with President Gorbachev to let them go. She, more than anyone in the West, seemed to have their interests at heart. Yet she was unable to get a better deal for them from her Community partners. Once again, it is a question of Britain having a different perception from that of our continental friends. It is a very valuable perception which should never be suppressed.

At the same time as the Eastern European countries became

candidates for joining the Community, the European Free Trade Association (EFTA) countries began to as well. Both Austria and Sweden have applied to join. Collectively they asked in 1990 for a new agreement with the Community. Their bid for a closer relationship between the two groups became known as the European Economic Space negotiations, now called the European Economic Area negotiations.

The EFTA nations had been prospering. Average annual real growth in EFTA as a whole over the decade 1980 to 1990 was about 2.6 per cent, whereas for the Community it was only 2.3 per cent. Finland and Norway had achieved 3.4 per cent, Britain 2.7 per cent, and Germany only 2.0 per cent. So EFTA had been doing better than the Community. Practising free trade to a greater extent than the Community had benefited them. They were concerned to secure more permanent access to the large Community market, on which all of them depended. They were apprehensive that the Single Market would in some way lead to 'Fortress Europe' and exclude their products. Apart from Austria and Sweden, they didn't really want full membership, but they wanted an agreement with the Community, in order to keep its market open to them for trade on fair terms.

At the time of writing, the European Economic Area negotiations have not been concluded. Is this is another sign that the Community does not really want to be an open market to the rest of the world?

These fears of EFTA that the Community might move in a protectionist direction and become 'Fortress Europe' were shared in many other parts of the world, including the United States. These fears were reinforced at the end of 1990 when the Community more or less wrecked the Uruguay Round of the General Agreement on Tariffs and Trade (GATT) negotiations. The Uruguay Round was a global negotiation aimed at securing free trade in many areas where protectionist policies had persisted. One of these was agriculture. The Community simply refused to adopt a position which led sufficiently to the phasing out of agricultural subsidies for it to be negotiable in the GATT round. As a result, the whole negotiation came to a halt. Margaret Thatcher tried as hard as she could to have the issue at least discussed at the Rome Summit in October 1990. They simply refused even to discuss it. This incident cast grave doubt on the genuineness of the Community's free trade protestations

This was an example of Margaret Thatcher pressing her vision of Europe as a community with its markets open to the world. Another example was her decision to go ahead with the construction of the

Channel Tunnel. The Government had throughout insisted that no public money should be spent on building the Tunnel. By 1984, when I was Secretary of State for Transport, it seemed that the private sector was ready to undertake both the construction and the financing of this immense project. She and I and Michael Heseltine were in the British Embassy in Paris one evening after a long day of discussions with our French opposite numbers. President Mitterrand had raised the subject with her that day and she wanted to respond to him the next day. There were about twenty officials in the room as well as we three ministers. The Ambassador supplied us all with whisky, and a spirited debate took place. We all came to the same conclusion, and the decision was taken to go ahead in principle, subject to the agreement of the Cabinet. We all had to have another glass of whisky to celebrate the decision before we were allowed to go to bed, exhausted though we were.

She saw the Tunnel as a contribution to free trade and open markets in Europe. In many ways it will play a greater role in 'building Europe' than all idealistic discussions about Economic and Monetary Union. It will be a concrete monument to her view of Europe.

So much for the 'substance' of Margaret Thatcher's European policy.

More insidious and difficult to rebut were the ceaseless accusations that her combative 'style' was counter-productive, that her belligerent manner and her tenacity merely stiffened the resolve of others to resist her. That charge was a large part of the case against her at the end. Indeed, it is said that after she no longer attended European councils the others all started to oppose the Commission's more extreme proposals in a way they didn't need to do before. She used to do it for them.

Some say that Margaret Thatcher's precise meaning got lost on occasion by the translators. We have never been very good at communicating, particularly with the French. One is reminded of Churchill's admonition to General de Gaulle during the war: 'Monsieur le General, markez mes mots. Si vous me doublecrosserez, je vous liquidaterai,' or of Mrs Neville Chamberlain's polite refusal of a request by the French Ambassador that she and the Prime Minister might dine at his Embassy: 'Mon mari est toujours occupé dans le Cabinet avec beaucoup beaucoup de papier.' The English language is constructed differently from both French and German, and although it is very clear and unambiguous, it can have an unexpected meaning unless expertly translated. Margaret Thatcher in full argumentative flight apparently sounded rougher than she intended, and the meaning of her words was not always properly understood. This is said to have been partly responsible for some of the difficult patches in her relationships with some of the other European leaders. She never attempted to speak in a foreign language; she always spoke in English.

I think the French and the Germans, in particular, did often try to bounce her, and also to thwart her, just as I experienced at a lower level. Behind her back they would arrange a common position, or to raise items not on the agenda and only inform her at the last moment. The most famous example of this was the Rome Summit of October 1990, when the Italian presidency added an item to discuss the end date of Stage II of the Delors Report at the request of President Mitterrand and Chancellor Kohl, and refused to allow the GATT talks to be put on it. Margaret Thatcher reacted to such tricks with considerable anger: she disliked most of all having traps set for her, or things being arranged behind her back, which she always regarded as 'treachery'.

Her forthrightness and her tenacity were alien to Latin politicians and they often reacted to her refusal to be circumvented by tricks of this sort with a certain amount of verbal abuse at the press conference afterwards. I believe deep down they resented her because she was so utterly unmanoeuvrable. As it was the interests of Britain for which she was fighting, we can be grateful for her resolution.

It was not a question of arriving at a compromise on the fundamental issue of the single currency. Where no compromise is desirable, and no compromise is needed, there is no point in compromise, and no point in failing to call a spade a spade. On the Delors Report issues there was no way Britain could be coerced. We could simply refuse to sign any new Treaty. All she had to do was to say 'No', and to go on repeating it. She had the country behind her. The argument that we should compromise, be more constructive and less negative, that we should be 'in there negotiating' so that we would 'influence the European Council from within' was always fallacious. Whenever we did make concessions, we got nothing in return. Such pleas were based on the premise that if we didn't say 'No' outright, we might be dragged each time a little bit further than we wanted to go. Margaret Thatcher's opponents over European policy wanted to keep her at the negotiating table not so that she might secure a better deal for Britain, but in the hope that she might be pulled along, inch by inch, in the direction she didn't want to go. In the end, they partially succeeded: we got stuck with ERM membership. It is not calamitous, and not irrevocable.

One of the arguments her critics used consistently was that by going along with the Community to a certain extent, we would buy the goodwill to enable us to protect our vital interests. This was the argument constantly used by Douglas Hurd and Geoffrey Howe, in various coded speeches. All the available evidence goes against this view. When Margaret Thatcher went to Madrid and announced Britain would join the ERM when the famous three conditions were met, she got not an inch in return by way of our partners abandoning EMU. When she went to Rome in October 1990, having just joined the ERM – and thereby performed an act of great 'Eurosolidarity' – her reward was to be humiliated and prevented from raising the issue of the GATT round at the Council. She got nothing in return. The evidence seems to be that the more she conceded to our partners, the more they believed she was weakening and the more they believed that Britain could be made to conform in the end, kicking and screaming. The Commission showed great lack of subtlety in saying these things. That in itself should have disillusioned those who criticized the soundness of her style and her tactics. But it didn't. Personal animosity to her and a desire to be loved in Europe were the motives of those who criticized her style.

In truth, Margaret Thatcher's policies had the right substance and she had the right style. Our partners in Europe are just as ruthless and determined to get what they want as she was. In fact, she achieved a great deal in keeping Europe moving in the right direction. Europe should be grateful to her for what she did, and so should we.

8

THE TREASURY UNDER
GEOFFREY HOWE

SIR GEOFFREY HOWE was Chancellor of the Exchequer from 1979 to 1983. The Chief Secretary, who deals with public spending and is also in the Cabinet, was John Biffen for two years, followed by Leon Brittan for two years. The Financial Secretary was Nigel Lawson for two years, followed by myself for two years. Others who were Treasury Ministers during this period were Arthur Cockfield, Jock Bruce-Gardyne, John Wakeham and Barney Hayhoe. Most of the main players in the economic events that followed had a spell in the Treasury. Margaret Thatcher regarded the Treasury as the only department where all the ministers had to be her supporters, and as the training college for future cabinet ministers. The only exception to this was Barney Hayhoe, who was known as our 'resident Wet'. In two key economic departments she also appointed firm supporters: Sir Keith Joseph was Secretary of State for Industry and John Nott was Secretary of State for Trade. In other departments she was content to have only one supporter, to put some 'backbone' into the Department; but the Treasury had to be fully manned. It wasn't a very practical idea.

I was the one supporter in the Foreign Office from 1979 to 1981. But there was nothing I could do either to hold the department's budget under control or to implant different policies. After all, I was only a Junior Minister of State looking after relations with the western hemisphere. In the Treasury, however, the faithful were congregated.

At the start of the new Government, the economic situation was indeed bleak. Inflation was running at 10 per cent and there was much more in the system still to come. It finally peaked at 21.9 per cent in May 1980 before the measures the Government took sent it all the way down to the low point of 3.7 per cent in May 1983. The taxation system was archaic – with top rates of tax on unearned income at 98 per cent and the top rate of income tax at 83 per cent. It was full of outdated and unnecessary tax reliefs. It discriminated against savers, married couples and developers of land. The Winter of Discontent had left the country demoralized and underscored the futilities of the last Government's income policy. The case for industrial relations reform was unanswerable. But the top priority was the defeat of inflation. The new Prime Minister saw this as essential. Inflation was an evil that continually robbed savers and pensioners. It led to a succession of wage claims and strikes which disrupted industry. It was debilitating for business and commerce. It set one group of people against another. It was a cancer that had to be eradicated.

Margaret Thatcher saw economic policy primarily as a question of good housekeeping. A Government must live within its means; and must spend no more than it could afford, just as with an ordinary household. Public expenditure must be vigorously controlled. To allow the national debt to get out of hand is dangerous, just as families must not overborrow. Governments must never borrow from the banks – that is a direct cause of inflation. The citizens should be asked to pay only the minimum amount of tax necessary to finance a minimum level of public spending. High tax rates were a disincentive which drove people to try less hard, or to go overseas, or to engage in tax avoidance devices. She believed markets would do the rest, and markets should not be interfered with: in particular, the Foreign Exchange Market should be left to itself. She believed passionately in the personal ownership of property by as many people as possible, and, of course, in the privatization programme.

All her Treasury ministers, and most of her Party, shared these simple economic objectives. But at the beginning of Geoffrey Howe's Chancellorship it was not a united Government and Party that set about tackling the economic problems of Britain.

It was also not broadly accepted within the Government – or outside – that monetary policy held the key to defeating inflation. Jim Prior was the only economic minister who has confessed to not being a monetarist, but there were other doubters, not in economic ministries. The experience of 1972–4, when the Barber boom unleashed the worst inflation Britain had ever known, had persuaded many of us that it was impossible to control inflation by legislating to stop the consequential rise in prices and incomes. But some of Margaret Thatcher's Government were not so persuaded in 1979. Both before and after Ted Heath's efforts in 1973, the Labour Governments had tried and failed to make such policies work. For decades we had been told that there was such a thing as 'cost-push' inflation – that the avaricious workers seeking after higher wages and the greedy manufacturers and shopkeepers forcing up their prices were a major part of the cause of inflation. Economic orthodoxy would allow nothing else. But the monetarists in the Government which came to power in 1979 were firmly persuaded that 'cost-push' inflation was a myth, and that inflation was caused by the Government allowing the money supply to be excessive.

Few who study these matters now disagree, but it was a radical and unorthodox policy to accept the monetarist doctrine at that time. However, so persuasive had the case for monetarism become within Whitehall that the Treasury, and, rather more reluctantly, the last Labour Chancellor, Denis Healey, had been following a basically monetarist policy since the 1976 International Monetary Fund (IMF) crisis. However, there was a vast difference between the Chancellor surreptitiously using monetary policy within the confines of the Treasury and openly espousing it as an essential plank of economic management, as Mrs Thatcher did in the 1979 election. It led to the Government acquiring the adjective of 'monetarist' – and it quickly became a term of abuse.

The Labour Party and some sections of the press used it as a form of insult to the Government. Monetarism became responsible for every evil under the sun – the state of trade, the lot of the feckless, the luckless, the homeless, and the jobless, even the weather itself. Everything bad was caused by this 'wretched monetarist Government'. It was a new demonology which our opponents had discovered.

The monetary theory is, in fact, merely a closer definition of good housekeeping, giving some important pointers as to how to translate 'living within one's means' in the family sense, into a Government living within its means too. To do so is infinitely more complex in the case of Governments than for the family budget – so vast is the scale of the Government's operations, and so great are the capital flows – both domestically and across the Foreign Exchanges. It is not enough for governments to keep good tally of the household income and expenses month by month. It is much more complicated than that.

Governments also suffer the same temptation as families – the temptation to spend more than they can afford. But it is within the power of Governments, unlike families, to live beyond their means by the simple expedient of debasing the currency. That is the mirror image, and the cause, of inflation. Throughout the centuries governments have debased the currency by various means; the Romans by clipping the corners off gold coins; the Victorians by printing excessive numbers of bank notes; the modern device is borrowing from the banking system. It is now all the fashion to say that an external 'discipline' is necessary to prevent governments from causing inflation in this way. I will return to that later. But it is worth remembering that there is such a thing as self-discipline – and it is self-discipline which most families have to exercise to keep themselves out of trouble. The Government used self-discipline in 1979.

The central principle around which all monetary thinking revolves is the Quantity Theory of Money. This is expressed most simply in the formula Money supply × velocity of circulation = prices × quantity of goods. According to this formula, with velocity and the quantity of goods fairly stable over short periods of time, increases in the money supply must result in a higher price level. The theory can be dated back to the fifteenth century, although it is commonly attributed to the American economist Irving Fisher. J.M. Keynes regarded the Quantity Theory as central to economic theory, and was one of its main proponents in the 1920s. He used it to explain the cause and cure for the slump of the late 1920s, when both the money supply and the velocity were strongly inadequate. Inflation became negative – prices and wages actually fell. The problem was exacerbated by the exchange rate policy of the time, on which J. M. Keynes held strong views which will become relevant later. But Keynes believed in the importance of monetary policy just as much as Margaret Thatcher and her Government – indeed, he virtually invented it. Her economic adviser, Alan Walters, was the current high priest of British monetarism. The difference was that Keynes lived at a time of inadequate money supply, whereas 1979 was a time of excessive money supply. If Keynes were alive today, I have no doubt that he would have pointed the way to cure inflation in a manner very similar to that which was used from 1979 on. To paint the continuing debate about economic policy as being one between monetarists and Keynesians is totally misleading and a slur on Keynes.

The debate in the early 1980s was between those who understood the functioning of the money supply in a modern economy, and those who still believed in cost-push and demand management.

Demand management had been the prevailing wisdom since the early 1940s. Broadly, the policy meant that when unemployment was rising, the Government injected some money into the system, through tax cuts and/or extra spending, to increase demand. When prices were rising, the authorities removed some money through tax increases and/or spending cuts to reduce demand. The overriding concern of every British Government since the war, scarred by the memories of mass unemployment during the 1930s, had been to maintain a policy of full employment through demand management. Indeed, this policy, which led to the jerky years of stop-go and which proved incapable of dealing with both runaway inflation and rising unemployment in the mid-1970s, remained in place up to 1976, when the Prime Minister, James Callaghan, told the Labour Party Conference in a celebrated speech that Government could no longer 'spend your way out of a recession'. It was a message that few in the Labour Party wanted to hear. In fact, demand management did much to exacerbate the original wound: if the economy was suffering from inflation, and at the same time unemployment was rising, then the wrong action was taken, and demand increased just when it should have been reduced.

The money supply figures gave a better (but by no means perfect) way of telling what the true state of the economy was. Margaret Thatcher's was the first British Government in post-war history to break consciously, deliberately and with conviction with the prevailing consensus of demand management and place all the emphasis in its economic policy on reducing inflation instead of manipulating the economy to maintain full employment. Low inflation – price stability – alone would produce a productive economy with the creation of real jobs and higher levels of employment in the long term. The argument that developed over managing the economy in 1980–1 was between those who wanted to employ demand management and those who wanted to kill inflation.

A convenient by-product of the demand-management policy is that it gives a good excuse for reducing taxes or spending more money whenever the economy is cooling off. There was even a smart name for it: 'countercyclical expenditure' it was called. Those compassionate politicians who always want to spend more money found this avenue blocked.

Throughout history there have been would-be alchemists who believe it is possible to turn base metals into gold. Modern-day alchemists believe it is possible for governments both to spend more money and to exact less in taxes. That never was possible. Although they pray Keynes in aid to justify themselves, they misunderstand his message. He identified that the money supply was inadequate to sustain the production of the nation in the late 1920s. He cannot be called in aid to justify an increase in the money supply in 1980 – when the money supply was already excessive. Keynes's theory of money fits both situations perfectly.

Thus the idea, still peddled by some critics and academics, that monetarism was a sort of experiment, a kind of evil creed invented by Margaret Thatcher in order to persecute the workers, was totally flawed. Monetarism was no more than an attempt to put economic policy on a logical basis. It was not revolutionary, it was a return to orthodoxy; it was abandoning alchemy in the light of the obvious evidence that alchemy was never going to work. One could say it was a return to good housekeeping.

Where difficulties and contention remain, and always will remain, is over the question of how to apply monetary policy and how to measure it. It is not an exact science. The time-lags between action and results are long – often two years or so. The analogy of the time it takes to turn round a 500,000 ton oil tanker, with a touch on the tiller, is all too apt. It was the problems of managing monetary policy which preoccupied both Geoffrey Howe and, later, Nigel Lawson. It was never doubted that demand management was wrong and that we had to get the monetary policy right in order to manage the economy properly.

Inflation was running at 10 per cent in 1979 and was expected to rise beyond 20 per cent. The Clegg Commission had recommended large pay increases to public employees even as the election was being fought. It was impossible to repudiate Clegg after accepting him during the election. Public expenditure was spiralling out of control. Geoffrey Howe was faced with a large and growing Public Sector Borrowing Requirement (PSBR). He had to raise more revenue in order to reduce it. He contained, rather than reduced, public expenditure and in his first Budget he raised extra revenue by increasing VAT to 15 per cent. He increased interest rates. But the Budget proved to be insufficient. The money supply was still growing strongly. In 1981 he produced a further sternly deflationary Budget. He raised another £3.5 billion by increasing taxes – principally excise duties. A very tight control was kept on public spending. The outside world was stunned. The effects of the 1980 Budget were already being felt in no uncertain manner. Unemployment had already risen to 2.1 million by November 1980. It reached 3 million in January 1982. Businesses were going under at an alarming rate. Profits and production and investment were falling back. Yet, instead of employing the traditional demand management policy of the post-war era, Geoffrey Howe read the monetary indicators as requiring a further reduction in demand, if inflation was to be beaten.

Alan Walters began advising the Prime Minister in January 1981 on economic affairs. He insisted that the diagnosis was correct. Demand was still too high. The Prime Minister is said to have hesitated much before agreeing to the famous 1981 Budget – the political reception of it was, indeed, highly critical. I was not, of course, privy to the discussions leading up to the 1981 Budget – I was still in the Foreign Office at the time. It did seem pretty draconian to any outsider, including me. But I had great faith in the efficacy of a monetarist solution to the problem of inflation. I was determined that we should not relax just, as it were, before the turning point was reached. I judged the 1981 Budget to be necessary. It was a very courageous act and both Margaret Thatcher and Geoffrey Howe talked later of it as the turning point in getting the economy under control.

The turning point it proved to be. Inflation started to fall soon after then. Production stabilized and started to grow again. Investment, productivity and profitability in industry all began to show improvements. It ushered in eight years of low inflation, improved industrial performance and economic growth averaging 3.5 per cent per annum. It was one of the most prolonged periods of steady economic progress in our history. Indeed, during the period from the trough of 1981 until the end of 1989, our manufacturing output rose by 32 per cent, manufacturing productivity by 51 per cent, profitability rose by 400 per cent, investment rose by 75 per cent and exports by 55 per cent. Employment rose to an all-time high of 27 million people, and the standard of living of a married man on average wages increased by 35 per cent. It was a halcyon period of economic success.

The dates I have chosen to show these figures are, of course, subjective. But I use them to illustrate the long-term benefits which flowed from Geoffrey Howe's first two Budgets and, in particular, the contentious 1981 Budget. Had he failed to heed the warnings from the monetary indicators and pursued a demand management policy in 1981, as many advised him to do, not only would inflation have persisted, but he would also have had to bring in a further deflationary Budget at a later stage. Both would have interrupted, with stop-go, that long period of success that followed. Historically, demand management had resulted in a succession of stop-goes. It would have done so again in 1981. By pursuing a policy with money supply as the indicator, we only had go.

There are three weapons in the armoury of a Chancellor – first, the fiscal weapon of putting up taxes to reduce demand; second, the monetary weapon of increasing interest rates to choke back demand; and, third, exchange rate policy, which involves trying, by various devices, to make the rate of exchange of the currency with other currencies different from what it would otherwise have been if left to the foreign exchange markets to determine. Geoffrey Howe used the first two of these weapons – fiscal policy and monetary policy. But he did not use exchange rate policy. He let the pound 'float' – that is, he left it to the foreign exchange markets to determine the pound's value. This in itself was a bold and innovative move. For much of the century the pound had been fixed at a certain value – first, to the value of gold on the Gold Standard and then, after the Second World War, to the value of the dollar through the international Bretton Woods Agreement which collapsed in the mid 1970s. Neither did the pound join the latest attempt to fix currencies at a certain static value – the European Exchange Rate Mechanism, started in 1979. Geoffrey Howe allowed the pound to float freely. It may have been a 'dirty' float (which means that the Bank of England was buying and selling pounds on the foreign exchange markets in order temporarily to affect its value), but the essential point is that in 1980–1 he defeated inflation without seriously interfering with the exchange rate.

The Labour Government in 1979 had declined to join the ERM. There was desultory talk of the desirability of our joining it in the early period of Geoffrey Howe's Chancellorship. I heard talk of it when I was in the Foreign Office, and I must confess that in the atmosphere of the Foreign Office I saw the political attraction of doing so, although I never really thought it was right to join. It is strange how the atmosphere in which one works can lead to one's views coming closer to those of others who have different basic beliefs. I admit the aberration, but I am now more than ever convinced that the ultimate decision to join the ERM was a mistake. It was not a hot issue during Geoffrey Howe's Chancellorship. None of us believed Margaret Thatcher would agree to it, and nobody felt strongly enough about it to get into a confrontational position over it. It was not an issue which came to the boil. The argument was between Foreign Office ministers, who saw it as a gesture of political goodwill towards the European Community and Treasury ministers, who saw it as inimicable to our economic interests. The Prime Minister was firmly opposed and the subject was dropped.

In fact, the advent of the new Government in 1979, and its convincing policies to squeeze out inflation, together with the growing oil revenues from the North Sea, caused the pound sterling to take off upwards in the markets. During 1980 the exchange rate rose by 12 per cent on average, compared with other major currencies, following a 9.25 per cent rise in 1979. This made it harder for British industry to remain competitive abroad, adding to the general difficulties.

One other reason why the pound rose in value in 1979 was that Geoffrey Howe abolished all exchange controls as one of his first acts on coming into office. Hitherto it had been necessary to get consent from the Bank of England to buy foreign currency. Apart from a sizeable administrative saving, it left businesses free to trade and invest all round the world as they saw fit. It seemed a dramatic thing to do at the time, but in retrospect one wonders what was the point of exchange controls in the first place. In fact, they were part of the armoury of distorting weapons necessary to support the value of the pound in the days of the Bretton Woods Agreement and before. But when they were abolished, the pound did not go down; it went up, because investors felt confident about putting their money into Britain, knowing they could take it out again if they wanted to in the future. Interest rates were high, and the pound sterling attracted much of the 'hot' money in the markets.

The high value of the pound in the early 1980s was not engineered by the Government. It reflected the market's view of its worth. Industry proved that it could compete, even at this high value. The trade balance was healthy. We ran trade surpluses of £6.7 billion in 1981, £4.6 billion in 1982, and £3.8 billion in 1983. Even after putting oil exports to one side, it was positive in 1981 and 1982. Although it added to industry's difficulties, it was not the same as 1991, when a pound kept artificially high greatly reduced our international competitiveness.

The squeeze of 1980–1, together with the high pound, caused a savage increase in unemployment, business failures and lost production. That is inevitably a price that has to be paid for tackling inflation. Whether the policy is labelled 'demand management' or 'monetarism,' it involves reducing demand in the economy. It is the reduction of demand that causes the unemployment. The difference between the monetary and the demand management solutions to the problems of 1979 was one of degree, not of principle. The demand managers would have relaxed the squeeze earlier, the pain might have eased a little, but inflation would have re-emerged.

Unemployment is a nightmare that haunts the British. The experiences of the 1930s are still deep in our consciousness, even the consciousness of those who were not then born or who, like me, were children at the time. In 1980 many people thought it was politically impossible to allow unemployment to reach the peak level of 3 million without taking early corrective action. The British remember the Jarrow marches and the great depression of the time. The Germans remember the Weimar Republic and the great inflation of the early 1920s. They rate inflation a greater evil than unemployment. I suspect in our heart of hearts we put it the other way round. This is a relevant point when we come to the events of 1990 and the question of European Economic and Monetary Union. But in 1980 it was regarded by many as unnecessary folly, and both cruel and pigheaded, to let unemployment go on rising unrelieved.

In the confines of the Foreign Office, I shared the sense of unease about the mounting numbers of the unemployed. I think that unemployment is an individual problem – each person without a job should be our concern. If the number is greater, the problem is greater, but the concern is not increased. It is a phenomenon which must happen in a modern society – subjected to an ever-increasing pace of change in industry and commerce. The solution is to make it at least tolerable for those who have to suffer a period out of work and to take the actions necessary to provide additional opportunities for them as best may be. But our concern should be for one human being unemployed and not heightened by 3 million. There is no such thing as an 'acceptable' level of unemployment if the unemployed suffer too much. In 1980–1 their lot was grievous, but in no way comparable to that of those who were unemployed in the 1930s. Those were the days of soup kitchens and real privation.

The point I want to stress is that governments hate causing unemployment – it is not a deliberate act to 'teach people a lesson.' It is an automatic result of a decision to reduce the level of inflation. Nor is it a satisfactory answer to say that inflation cannot be reduced because it would cause unemployment. Inflation, if it is allowed to persist and accelerate, is an even greater evil, resulting in unemployment in the end too. I think any leader is right – and that Margaret Thatcher was right – to put the defeat of inflation as the top priority.

Inflation had demonstrated its evil effects in both 1974 and 1979. Those in charge of the new Government in 1979 were all too well aware of them. People who had saved for their retirement found their savings diminishing rapidly and the income from them dwindling in terms of what it would buy. Those on the State pension were constantly losing purchasing power as each month went by after the last annual uprating. Many private sector pensions were not even indexed. All of these groups and many more, mostly among the least well off, suffered greatly. The wage earner too found his wages buying less between annual wage settlements and as a result pressed for higher wages to compensate. Employers, battling to contain their costs, resisted these demands. This led to more and more strikes, with mounting bitterness. Wage earners were often able to do better as a result of the strike weapon. The pensioners in turn resented those who could maintain their own position through striking and saw it as being at their expense, as prices of goods and services rose. The only people who did well were clever speculators who could anticipate where the largest price rises were to come. When the Labour Government in 1978 tried to moderate all this through attempting to control prices and wages by law, it merely exacerbated the situation without curbing the inflation and the result was the Winter of Discontent. In the end, the public sector unions caught up what they had lost as they were determined to do.

Inflation greatly weakens industry and commerce too, because it has to be allowed for in tendering and pricing policy. If inflation was accurately predicted, the contract was likely to be lost. If it was underestimated, the contract would result in a loss. The whole business of estimating and cost control becomes infinitely more difficult. There are few in business who do not put the defeat of inflation highest on their list of political priorities.

Thus, both unemployment and inflation are evils. The ideal policy is one that steers so straight a course that both are avoided. Seldom can that be achieved and it was a great triumph to achieve it from 1981 to 1988. But there can be little argument that when inflation does break loose it must be reduced, and that inevitably leads to a loss of jobs.

There was a growing chorus of criticism as unemployment rose and inflation was squeezed out of the system. The Labour Party naturally mounted the biggest onslaught they could. Michael Foot, the Labour Leader, quoted Keynes: 'Every puff of Mr Baldwin's pipe costs us thousands of pounds.' He went on, 'Well, every shake of Mrs Thatcher's head costs this nation tens of thousands of jobs; many of them jobs that are never going to be recovered.' (How wrong he was!) The press became more and more censorious. Academics joined in. On March 30 1981, 365 economists wrote to *The Times* demanding a relaxation of the squeeze: 'There is no basis in economic theory or supporting evidence for the Government's belief that by deflating demand they will bring inflation permanently under control and thereby induce an automatic recovery in output and employment.' (They were wrong too.)

Equally predictably, many in the Government and the Tory Party in the House of Commons became first anxious, and then downright critical. They became known as the 'wets'. 'Wet' is, I think, a schoolboy word to describe some wretched boy who doesn't dare do something either athletic or naughty. The zenith of wetness is when somebody is described as 'so wet you could shoot snipe off him.' Those who held firm become known as the 'dries'. I remember finding a device in a garden shop which you stuck in a plant pot and it recorded by the colour it turned whether the soil was wet or dry. I sent it to Ian Gow, the Prime Minister's Parliamentary Private Secretary, who promptly asked for twenty-one of them, in order to test the humidity of each member of the Cabinet. I don't expect this little joke ever reached Margaret Thatcher. She would not have been amused.

Among the wets there were a number of categories. First there was Ted Heath, who rarely missed an opportunity to join in any criticism of the policies of his female successor. Part of his animus towards Margaret Thatcher might have stemmed from the fact that he himself had tried to introduce many of the reforms in 1970 that she was later to achieve in 1979 – with the difference that he had been forced into a humiliating U-turn in 1971 and we could rightly point to the catastrophic consequences of it. Those of us who lived through those days were determined not to embark on the same tragic path. Indeed, many of us thought that if Ted Heath had held his nerve for a few more months in 1971, he would have succeeded in achieving an inflation-free economy with a long period of stable growth ahead. That it worked ten years later lends credibility to that point of view. Ted Heath was at the forefront of those denouncing Margaret Thatcher for the growing unemployment in 1981. As he continued to denounce her even when the policies were succeeding his criticisms carried less and less weight, as he appeared to be trying solely to settle old scores.

A much more formidable group of wets were the old-fashioned Tory patricians – Peter Carrington, Jim Prior, Ian Gilmour, Christopher Soames and Francis Pym. They were all members of her first Cabinet and all showed concern as the squeeze began to have effect. With experience of running large estates or large companies people like these had always managed to cushion their tenants and employees from the worst effects of a depression, and also to provide for them in sickness or old age over and above that which the State could do. They never could see that the Government itself has far wider responsibilities and far fewer resources per capita to provide for those responsibilities. The Government too, unlike them, has to deal with inflation and to put pressure on industry to improve efficiency. It was because their predecessors like Harold Macmillan, Alec Douglas Home and Ted Heath had this instinct never to push it too far in economic policy, that inflation had become more and more endemic in the system. Demand management and 'counter-cyclical policy' was a useful argument for allowing them to relax with honour when any squeeze appeared to be working. John Major said in October 1990, 'If it isn't hurting, it isn't working.' The patrician Tory always says 'If it's hurting, we had better stop it working.' It was a beguiling theory and an attractive policy, but unfortunately one of the main contributors to stop-go through the 1960s and 1970s and to Britain's worsening inflation and general economic performance.

Nevertheless, their political fears began to mount as unemployment rose. Second-in-command at the Foreign Office was Ian Gilmour, who was in the Cabinet as Lord Privy Seal and was perhaps the most open in what he said in public. He stayed just within the bounds of what was permissible, but in private conversations he was openly critical and disparaging of the squeeze and its effects. An accomplished political writer, his belief on all matters political was that one should do nothing until the necessity to do something became irresistible. He carried to extremes the political maxim that change is undesirable unless change is inevitable. No doubt he would agree with Lord Salisbury's definition of the ideal foreign policy as 'drifting down a river in a punt, doing nothing until it is necessary to fend the punt off from getting too near to one bank or the other.' That was certainly Ian Gilmour's attitude to economic policy and he thought we were already in collision with the right bank of unemployment.

Similar thoughts were probably in the minds of Peter Carrington, Jim Prior, Christopher Soames and Francis Pym. They would never have allowed so many of their tenants and employees to lose their jobs. Yet they were uncertain of their ground. They suspected that there was at least some truth in the monetary theory; they did not feel bold enough to press the alternative policy. Jim Prior described their dilemma in his book, *A Balance of Power*: 'We pragmatists were on a very difficult wicket, because we could not prove in a short time that their ideas were wrong. We could not even say that ours had been particularly successful, because in the 1970s they undoubtedly had not succeeded. Only the passage of time would prove our point, but by then a great deal of damage could have been done to the country, and to our party.' Eventually, they responded to the call for strong support for Margaret Thatcher and Geoffrey Howe which Willie Whitelaw demanded of them. They thought discretion was the better part of valour.

Willie Whitelaw, himself a Tory patrician, but one who had vowed support to Margaret Thatcher, never wavered. He decided that loyalty, and his sixth (political) sense, required that his colleagues saw the 1980–1 squeeze through – and he was right. His political instincts convinced him it would come right in the end and his authority prevailed upon his patrician colleagues. Peter Carrington never felt confident in his own economic judgement. Ian Gilmour and Francis Pym and Christopher Soames and Norman St John Stevas preferred not to push their fears too far; they did little more than grumble privately.

Peter Walker was of an entirely different school. No patrician, he was supported by a phalanx of backbenchers, much more numerous than the backbench supporters of the patricians. They were the professional men, the Tory fixers, the accountants and lawyers and merchant bankers, who believed in the need to win elections whatever principles had to be sacrificed in order to do so. The important thing was to be loved, to be popular, to be re-electable. The Government did not seem to be re-electable in 1981. Good political management should not expose one to such hazards. They yearned for the old politics of fudge, consensus and compromise. Peter Walker was the chief exponent of this philosophy. First elected in 1960, flushed with success both financially and in terms of reputation by having been the Walker of Slater Walker Ltd, he quit the City in order to scale the political heights. Violently anti-common market in 1961, he later accepted high office under Ted Heath in order to further Britain's bid to join it. He was never at ease with the policies of Mrs Thatcher's Government, nor, indeed, with her personally: I suspect the feeling was mutual. But he nevertheless continued to remain a member of her Cabinet until he resigned in order to 'spend more time with his family' in January 1990.

The members of his sizeable following on the backbenches were the ones who began to make their voices heard in protest at the squeeze. They were also the ones who were always pressing for more public money to be spent on good causes. Others joined them as time went by; often those whose talents had not been recognized by promotion, or who had been dropped from the Government. The longer Margaret Thatcher remained Prime Minister, the more their numbers inevitably increased. It is one of the hazards of such a long period of rule in British politics that the number of malcontents grows steadily with the passage of time – this was a major factor contributing to her eventual downfall.

Despite the pressure from all these critics, Margaret Thatcher and

Geoffrey Howe held firm to the strategy. By 1982 the beneficial results began to be discernible and the wets became more muted. By 1983 they were nearly all silenced. Chris Patten was one of the joint authors of a pamphlet in 1981 entitled *Changing Gear*, which pronounced its purpose as: 'to halt the decline of the economy, to make the re-election of Mrs Thatcher's Government more likely, and to rescue the moderate Tory cause from the broom cupboard to which it had been confined.' When questioned by an interviewer much later as to why he had abandoned the wet cause, Chris Patten replied that by then he realized he had been wrong. Would that many other of the Government's critics, who made life so difficult at that time, had had the grace to admit the same. They made the painful task of squeezing inflation out of the economy more difficult still: they added to the intense strain which those who were in control must have felt, while enjoying the benefits which success brought to the Party in two subsequent General Elections.

Those of us who supported Mrs Thatcher's economic policies knew that to bow to the criticism of the wets and others in 1981 and to reverse engines would have led to disaster. We had learnt from the unfortunate economic consequences of Ted Heath's U-turn in 1971. I believe this thought fortified the Government and caused the older wets to steady. Mrs Thatcher never wavered in her determination to see it through. As Jim Prior admitted, he 'grossly underestimated her absolute determination.' In her speech at the Tory Party Conference in 1980, she made it abundantly clear that there was not going to be a U-turn. 'You turn if you want to,' she said. 'The lady's not for turning.'

I viewed these events from afar in the Foreign Office, dealing with the problems of the Caribbean and South America, including the Falklands. But in September 1981 I was moved to the Treasury and was appointed Financial Secretary. I was delighted with this appointment. I felt away from politics and away from economic policy in the Foreign Office. The Treasury job would bring me back into the mainstream of politics. The job of Financial Secretary was said to be the threshold to promotion to the Cabinet – in fact, all of Margaret Thatcher's Financial Secretaries made it. I was shown a list of the Financial Secretaries going back a hundred years and was delighted to see that my own great grandfather had held the post in the 1890s.

It was an awesome day when I first walked into the Treasury. It inhabited that dreadful ponderous Victorian building in Great George Street, with its scrubbed red linoleum floors, its endless stone staircases, and its atmosphere of carbolic and parsimony. It was said that the Treasury had to set a Spartan example itself in order to encourage economy in the rest of Whitehall – but its only effect was to depress the inmates.

The Treasury officials all had double firsts; their reputation was daunting. I had to manage the Inland Revenue, the traditional role of the Financial Secretary to the Treasury. Revenue officials were said to be people with moral fervour. To be as knowledgeable about taxation as they were, and yet not to desert the Revenue for the offices of the lucrative 'tax planning' firms required an unselfish devotion to squeezing the taxpayers which could only be based on a certain grim morality, I was told. Certainly understanding the minutiae of tax policy required an intellectual effort of academic proportions. In practice, they were dedicated, charming people, of a high calibre, trying only to do their jobs, although they did have a very purist attitude towards the taxpayer. I enjoyed my two years in the Treasury and ended up with a great respect for the devotion to duty and the ability of those who worked for me. I suppose the Treasury has to show that austere face to the outside world as a contribution to preserving its mystique or sublime integrity and total infallibility. Whether or not it frightened the lobbies, it certainly frightened me.

My particular responsibilities were with the detail of taxation policy, the European Community Budget and the privatization programme. The latter was a secondary function. The sponsoring departments were responsible for preparing industries for privatization and the Treasury ministers mainly came into the act at the time of placing the shares or fixing their price at the time of flotation.

The taxation work was intellectually very difficult – closing loopholes, thinking up minor 'goodies' for the Budget, dealing with casework, and listening to both individuals and interest groups who were looking for a better deal than the tax system offered them. We worked up the Business Expansion Scheme, laid the groundwork for abolishing life insurance premium relief, and worked on plans for abolishing other tax reliefs. I examined in great depth the possibilities of combining tax reliefs for the less well off with the social security system – with the object of finding a system of Negative Income Tax, as it was called. None of them ever seemed to me to be convincing. I firmly believe it is better to operate the two systems independently. I suppose I worked over a lot of ground in the taxation field which had been worked over many times before and would be worked over many times again in the future. I produced few useful results for my trouble.

Geoffrey Howe was primarily preoccupied with economic policy during his Chancellorship. He hardly had much time to spend on tax reform. Moreover, it was not an easy time for reforming taxation. Taxes had to go up in his first two Budgets, and there was little to give back in his second two. It is easier to reform taxes against a background of being able to cut them.

Nevertheless, he removed some of the worst excesses of the Labour Government before him. He cut the top rate of income tax from 83 per cent to 60 per cent. He also laid the foundation stones for many of the major tax reforms which Nigel Lawson was able to implement later. They were already being discussed at this time. We began work on the reform of company taxation and of separate taxation for husbands and wives. We were particularly concerned to bring to an end the many tax reliefs which complicated income tax and made it unfair. I became totally persuaded that there should be as few tax reliefs as possible. A tax relief, however worthy its objective, is of different value to taxpayers on different incomes and of no value to those who do not pay tax. If one wants to help the disabled, or savers, or home buyers, or those with children, it is better to give them grants than tax relief. The grants can be tailored to meet the need – more for the less well off. Tax reliefs usually mean more help for the better off, and no help for the less well off.

Children's tax allowances had already been turned into child benefit. We abolished one or two minor tax reliefs. It was left to Nigel Lawson actually to get rid of life insurance premium relief – surely the most anomalous of all. But there was one tax relief where we failed – mortgage interest relief.

Up until the 1960s, it was seen as perfectly logical to tax interest received and to relieve interest paid, on the basis of symmetry of treatment. The previous Labour Government removed this relief. Tony Barber, the Chancellor in 1971, restored it. As a backbencher on the Finance Bill at that time, I spoke against its restoration. It seemed to me that borrowing money and having to pay the interest was just as much an expense voluntarily incurred as hiring a gardener and having to pay his wages. It was just another expenditure. It had the economic effect of subsidizing borrowing, leading to an increase in borrowing.

When Labour came back to power in 1974, they resolved once more to end tax relief on interest paid. But they exempted mortgages, and allowed interest on a tight definition of a mortgage to be tax relieved up to a ceiling of £25,000. This was to assist home buyers to acquire their houses. It was hard to argue against it, although the 'impurity' of the scheme offended me. I also believed it would spill over into a general relief for interest on borrowed money, which to some extent it did later on. The other defect was the arbitrary limit of £25,000, which was not indexed to rise automatically with inflation. It became a natural Opposition ploy to seek to raise this limit in each year's Finance Bill, so as at least to maintain its true valuation. In this ritual, we all partook.

In 1981, however, things looked rather different. The number of house buyers had increased greatly, partly as a result of the right to buy council houses. The cost of the relief was growing apace. It began to be exploited by using it to obtain cheap credit for purposes other than home buying. Finally, as a tax relief, it was worth a lot to the better-off and less to standard rate and non-taxpayers. Treasury ministers were united in wanting to see it go, at least for future mortgages. Margaret Thatcher was determined to retain it, and even to increase it by restoring its real value. She was adamant, but we pressed our case. The matter was resolved at a meeting between her and all the Treasury ministers in her study at Number 10. She quoted from speeches which each of us had made during the Finance Bill debates of the 1970s, advocating increases in the £25,000 limit. We were routed. It was agreed to leave it in place, but not increase the limit. In 1983 the limit was increased to £30,000, but it is now worth only a fraction of its 1975 value. It is, in fact, 'withering on the vine.'

Who can say who was right? Margaret Thatcher passionately believed in home ownership and was prepared to subsidize it, even for the well off. We wanted to save the cost of it, get rid of its economic ill effects, and remove the distortion it caused. I came to be more and more conscious of this distortion when working on housing policy as Secretary of State for the Environment.

In a sense it may have been the right solution. It has 'withered on the vine' in terms of its value, partly as a result of the reduction in income tax rates, and partly as a result of inflation. Norman Lamont, in his first Budget in 1991, removed the relief for the higher rate of income tax.

It is now worth some £1,125 a year for a standard rate taxpayer. This is a helpful sum, but not so significant when set against the current price of houses. The affair was an interesting clash between a logical tax policy and the political convictions of the Prime Minister.

Geoffrey Howe was not an easy person to work for. Delegation was not a word he understood. Try as I did to find solutions to the problems on my desk, he would insist on crawling all over the problems himself again. He worked through the night, redoing what his junior ministers had done, and often coming to the same conclusions. He spent hours satisfying himself that the presentation was right. I used to wonder whether I performed any useful function at all if all had to be done again. He was careful, thorough and lugubrious. It was my experience under Geoffrey Howe which persuaded me of the vital importance of delegating to junior ministers when I later came to run a department of my own.

When it came to the major questions of economic policy, although he wanted to hear them, the thoughts of his junior ministers mattered little. We had frequent meetings throughout the week when he would bare his soul about the grisly problems with which he was grappling. But what we said seemed to have little impact on the ultimate agonizingly arrived-at decisions. I made no complaint about this – he who has alone the ultimate responsibility must be free to take the final decisions.

The licence he afforded himself as Chancellor to take the ultimate decisions he was not prepared later to afford to the Prime Minister herself in exercising her responsibility to take her ultimate decisions. For my part, although I found his lack of reliance on his juniors irritating, I bore with it contentedly because I realized the awesome nature of the responsibilities he carried. It was Geoffrey Howe's head that would be on the block if he got it wrong, not mine. In the exercise of taking decisions that affect the lives of millions of ordinary people, their jobs, their livings, their savings and mortgages, if the buck stops with you, then you have the right to take the ultimate decisions. Would that Geoffrey Howe had extended the same understanding to his own superior later on.

I believe Geoffrey Howe was firmly convinced of the primacy of the need to control the money supply. But he still had a sort of vestigial urge to make a direct impact on prices and wages; he could never quite recant from his days under Ted Heath as Secretary of State for Prices and Incomes. Jim Prior records him as being prepared to sign a document in the late 1970s which contained the phrase: '. . . the Government must come to some conclusions about the likely scope for pay increases . . .' Luckily, as he records, Margaret Thatcher vetoed its publication. I remember talking to him in 1973, after I had resigned, and asked him how he could reconcile himself to operating such a policy. He responded with total conviction that it was essential to use the law to limit price and wage increases as a contribution to moderating inflation. He by no means gave the defence that as a skilled barrister it was natural for him to take up any brief he was offered: he defended his role with enthusiasm. From 1979 to 1983 he still hankered after finding ways of talking down wage increases, of using the nationalized industries to set an example of wage restraint, of browbeating them to hold their prices below what was really necessary. He (and Nigel Lawson too) persisted in a policy of grossly under-rewarding nationalized industry chairmen and board members in order to encourage their private sector equivalents to moderate their salaries. It didn't work. We found it harder and harder to recruit managers of nationalized industries of sufficient calibre, and some private sector bosses continued to behave with reckless greed in relation to their own pay. One of the worst things that happened during Margaret Thatcher's Government, in my opinion, was the way some indifferent businessmen paid themselves ridiculously high salaries, despite the huge tax reductions they received. It also made Geoffrey Howe's itch to work directly on wages look mean by comparison.

I regarded his instinct to massage wage demands not so much as mean, but as misplaced. We believed – and I still do – that inflation is caused by excessive money supply. If the money supply is controlled, then surely what can be afforded in paying the wages is no concern of the Government? Of course, if the Government is paying the wages, it must pay what is necessary to 'recruit, retain and motivate', in the words of the McGaw Report on civil service pay of the time. It should pay no more than that – to do otherwise is to overburden the taxpayers. I drew a strong line between the Government's activities as an employer – where it must pay the going rate – and its attitude towards the private sector, where it must leave it to the market in conditions where the money supply is firmly under control. Both Margaret Thatcher and Geoffrey Howe tended to try to force public sector pay too low in comparison with the private sector and this led to a number of strikes.

Jock Bruce-Gardyne was the Economic Secretary. He was a lifelong friend of mine. He had been a journalist on the *Financial Times*, and spent some years in Paris as the *Financial Times*'s correspondent and there he had learned to speak perfect French. He had a very clear grasp of economic principles and great courage and resolution. He was one of the few who stood up against the follies of 1972–4. He was also a considerable eccentric. He used to go everywhere on a bicycle, strapping his red boxes on the back. One day a red box fell off in Kensington High Street, scattering its papers far and wide – from then on the box had to follow him home in his chauffeur-driven car behind the bicycle. It was a tragedy when Jock Bruce-Gardyne died of a brain tumour early in 1990.

Jock Bruce-Gardyne and I had many discussions with Geoffrey Howe about economic policy. Geoffrey Howe was much concerned by the difficulty of measuring the money supply. With Nigel Lawson's help in 1980, he published the first of a series of annual documents called 'The Medium Term Financial Strategy' – the MTFS.

The various definitions of money supply fall, broadly speaking, into two groups: the narrow measures of money – M0 and M1 – and the broad measures of money – M3, Sterling M3, M4 and PSL2. Narrow in this context means restricting the measure to the most liquid forms of money, like cash and bank notes. The broader measures include bank deposits. Some go further and include non-bank holdings of treasury bills and investments in building societies or local authorities. The broader the measure, the more illiquid the money becomes: that is, the harder it is to use it quickly. Money tied up on a 3 month deposit, for instance, is less liquid than a £5 note.

The original MTFS in 1980 explained that 'No single statistical measure of the money supply can be expected fully to encapsulate monetary conditions, and so provide a uniquely correct basis for controlling the complex relationships between monetary growth and prices and nominal incomes.' Nevertheless, the Government selected only one monetary indicator for which to set a target. This was Sterling M3 – a broad measure. It was a slightly odd decision, because the paper admitted that 'No one aggregate is by itself a sufficient measure of monetary conditions.' In practice, Sterling M3 was probably indeed the most important of the aggregates, although later it came to be regarded as wayward owing to its tendency to show higher growth than appeared to be justified by the evidence. Geoffrey Howe accepted the signal that M3 gave in his 1981 Budget. It was then rising fast, and he reduced demand in accordance with the MTFS policy. But M3 persisted in growing later on, and he began to regard it as 'wayward' towards the end of his Chancellorship. He discounted it more and more. He was probably reluctant at that time to drop it altogether, for fear of being accused of shooting the messenger that brought bad news.

There was endless discussion of these issues, both in public and in private. The main change that Geoffrey Howe actually made was to assign a role to the exchange rate, without letting it rule the roost.

These changes in monetary policy gave much scope for criticism. It was hard to justify raising interest rates or taxes on the basis of a money supply indicator which soon afterwards was questioned or even later, rejected. Jock Bruce-Gardyne and I felt all this was far from convincing, and I believe it greatly undermined Geoffrey Howe's confidence in the system he was trying to operate. This is what probably led him to look for some more permanent benchmark, something fixed against which to measure progress, rather than to rely entirely on mercurial and unreliable monetary indicators. It was probably at this time that he began to see the Exchange Rate Mechanism of the European Community as having some merit. It probably wasn't until after he ceased to be Chancellor that he became convinced that we should join, but I suspect the difficulties in interpreting the MTFS policy played some part in persuading both him and, in due course, his successor Nigel Lawson that we should join.

For my part, with some support from Jock Bruce-Gardyne, I didn't like the increased role assigned to the exchange rate. Monetary policy was not an exact science and no economy behaves exactly as expected. It was natural that the monetary indicators should behave differently – after all, they measured different things and, at any given stage in the economic cycle, those different things were clearly going to behave differently. I believed that all of the indicators, together with all other evidence, should be considered carefully, but at the end of the day, taking action must always depend on a Chancellor's judgement. It had always been so – Chancellors have always had to take a subjective view of how fast an economy was heating or cooling, and to take action when they judged it right to do so. Even those who believed in demand management had to take such decisions. That, indeed, was what both Geoffrey Howe and Nigel Lawson actually did themselves – they used their own judgement, in the light of all the information, about whether the money supply required to be curbed or not. Equally I thought it was a mistake to ignore any signal which any of the indicators gave.

Indeed, one day in September 1981, only a few days after I had entered the Treasury, I happened to be the only Treasury minister in London. Both the Chancellor and the Prime Minister were abroad. Peter Middleton, the Permanent Secretary in charge of economic policy, came into my room and suggested that interest rates should go up 2 points. Having cleared it with my superiors abroad, I duly agreed. It was then generally thought to be a right and necessary step. But it was a decision based on a judgement of the facts at that time; the MTFS was no more than the framework within which we were working. I remembered irritating Geoffrey Howe one day by saying I thought he would do better to manage the economy 'by the seat of his pants' rather than trying to read too much into M0, M1, M3, the exchange rate and the rest of them. In the second half of the 1980s Chancellors more or less did this. The MTFS remained in place and targets for the growth of one or other of the monetary aggregates continued to be set, but decisions were taken on the basis of all the available evidence, not on just one monetary indicator. I don't think any of us fully appreciated the significance of the wayward behaviour of M3.

Nevertheless, Geoffrey Howe presided over the renaissance of the British economy. His four Budgets between them set the scene for six years of uninterrupted growth after 1983. His was a record of good management of the economy which few Chancellors, if any, can match.

THE ADVISERS

(Below) Charles Powell. 'Entirely loyal as well as discreet.'

(Right) Alan Walters. 'He was no politician: indeed, he was a person who despised politics. He it was who led me to define an economist as "a politician who doesn't have to be elected".'

(Foot) Bernard Ingham selects questions for Margaret Thatcher at a tumultuous press conference at the EEC Summit at Luxembourg, 1980. 'A bluff, blunt Yorkshireman, with a growling voice, he looked the least likely person to manipulate the press. Yet he proved invaluable to her.'

An 'informal' meeting with
President Mitterrand in Paris,
1990. 'I can remember very
jovial meetings with both
Chancellor Kohl and
President Mitterrand. It was
when they got together behind
her back to try to get their way
that things got more difficult.'

Meeting Chancellor Helmut
Kohl at the European Summit
at Fontainebleau, 1984.

Margaret Thatcher
applauds Nigel Lawson at
the 1988 Party conference.
'It would have been
possible to salute him as
one of the greatest
chancellors of our time,
were it not for his
management of monetary
policy.'

Nigel Lawson at the time
of his resignation.

The Czech President Vaclav Havel at
Downing Street, 1990.

(Above) King Fahd of Saudi A
is welcomed to Downing Stree
1987.

Margaret Thatcher welcomes
President and Mrs Reagan to
Downing Street, 1989. 'Worl
politics for much of the 1980s
dominated by Gorbachev, Rea
and Margaret Thatcher.'

President Gorbachev and
his wife Raisa with
Margaret and Dennis
Thatcher before a dinner
at 10 Downing Street,
1989.

Margaret Thatcher meets
enthusiastic crowds
during her official visit to
Moscow, 1987.

Nigel Lawson and Sir
~~rey~~ Howe – architects of 'the
~~id~~ Ambush'.

~~w left)~~ Margaret Thatcher and
~~eoffrey~~ Howe at Madrid.

~~t)~~ Michael Heseltine with
~~alists,~~ November 1990. 'Ever
~~he~~ resigned over Westland, he
~~een~~ waiting for his opportunity
~~for~~ the leadership.'

~~w)~~ Douglas Hurd and John
~~r.~~ 'After the second leadership
~~, Michael~~ Heseltine and
~~las~~ Hurd immediately
~~rew.~~ John Major was the new
~~Minister.~~'

Margaret Thatcher was in Paris during much of the leadership campaign. Here she attends the great dir at Versailles, 20 November 1990.

Margaret Thatcher delivers her 'immortal last speech as Prime Minister' during the Commons Vote Censure.

9

THE TREASURY UNDER NIGEL LAWSON

AFTER THE 1983 election, Margaret Thatcher made Geoffrey Howe Foreign Secretary and Nigel Lawson Chancellor. Geoffrey Howe had christened his dog 'Budget'. The shock of the transfer was too much for Budget, who died. He proceeded to call the replacement 'Summit'. I was hoping that perhaps my time had come for a change – I had been Financial Secretary for two years. Soon after the election, Ian Gow telephoned me on the Prime Minister's behalf and said I could choose between staying as Financial Secretary and becoming Minister for the Arts. This was the second time I had been offered the job of Minister for the Arts and for a second time I turned it down. I always saw it as a sort of goalkeeper's job, where the many Arts lobbies kept the poor minister under constant siege for more money. The Arts had articulate and powerful lobbies with many friends in high places. Although the Arts budget increased by 38 per cent in real terms over the decade, it was a limited budget and there was little scope for meeting their extra demands. I believe state funding is necessary for some aspects, but I believe painters, poets, writers and sculptors should get their living from their customers, rather than from the taxpayers: otherwise, government is in the business of 'backing winners'. Operas, ballets, theatres and orchestras should, I think, get a much higher proportion of their income from their audiences and customers than they do. I would also prefer to see any public subsidy for these activities go to the less well off members of the audience, as opposed to the institution itself.

I never felt any sympathy with the highly organized, highly precious Arts lobby, which thrived on its very successful campaign of lobbying for public funds from the taxpayers. I love beautiful things; I have even tried to contribute my own best in this respect as a water colourist. But I am more than content with the verdict of the market; and if the market had not appreciated my works it would never have occurred to me to seek extra income from a compulsory levy on the taxpayers.

There is a better case to be made for public money to be used in support of our incredible heritage of paintings, buildings, sculpture and furniture. But even that case is predicated on the assumption that these treasures have to be in public ownership.

These views would not have made me a happy or successful or popular Minister for the Arts.

I told Ian Gow that I would prefer to stay at the Treasury. As it turned out it was for only four months. In October, following Cecil Parkinson's resignation, I was made Secretary of State for Transport. During those four months there was the Long Recess, so my actual period of working with Nigel Lawson and the new Treasury team was very short. Thus, once again, I observed the workings of the Treasury from outside.

Peter Rees was Chief Secretary; John Moore was Economic Secretary (and Financial Secretary following my departure). We also still had Barney Hayhoe.

I had known Nigel Lawson for many years and we had been companions in arms together over many issues. We shared the same basic political and economic philosophy. We were friends, friends who had embarked on a common cause: the establishment of a free enterprise culture. We had been together on numerous Finance Bill committees when in opposition and were used to working together. He had a habit of suddenly starting to roar with laughter in the middle of making a speech, anticipating a joke he was about to make. As the rest of the committee had not heard the joke we could only laugh at him, not with him. It was an eccentricity which endeared him to his colleagues. In Government he was not a humorous or easy person to work with – a man of strong personality and strong views and when convinced of something it was very difficult to change his mind. Like Geoffrey Howe, he was not a good delegator, preferring to examine and satisfy himself as to the correctness of every detailed decision. Nor did he share his thinking to a great extent with his juniors. He had a very powerful mind and was both clever and firm. He did not suffer fools, or foolish ideas, gladly.

His qualities made him a natural choice for Margaret Thatcher to appoint him as her Chancellor. She had schooled him from the beginning – first as Financial Secretary, and then as Secretary of State for Energy – to reach the top of the ladder early and to acquire the necessary experience. It was an appointment towards which she had been working since 1979. It was a marvellous opportunity for him when he moved in to Number 11 Downing Street in June 1983. He had his leader's full confidence and respect. He was young, extremely well equipped for the job, and he had the support of the Party and the City.

Nigel Lawson returned to the Treasury with the economy in good and improving shape. Inflation was coming down rapidly, the money supply was well within last year's target range and output was rising. Unemployment was still high, but beginning to fall. In fact, employment was rising quite fast but the number of people seeking work was also rising. He inherited a healthy situation.

Policy changed but little with the change of Chancellor. He continued to exert as much downward pressure on public spending as he could. When it was necessary to increase spending in an emergency, or on some new problem, he was always firm but not unreasonable. Public spending fell under his Chancellorship from 46.5 per cent of GDP to 39.5 by 1989, but this was mainly because of the steady and impressive growth of GDP over which he presided, rather than of any reduction of spending. In fact, spending increased in real terms by 4 per cent during his period in office. He was particularly successful as a tax reformer. It is possible to question some of the legacy he left by the end of his time in the context of all the other imposts on the citizen, like the Community Charge, which I have described. He replaced the system of corporation tax he inherited, which had a high rate of tax and very high levels of investment relief with a new system, based on realistic rates of depreciation and a much lower rate of tax. He got rid of a number of taxes altogether. He turned the Capital Transfer Tax into an inheritance tax which exempted most small estates, but was sufficiently bearable for the large estates for them not to seek to avoid it altogether. He cut out most of the remaining income tax reliefs. He eventually succeeded in establishing totally separate taxation for husbands and wives. Over time he brought the standard rate of income tax down from 30 per cent to 25 per cent and the higher rate to 40 per cent. He did much to encourage savings and personal pensions. It was a major achievement. The gratifying thing was that tax yields often increased rather than diminished as he transformed the taxation system into one which the taxpayer thought was fair.

He was a passionate believer in privatization and during his Chancellorship the vast bulk of the remaining publicly-owned industries passed into the private sector. It would have been possible to salute him as one of the greatest Chancellors of our time, were it not for his management of monetary policy – the area in which he came to the Treasury with a reputation second to none.

His attitude to monetary policy at the beginning was almost identical to Geoffrey Howe's. They had together, with help from others, invented the Medium Term Financial Strategy, and Nigel Lawson further developed the concept in his first few Budgets, with the benefit of the experience of the last four years. He continued to wrestle with the problem of which of the monetary indicators was most important. In his first three Budgets, he set targets for M0 and M3; in his second three Budgets he abandoned M3 and came to rely upon M0 alone. The problem that Geoffrey Howe had come up against was still as intractable as ever. Which of the indicators gave the Chancellor the best indication of what was happening in the economy?

Financial deregulation and the changing world market conditions were in themselves altering the way these indicators behaved. Over the years, M3 – the measure of broad money – was thought to behave so unreliably that Nigel Lawson eventually decided it was no longer suitable for using as a target. M0, the narrow measure, came to be relied upon alone. First, he thought it gave the most up-to-date picture of what was happening in the economy and, second, with the advantage of hindsight, it seemed to have given a fairly accurate picture of the state of the money supply. It remains the only monetary indicator which is targeted to this day.

In late 1985 M3 was growing fast. Interest rates were high, and the corporate sector was in heavy surplus. Large amounts of money went into bank deposits – at that time the best haven for surplus funds. This was the reason for the fast growth in M3. There was no sign of inflation returning and M0 was staying well within target. It therefore seemed reasonable to conclude that M3 was of no significance and Nigel Lawson dropped it as a target.

The effect of the funds piling into bank deposits was to give the banks a much increased potential to lend. Money was advanced in ever-increasing quantities for property purchase and for company takeovers. Asset prices started to rise. Inflation first appeared in the mid-1980s in the price of houses, land and other assets. Many would argue that this asset price inflation inevitably transferred itself into wage and price inflation after the normal time lag; in other words, that the growth of M3 in 1985–6, far from being irrelevant, was the warning signal of the latent inflation in the system that manifested itself three years later. There were other factors in play by then, as I shall show, but it is arguable that the downgrading of M3 in 1985 was Nigel Lawson's first error.

As I described in Chapter 8, the absence of credibility in relation to the value of the monetary indicators in the mind of the authorities became a very serious problem. It enabled critics to ridicule the whole concept of controlling the money supply, as the measuring rod for assessing progress was continuously being changed. If the performance of different motor cars was to be measured by the miles they ran per gallon of petrol consumed, then one must not change the definition of the length of a mile at frequent intervals. Critics could make a superficially good point in ridiculing the changes in the indicators most in favour.

Of course, measuring miles per gallon is an exact science, whereas measuring monetary growth can never be so. It was fruitless to try to seek too exact and scientific a measurement of something which is always changing and can never be precise. The growth of the monetary indicators, as I have said, should only be seen as one of the many factors to be taken into account when making an economic judgement. It is also necessary to look at retail sales, manufacturing output, wages and prices, the exchange rate, the trade balance and a host of other things, including anecdotal evidence. This became, I think, Nigel Lawson's view as well. But this perceived deficiency in the reliability of the various measures of money supply, together with the criticism of the frequent changes, greatly worried the Treasury experts and in turn they extended their worries first to Geoffrey Howe and later to Nigel Lawson. They both hankered after some lodestar, some fixed point, against which to measure progress and to assess the need for policy changes.

Nigel Lawson had for some time been attracted to the idea of joining the Exchange Rate Mechanism and because of this uncertainty he in time began to put greater emphasis on the exchange rate as a possible answer to his dilemma. The first reference to it is in his 1985 MTFS, which stated, 'Significant changes in the exchange rate are also important. It will be necessary to judge the appropriate combination of monetary growth and the exchange rate needed to keep financial policy on track: there is no mechanistic formula.' Similar statements were included in all subsequent MTFSs produced by Nigel Lawson, but with growing emphasis on the importance of the exchange rate. The 1987–8 MTFS said, 'Monetary conditions are assessed in the light of movements in narrow and broad money and the behaviour of other financial indicators, in particular the exchange rate. There is no mechanical formula for taking these factors into account; a balance must be struck between the exchange rate and domestic monetary growth consistent with the Government's aims for money GDP and inflation.'

The significance of this growing preoccupation with the exchange rate is profound. In effect, the kernel of the concept was to use the value of the pound in the foreign exchange markets as a measure of the state of the economy. If the pound was going down, policy was too lax. If the pound was going up, policy was too tight. By using the value of the pound as a form of measurement it was easy and natural to slip into using it as a target. With the monetary indicators, it was possible to set a target for their growth, and then adjust policy according to whether the target was being hit or missed. With the exchange rate, the same was possible; policy could be adjusted as to whether the target was being hit or missed. But then, why stop there? It was possible to make sure the target was always hit, by intervening in the foreign exchange market to achieve a certain predetermined exchange rate, or even to go further and in some way 'fix' it at the preferred value. Thus over the years Nigel Lawson became attracted to the policy of targeting a certain exchange rate for the pound; and then later he pursued the idea of using both policy change, and intervention by the Bank of England, to achieve a preferred rate of exchange for the pound. The fatal error had now crept into policy-making of going back to fixed, or at least semi-fixed, exchange rates – the same policy that Geoffrey Howe had eschewed in 1979.

I do not know precisely when these ideas crystallized in Nigel Lawson's mind – but it was probably about 1985. Nor do I know who influenced him. The Treasury, at least in the days when I was there, were weaned of their normal obsession with fixed exchange rates. The Bank of England never has been weaned and never will be, I suspect, unless Alan Walters were to be appointed Governor: a desirable, but unlikely, proposition. Nigel Lawson may have listened to the Bank. It may be that on his international travels, particularly in Europe, he was impressed by what he heard. It is not for me to judge. But he was not known for listening to advice he received, unless it was advice with which he agreed. Most probably he came to his own conclusion, living as he did daily with the problems of running the economy. Having come to his conclusion, he believed in it unshakeably.

What is curious about his conversion is that from 1983 to 1987 the economy was running extremely well, and smoothly. Everything was behaving – we were even chalking up steady 3.5 per cent annual economic growth. There wasn't a cloud on the economic horizon (if we ignore the growth in the discredited M3). It was the least likely time, in decades of economic turmoil, for it to seem necessary to change one of the fundamentals of economic policy. For once, economic policy was delivering the required results.

As this is one of the most crucial considerations in managing any economy, and it was probably the most important single factor contributing to the eventual departure of Margaret Thatcher, I fear I must take the reader through the complex arguments on both sides of the question of exchange rate policy. The fact that even the mention of the words 'exchange rate' may induce an immediate turn-off merely heightens its importance: it is because people find the subject turns them off that it has aroused so little controversy and its importance has not been understood. For this reason alone, I must try to make it easy to comprehend.

The exchange rate is merely the price at which one can swap pounds for dollars, or Deutschemarks, or any other currency. As we all know, it varies from day to day. The exchange rate is determined by foreign exchange dealers in markets who make their living by making a tiny profit, overall, in the business of exchanging one currency for another. They have to cover their losses when they exchange two currencies for what turns out to be the wrong rate by their profits when they get it right. By the nature of their trade, they are cautious speculators; they have to speculate on where the values of the different currencies are going to be tomorrow, but cautiously.

Moreover, there is, of course, a cross rate between each of the independent currencies of the world. Currency A may be worth two of currency B and four of currency C: in that case, currency B is worth two of currency C. It is a market in which many independent currencies are all moving up and down against each other.

Foreign exchange dealers have to have reasons for expecting one currency to rise or fall against the rest. The reasons are manifold. The discovery of gold, or oil, or uranium, for instance, and the relative changes in the prices of such commodities, obviously affect the value of the currencies of countries where they are found. War, civil unrest, or adverse political change can destabilize a currency. Peace, civil tranquillity or the election of a good government can enhance a currency's value. These are exceptional events which do not happen on the great majority of trading days.

In uneventful times, the market prices the various currencies on the basis of which currency is the investment in which the holder of funds should best invest. The investor looks for two things: what interest rate he will receive on the investment, and what loss of capital value he will suffer owing to the currency in which he invests depreciating in the foreign exchange markets over time. He looks for the highest real rate of interest – that is, the gross interest he is paid in the year, less the capital loss due to capital depreciation. If the real rate of interest looks right, he will invest in a currency. The gross rate of interest is easy to determine: it is public and a precise figure. The element of guesswork comes in relation to the capital depreciation; that is, the future rise or fall in the value of the currency against that of his own currency.

For this latter purpose, the best surrogate is unit labour costs. This is the index which combines the rate of inflation in any economy with changes in its labour productivity. Looking back on any period when exchange rates between two currencies have changed (and barring erratic events of a mineral or political nature), it is usual to find the changes in currency parities mirror very closely the changes in unit labour costs (ULCs). Thus, for the main European countries over the period of the decade 1980 to 1990, the changes were:

	Currency Change	Unit Labour Cost Change
German DM/French Franc	−47%	+45%
German DM/Italian Lira	−64%	+71%
German DM/British Pound	−25%	+23%

Despite the fact that they were both members of the Exchange Rate Mechanism the changes in the value of both the franc and the lira in relation to the DM followed closely the relative changes in the unit labour costs of France and Italy on the one hand and of Germany on the other. Apart from 'erratic' developments, it is the change in ULCs, which, over time, causes changes in parities. Foreign exchange dealers therefore look always at factors contributing to changes in ULCs in order to determine whether to mark a currency up or down against other currencies.

If the markets take a gloomy view of a country's ULCs, it is necessary to increase interest rates, or otherwise the value of the currency will decline. Investors will see a depreciation coming, which signals a fall in real interest rates. This can be compensated for if the authorities raise interest rates. The exchange rate is therefore just the price the market puts upon the value of a currency, taking all those factors into account, at any given moment of time.

Any decision to try to affect the exchange rate and to fix it at some predetermined value in relation to the value of other countries' currencies is a fundamental one. It forces the authorities to use interest rates, or fiscal policy, or both, for the purpose of making sure the currency achieves the predetermined exchange rate. The economic weapons are thus not deployed for the purpose of controlling the money supply, but for the purpose of achieving a certain exchange rate.

The first argument in favour of doing this is that if country A is controlling its economy exemplarily, then to align and maintain the currency of country B at a constant rate of exchange between the currencies of country A and country B, must mean that the money supply of country B is controlled at the same level as that of the exemplary country A. The argument is, in fact, false, because it assumes identical rates of productivity growth in the two countries, as I will demonstrate. It would hold if inflation were the sole criterion: but it is not. It is relative changes in ULCs, which are a combination of inflation and productivity changes, that determine changes in currency values.

This leads on to the second argument used to justify fixed exchange rate policies. They are said to provide a 'discipline' on the authorities to manage the currency in a non-inflationary way. From the previous paragraph, it is immediately obvious that it can be a very perverse discipline. If country B's ULCs are doing better than country A's, the only way for it to prevent its currency rising against country A's is to lower interest rates, and thus inflate! But this argument is even more fundamentally flawed. It assumes that an external discipline is needed and that there is no such thing as self-discipline. Some governments in the past have, indeed, inflated deliberately; but for the last decade or so, that bad habit has come to an end in civilized economies. Inflation nowadays is normally caused by mistake, not by a lack of self-discipline.

Nigel Lawson did not need discipline, nor did he lack it. He did not want to inflate the British economy. He had all the self-discipline necessary. What happened was that he got it wrong – not because of any lack of discipline, whether internal or external, but because he ignored the signals from M3, and second, because he pursued a policy of trying to fix the exchange rate, at a time when it was being moved up by the market.

The third argument of the advocates of fixed exchange rates is the most absurd of all. The argument is that 'devaluation' of the exchange rate causes inflation. It was even spelt out for the first time in the 1990 MTFS, where it said: 'But appraised carefully with other evidence, the exchange rate is a sensitive and timely indicator. Moreover, it can also play a direct part in raising inflation; a *lower pound tends to lead to higher import prices in sterling terms* as well as giving more headroom for domestic producers to pass on increased costs. A higher pound has the opposite effect.'

For the first time since the 1970s the old fallacy of cost-push inflation was actually trotted out in an official document. Because imports would cost more, that would 'play a direct part in raising inflation.' It might as well have said, 'if wages or prices go up, it would play a direct part in raising inflation.' The statement flies in the face of Keynes's monetary theory – which is that inflation is caused by an increase in the money supply, not by rising prices. Surely, if the money supply is firmly under control, an increase in import prices has the simple result that we can afford to buy fewer imports?

The fourth argument for fixed exchange rates is one of general goodwill towards the international community and the business section of the domestic economy. Everyone wants stable exchange rates. In themselves, they are obviously desirable. Other nations want them too. They are like motherhood and apple pie. Unfortunately, the way to achieve them is for each nation to pursue economic policies which lead to convergence between the economic performance of nations, not to try to fix the results in advance by decreeing what a currency is worth, in defiance of the markets.

Britain has run its economy with some form of fixed exchange rate mechanism for a century or more. The most famous example was in 1925, when Churchill, as Chancellor, took sterling back onto the Gold Standard. He took us in at far too high a rate, and since the pound was irrevocably valued at £4 15s 6d per ounce of gold under the Gold Standard, there was no way of adjusting the currency value in order for Britain to become competitive. Industry could no longer export and imports flooded into the country. Industry tried desperately to cut its costs and wages. Wages were cut by up to two-thirds – but still we could not compete. It was not until 1931 when we left the Gold Standard that industrial recovery began and unemployment began to fall.

Later, a similar form of fixing of our currency took place under the Bretton Woods Agreement. At least sterling was not over-valued at the time we joined it, and for a while we remained competitive. But later we again became uncompetitive and British industry began to suffer once more. We formally 'devalued' in 1949 and had to do so again in 1967. Industry suffered for a long period before each devaluation actually happened.

By contrast, Germany and Japan since the war have always managed to avoid this mistake. The desire of the British and Americans to keep up the value of their currencies has as its mirror image the result of keeping the DM and the yen always more competitive than sterling and the dollar. This, in my view, is the major reason for the relative success of Germany and Japan in the industrial field, as I have described.

The crux of the argument arises out of this. It is generally agreed that Britain historically has had a tendency to be more inflationary than Germany and Japan. The experience of inflation in the 1960s and 1970s perhaps built in the tendency for employees to press for, and on the whole to receive, higher wage and salary increases than their productivity increases properly allowed. As this has increased our ULCs the markets have tended to drop the value of our currency to compensate. The advocates of fixed exchange rates claim that the refusal to drop the currency value to accommodate such wage increases will in due course change the tendency to give in to unjustified wage claims – the so-called 'external discipline'. The floating currency advocates believe it is necessary only to control the domestic money supply and that this discipline will bring wage increases back into line with productivity increases. As Karl Otto Pöhl has put it, 'Interest rates should be set according to domestic monetary conditions and the exchange rate should be left to go where it will.' To persist with an over-valued exchange rate is an extra and unnecessary burden over and above the restriction of the money supply caused by the interest rate. Too high a currency value cuts into industry's competitiveness, on top of the already serious difficulties which high interest rates impose upon it. Geoffrey Howe in 1979–83 demonstrated during his Chancellorship that it was possible to bring inflation down from 22 per cent to 3 per cent by controlling the money supply alone. Although he intervened in the foreign exchange markets, there was no attempt to fix the exchange rate during his Chancellorship. The pound was indeed very high during much of this period, but that was due to the judgement of the market, not to intervention. Despite the high pound, industry started to increase its sales and exports long before the squeeze came off because it was not priced out of world markets by an over-valued pound, in addition to the pressures caused by high interest rates.

It is against that background that I will consider Nigel Lawson's conduct of economic policy. I realize that many would not accept my analysis – and certainly Nigel Lawson would not, but then they must explain what went wrong about 1987, because 1987 is when things did start to go wrong. The reason why they started to go wrong can be easily explained by my analysis.

The precise timing of when things began to change is hard to determine, but it is not important. Certainly the years between the 1983 and 1987 elections were happy and prosperous ones. Employment continued to rise and overtook the increase in those wanting jobs. Unemployment peaked in 1986, and fell steadily from then until the end of the decade. Inflation remained low, and economic growth was running at a steady 3.5 per cent per annum. Industry began to invest and expand, helped by the tax reforms and the policy of deregulation, over which Nigel Lawson presided. Productivity increased dramatically. Small businesses started in increasing numbers and more and more people became self-employed. They were the halcyon years.

The one small cloud upon the horizon was the escalation of land and asset prices, which at the time merely had the effect of increasing the feeling of well-being. The 1987 Budget was a pre-election Budget. Things were going so well that there was no need for the usual so-called 'give away' Budget – it was possible both to cut the borrowing requirement and to reduce taxes without adding to demand in an irresponsible way. Nigel Lawson budgeted for a Public Sector Borrowing Requirement (PSBR) of only 1 per cent of GDP – £4 billion. The year before he had budgeted for 1.75 per cent. He was able to reduce the standard rate of income tax from 29p to 27p at the same time. He could afford £2.5 billion in tax cuts as well, so buoyant was the economy. No one could describe this as an inflationary Budget. Indeed Retail Price Inflation remained low in 1988.

It could be said that Nigel Lawson's first four years as Chancellor were exemplary. The Tories were re-elected in the 1987 election with a handsome majority. Nigel Lawson appeared to play a vital role in that victory by his masterly demolition of the Labour Party during the campaign. He played the old game of costing their programme and working out the consequences in increased taxes. An old game it may be, but it is a fair game, and as usual it worked. It will probably always work if Labour insists on going into elections with absurdly high spending plans.

So high was his stock after the election that Margaret Thatcher immediately asked him to continue as Chancellor. There was no higher job for him to go to. I doubt if he wanted to be Prime Minister. He may have wanted to be Foreign Secretary. He and I had both been turned down for the diplomatic service by the Foreign Office after leaving university.

So it was natural for him to stay as Chancellor. I myself continued at the Department of the Environment where there was still much unfinished business to discharge. I saw more of him in the period after the 1987 election – I was busy getting the Community Charge legislation through Parliament and privatizing the water industry, both of which brought us into frequent and amicable contact. We had no differences over water, and although he was never in favour of the Community Charge, our mutual business on that topic was conducted cordially.

Where we began to share mutual alarm was over the rising prices of land and houses, particularly in the south of England. The cause of this was probably the high level at which M3 had been running. The huge bank deposits of surplus funds were being lent on to property companies who bid the price of land up in a shortage situation. Asset price inflation in due course gave way to retail price inflation. I charged Nigel Lawson with having allowed such credit to become too freely available, and he charged me with having allowed planning permissions to be not freely available enough. We both questioned the effect of keeping mortgage interest relief. I still think this was a crucial signal in the development of inflation.

Nigel Lawson had by then become a major figure on the international finance ministers' scene. Of long standing, high stature, and wide reputation, his voice became important at meetings of the finance ministers of the top countries: the Organization for Economic Cooperation and Development (OECD), the Group of Seven, and the Group of Six and the Group of Five, as they were called.

These international meetings had been regular events for many years, but a crucial one took place in September 1985. It was called the Plaza Agreement. In addition to the normal review of the world economic situation, the finance ministers came to the view that the major world currencies were undervalued as compared to the dollar. They made an agreement to use coordinated intervention to redress this deficiency. In other words, they ganged up to push the dollar down. Whether they were right and the dollar was too high and the markets were wrong seems highly questionable. Nevertheless, they acquired a taste for combined intervention in the foreign exchange markets, which certainly had the results they desired.

They continued to intervene when they thought it appropriate to do so through 1985 and 1986. In February 1987 there was a meeting of the Group of Six in Paris. The resulting agreement acquired the name of the Louvre Accord. At that time, the US deficit was still far too large, and investors were beginning to despair. The dollar continued to decline against other major currencies. For some unaccountable reason at the Louvre Accord they decided to arrest its fall. The official reason given was to ensure exchange rate stability. The others intervened massively to support the dollar, and European and Japanese interest rates were cut, while US rates were increased. The result was a success – the decline in the dollar was arrested and it rose quite sharply. Investors, taking the Group of Six at their word, believed that there would be exchange rate stability. If it was to be the case that the dollar would not be devalued, the obvious safe haven for funds was the dollar, by then paying a much higher rate of interest than the yen or the DM. Vast funds crossed the Atlantic in response, and the dollar rallied.

It didn't, of course, last. The US was inflating faster than the others and in little over a year's time, the markets re-asserted themselves. As Martin Feldstein wrote in the *Financial Times* on 29 March 1990: 'The Louvre Accord has been unsuccessful because the goal of fixed nominal exchange rates is a mistake in a world in which inflationary rates differ.'

Nigel Lawson was a leading advocate of the Louvre Accord. I became suspicious of these events at the time. It seemed to me that we were ganging up with the Japanese and the Germans and the Americans to prop up the ailing dollar – in order to engineer keeping it above its market value. Even in 1985, Nigel Lawson had begun to support moves internationally to interfere with currency values on a more substantial basis than merely day-to-day intervention. The Louvre Accord was the first attempt to fix an exchange rate – that of the dollar – at a higher level than the market wanted. The United States was still running a huge budget deficit, which resulted in a huge trade deficit. It was natural in these circumstances that the dollar should be weak – and good for the United States too. A weak dollar would have helped them to price their exports back into being competitive and to displace imports. But the Americans, as they still do, were blaming all their problems on the Japanese instead of on their budget deficit; they thought their dignity and importance required a higher dollar value than the markets were offering. So they were keen to avert the decline of the dollar, which was actually to prevent the only thing which would have helped them, given that they were not prepared to reduce their budget deficit. Although on this occasion it was beneficial to the British economy to keep the dollar high – it meant we could sell well into the States, and we did – I did not like the principle of Plaza, let alone of Louvre.

On 16 October 1987 there was a huge hurricane, which did great damage in southern England. But the economic skies were clear, until suddenly, three days later, on Monday, 19 October 1987, came the stock market crash. Wall Street tumbled overnight. London fell by some 15 per cent: Tokyo and Frankfurt crashed in unison by roughly similar percentages. There was pandemonium and panic. There was wild talk of 1929 repeating itself. Nobody quite understood why the stock market had tumbled in this way. The conventional wisdom emerged that it was indeed a repeat of 1929, when a similar dramatic fall in stock market prices had ushered in a long period of severe depression on both sides of the Atlantic.

There is a much more convincing alternative explanation of the October 1987 crash. It happened partly because world stock market prices were too high, but partly it was caused by the Louvre Accord. Investors in US stocks, having hoped for a reduction in the dollar in order to enable their companies to compete and prosper, found their hopes frustrated by the action which followed from Louvre. The prospects for the profits of US corporations suddenly became questionable. It was much more profitable to put money into the dollar than into US stocks. Louvre had killed any hopes of the necessary and expected devaluation of the dollar, and they collectively decided to get out. They did. When such things happen the first few who make a move to exit spark off a stampede by the masses, who had been waiting only for confirmation of their growing doubts, which are confirmed when a few substantial investors decide to sell.

The stock markets have become more or less worldwide and instant communication enables all the world's markets to adjust simultaneously. So Tokyo, London, Frankfurt and Paris all fell. The markets were too high, and the Louvre Accord was probably the trigger that set them tumbling. But the one explanation which could not have been right was the one that said we were suffering a liquidity crisis similar to that of 1929.

In 1929 the US and the UK were newly aligned to the Gold Standard, at exchange rates which made it impossible for either of us to remain competitive. In order to maintain our currencies at the predetermined values, both of us applied severe monetary squeezes resulting in the famous collapse of equity values of the 1929 crash. The problem at that time was grossly inadequate money supply for the familiar reason of trying to maintain an impossibly high exchange rate.

In 1987 it was simply not credible to believe that the British money supply was grossly inadequate. M0 was growing healthily, although not excessively, by about 5 per cent in 1987. Broad money (M3) was growing a great deal faster. There was no shortage of demand or liquidity in Britain in the autumn of 1987 – indeed, there was probably too much. How anyone could think that we faced a situation similar to 1929 I cannot understand. Whatever may have been the cause of the trouble in the US, it wasn't that in Britain.

But Nigel Lawson apparently came to the conclusion that Britain was suffering from a liquidity crisis. He feared another 1929.

I believe there was more truth in my alternative explanation, which I offered at the time and which laid some blame on the Louvre Accord. We agreed to differ. There was nothing more I could do but to register my doubts. He turned his beliefs into action in due course. He took major steps to stimulate the British economy in the 1988 Budget, in order to save it from what he thought was the coming severe depression, redolent of the 1930s, and the dole queues. To be fair, I suspect he was influenced by some very poor Treasury forecasting and by the rest of the top finance ministers who certainly took the same view. A meeting of OECD was even called to discuss the expected recession. I could not persuade him otherwise. I had put the alternative view; I had suggested the crash was at least partly caused by interfering in the value of the dollar.

The Plaza and the Louvre discussions, however, confirmed another thought in Nigel Lawson's mind. If the international community felt it right to push down, or push up, the dollar, why should not he intervene to affect the rate of exchange of the pound? I don't know when he first came to believe we should join the ERM. In a speech in 1990 he said he believed we should have joined at least five years earlier. The first encounter with the Prime Minister probably came about 1985 or 1986, when both Nigel Lawson and Geoffrey Howe joined forces to try and make her agree to join the ERM. The other member of the small group formed to consider the matter was Willie Whitelaw. He apparently came to the conclusion that it was wrong to do so, and he sided with Margaret Thatcher. She was thus able to resist the first attempt by Nigel Lawson and Geoffrey Howe to force her to join. This was to be robustly maintained until long after Nigel Lawson ceased to be Chancellor.

Queen Mary Tudor recorded, 'When I am dead and opened, you shall find "Calais" lying in my heart.' When Margaret Thatcher is dead and opened it will be those three letters 'ERM' that will be lying in her heart. They were to come back and plague her ever more intensively until she fell – indeed, they were probably the underlying root cause of her fall. In my view, she was right to resist our joining the ERM as strongly as she did. Joining it represented a move towards fixing the exchange rate – not irrevocably – but in such a way that monetary policy was expected to be directed towards maintaining the pound's value within its band of the ERM, rather than 'according to domestic monetary conditions' to re-quote Herr Poehl. In the ERM, the dilemma I described earlier becomes a reality. Is the domestic economy or the exchange rate to be the top priority? Margaret Thatcher was rightly suspicious of getting herself into this trap. Her instincts told her that since foreign exchange was a market, it was unwise to interfere in the workings of the market. She was dead against it, and she was fortified in her opposition by Alan Walters and a number of cabinet ministers, myself included. Margaret Thatcher told Nigel Lawson that she would not agree to our joining the ERM. Unable to prevail, but far from persuaded, he resolved to join it unilaterally and unofficially. In early 1987 he started to 'shadow the DM'. He sought to keep the pound at a value of around DM3.00. He used massive intervention by the Bank of England to try to achieve his aims. Indeed, he had no other weapon. He could not call on other ERM members to support the pound, since we were not members. He could not declare a band of values, out of which the pound would not be allowed to move, for the same reason. So he commissioned the Bank of England to chuck the reserves at the pound if it went below the magic figure of DM3.00 and to sell it short if it went above. The Bank was a willing, nay, keen, accomplice: they had always longed for the good old days of fixed parities, and this at least was a step in the right direction. Fixed parities make central bank governors feel important – they give them a *raison d'être* to maintain them. Otherwise they don't do anything very important. It is rare to find a central bank governor who understands the need to let the exchange rate 'go where it will'.

Margaret Thatcher could do little about all this. Nigel Lawson's stock was riding high. Although she no doubt disapproved, the Chancellor and the Bank alone were responsible for managing the currency day to day. Nor were we ERM members – it was a sort of do-it-yourself private enterprise membership, in theory easily aborted if it didn't work. I suspect Nigel Lawson just did it and bolted his door against the protests coming from his neighbour at Number 10. Shadowing the DM was not a policy that had been agreed by the Cabinet.

It so happened that, in 1986–7, British ULCs in manufacturing were growing at 0.7 per cent per annum and German ULCs at 7.2 per cent per annum. Not only did we have marginally lower inflation than the Germans, but our labour productivity was growing much faster than that of Germany. As a result, the pound was pressing upwards in the markets. At the end of 1987 a pound was worth DM3.00, and it reached DM3.25 at the peak in early 1989. So the new DIY ERM member had to get the pound down – an experience very different from the usual one of trying to prevent it falling. How were the Chancellor and the Bank to achieve this? There was no way they could stop our productivity growing so well. The only way was to lower interest rates, thus causing sterling to be less attractive to international investors. This in turn should have had the effect of bringing sterling down. His determination to shadow the DM, a policy which had few friends, had never been approved by Cabinet. It cannot have pleased his own Prime Minister and led him to the conclusion that interest rates should be cut. The two misconceptions came together: there was a 1929-type slump coming; and the pound must be kept at DM3.00 instead of appreciating. The answer to both problems was to slash interest rates. He could kill both birds with one stone!

This was the first time under Margaret Thatcher that a Chancellor decided to cut interest rates when the money supply appeared not to be signalling that any change of policy was needed – or, if one takes M3, that policy was too loose. It was, in fact, 'demand management' all over again. He feared a recession was coming and wanted to maintain the parity of the pound. So he took action to stimulate the economy. In fact, no recession was on the way, but the economy was certainly stimulated.

In his 1988 Budget, Nigel Lawson cut the standard rate of income tax again, from 27p to 25p, and the higher rates were amalgamated into a rate of 40p – the highest having previously been 60p. He nevertheless was able to propose a balanced budget – the PSBR was zero. It was a remarkable achievement.

The substantial tax cuts appeared to me to be justified. He predicted and achieved a budget surplus during the year. I would not argue that the tax cuts were excessive, although many did at the time. I suspect there was a certain mixing up of the arguments here. Egalitarians objected strongly to the cut in the top rate of tax to 40 per cent, and sought to criticize that decision by saying it represented a bigger tax cut than the economy could afford. In fact, in terms of the amount of money it cost – £1,025 million – it was almost insignificant, as against the total yield of income tax of £42.1 billion. It may or may not have been sound politics, but it was not unsound economics.

Between October 1987 and May 1988 he also brought interest rates down to 7½ per cent. He did this because of his fear of a liquidity crisis, and because he wanted to arrest the upward march of the pound. The pound was strong and he tried to use intervention to prevent it rising above DM 3.00. Margaret Thatcher took a different view: this was when their disagreement first became acute. I felt he was greatly overdoing it, and told him of my alarm. He had not listened to the counter-explanation for the October crash, nor had he let himself be guided by the state of the monetary indicators, nor by the growing level of demand in the economy, nor by the rising levels of borrowing, and of house prices. He was determined to keep the DM3.00 parity. It was impossible to change his mind. I mentioned my fears to him, but he dismissed them. He was the miracle Chancellor who had cut taxes and interest rates at a stroke, and this was not even a pre-election Budget.

Time-lags are notoriously difficult to estimate in assessing economic policy. Something is done at Christmas – when will the results show up in the real economy? Usually it takes eighteen months to two years. But on this occasion, the markets reacted quickly and savagely. The money supply indicators started very soon after the Budget on their upward march. The credit boom gathered pace; the price of land and houses really took off. Credit was obtained on the security of escalating house prices, credit was used to finance a spending spree, mainly on imported goods. The balance of trade swung violently into deficit, reaching an annual level then measured at about £20,000 million at the peak, as the copious cheap credit found its way into consumption of imports. There was also an industrial investment boom, as industry sought to take advantage of the cheap credit and the expanding domestic market. But despite rapid industrial expansion, it was imports which took the lion's share of the surge in demand. Nigel Lawson could not fail to see the danger signals. He increased interest rates in steps to 13 per cent by November 1988. The astonishing thing in 1988 was how quickly the red lights started to flash in Great George

Street. I suspect that the explanation was that the assets inflation sparked off by M3 was by then transforming itself into retail price inflation. Only a few months after the glory of the 1988 Budget, the Chancellor himself was forced to slam on the brakes. Inflation was starting again on its upward march. Nigel Lawson came to refer to it as no more than a blip. Some blip!

There was never a word of apology, or humility. Many Chancellors would have resigned after presiding over such a disaster. Nor did he learn the lessons. His policy of shadowing the DM continued (although we heard nothing more about 1929-type slumps by early summer 1988). Margaret Thatcher was appalled. She must have felt bitterly disappointed that the top priority of all her ambitions – an end to inflation – should suddenly have gone seriously wrong. Where they both agreed was that the boom had to be cooled, and she supported him strongly in that. She identified that shadowing the DM was, and continued to be, the root cause of the problem, but she could not prevail upon Nigel Lawson to abandon this policy. Their personal relationship deteriorated. He went on pursuing the same policy remorselessly. She assailed him from next door at Number 10, coming up always against the same refusal to change. Their strong difference of opinion was not about the need to squeeze the economy through high interest rates, but about his fatal attachment to the magic DM3.00 benchmark. The markets took little heed either of his wishes or of the Bank's intervention to sell sterling. Stimulated by the high interest rates, the pound continued to battle its way upward against the DM, reaching a peak of DM3.25 in early 1989, before the market got the message of the inflation that Nigel Lawson's policy had sparked off. Thereafter it pursued an equally relentless downward course, as inflation reappeared on the scene, bottoming out at DM2.75 a year later.

This impossible tension between Prime Minister and Chancellor first reached the public consciousness in her (now) famous answer to a question in Parliament on 10 March 1988. Questioned by Neil Kinnock on the policy of shadowing the DM, she told the House, 'There is no way in which one can buck the market.' It was the first public recognition of their disagreement. It was at this point that the argument emerged, at the peak of Nigel Lawson's career. It was in language that people could understand; and it was frank, and it was right. But it was interpreted as the words of a fractious woman impeding her brilliant Chancellor's policy, not as one who was right, being undermined by his doggedness. In his stubborn way, it caused

Nigel Lawson to become even more obstinate. The truth, spoken in public, not only made him fight harder, but he was hurt by her public rebuke. She refused to make amends by saying she didn't mean it, because she said she did mean it.

At this stage in the saga, there are two lessons to be drawn. The first is the obvious one that a Chancellor and a Prime Minister must be agreed on policy and must work together. If they don't, one or the other has to go, and it has to be the Chancellor. The constitutional position is that the Prime Minister is First Lord of the Treasury, and as such has ultimate authority over the Chancellor. If a Treasury minister – even her Chancellor – differs from her in the ultimate, he either has to give way or to resign. Nigel Lawson did neither. He persisted with his policy. He left her with no option but to suffer him or sack him. I suspect he thought she would sack him. But she didn't. I have often wondered why she didn't. She hated sacking people. She had already had to sack a number of ministers over the years. I suspect that she shrank from dismissing so redoubtable a figure as her Chancellor, particularly one with Nigel Lawson's reputation, still relatively untarnished at that time. He was still the darling of the Parliamentary Party. It was a cruel dilemma; either to cause a major row by dismissing her Chancellor, or to stand by while she watched him drive the economy onto the rocks. He left her no other option, and she chose the latter course. I believe it was the greater of the two evils.

The second lesson is less topical – but perhaps equally important. Nigel Lawson did not lack discipline – he did not want or mean to set inflation in motion again. He just got it wrong. Those who talk about 'discipline' in running an economy tend to think that there are those who want to create inflation and those who don't. In fact, there is another category – those who don't want to create inflation, but who do so by mistake. Nigel Lawson fell into that category. It is worth remarking that even central bank governors might get it wrong. There is every evidence that the Bank of England supported his policy. Again, I quote Herr Otto Poehl, who said, speaking in 1991, 'In my view it would therefore be desirable to embody in the Statute of a European Central Bank a clause to the effect that domestic stability must have priority over Exchange Rate stability.' That encapsulates the mistake that Nigel Lawson, and the Bank, made in 1988 and 1989 – it wasn't a lack of 'discipline', it was an error caused by a mistaken judgement about the value of M3 compounded by giving priority to the importance of a given exchange rate. It was an error which was to have disastrous consequences.

Despite the rapid rise in interest rates following the 1988 Budget – there were nine separate hikes, taking base rates to 14 per cent – the inflation unleashed in the economy grew apace. Inflation was running at 3.5 per cent at the time of the 1988 Budget; by the end of 1988 it had reached 6.8 per cent. It went up to 10.7 per cent in 1990 before it started to retreat. The medicine to cure it was savage too. Base rates at 14 per cent caused severe distress to people with large mortgages, and both company order books and company profits began to suffer and then to decline. After the usual time lag, unemployment began to increase.

The 1989 Budget was a neutral one. Nigel Lawson made some useful relaxations in the burden of National Insurance contributions paid by the less well off, but no major tax changes. He again forecast a budget surplus, this time of £14 billion. It was, in macro-economic terms, a no-change Budget. He had eschewed the fiscal weapon by then as an instrument of economic policy. The old concept of raising or lowering taxes as part of squeezing or relaxing the money supply was out of fashion: I never quite understood why. It certainly would have helped to take some of the strain of the reduction of demand by increasing taxes, both in 1989 and 1990. The interest rate is a weapon which hits borrowers and investors; it actually assists lenders. Taxes reduce demand across the whole population, imposing a more equal level of sacrifice. I think there were two reasons why Nigel Lawson rejected serious tax increases in 1989. One was because he was already running a considerable budget surplus. To have added further to that surplus seemed to him perverse. He used his budget surplus to repay the National Debt, which in turn he thought added to the purchasing power of the holders of redeemed debt. He was inclined to argue that there was no point in such a transfer of resources from taxpayers to the holders of government stocks – it hardly reduced demand at all. I doubt this myself. Individuals are much more likely to spend money than the holders of government debt. Nor did he have to use the surplus for this purpose. He could have bought foreign government bonds, and shipped the money out of the UK economy, thus reducing demand. I believe forswearing fiscal policy, and relying totally on a high interest-rate policy, was misguided: it did more damage to our productive capacity through slowing down industrial investment than was necessary for the defeat of inflation.

The other reason why he probably chose not to raise taxes was that he saw himself as a tax-cutting Chancellor and the last thing he wanted to do was to be forced to put them up again. Thus he did, indeed, eschew the fiscal weapon.

Nigel Lawson persisted with another and more important policy which also damaged our productive capacity. He continued to shadow the DM. Although he initially failed by his interest rate cuts to stop the pound appreciating against the DM – it reached DM3.25 in late 1988 – he succeeded in due course when the full inflationary effects came through to the markets. The pound started to fall. He increased interest rates again and massive intervention was used to stop the pound falling. It was a curious consequence of his exchange rate policy that he had to increase interest rates as the pound rose above DM3.00. He also had to increase them as the pound fell below DM3.00! Such a paradox is bound to happen unless interest rates are used solely to maintain domestic monetary stability. They were on the first occasion – but not on the second!

He came to the conclusion that his policy of unofficial DIY membership of the ERM left him without much-needed help from his European counterparts, and without the so-called 'discipline' provided by official membership. He returned to the attack against Margaret Thatcher to try to get her agreement to full membership of the ERM.

In this renewed attack on Margaret Thatcher he returned to his old ally. Geoffrey Howe had been looking at the same question through Foreign Office eyes. The European side of the Foreign Office had long yearned to join the ERM. To do so would prevent us from always being 'isolated' in the Councils of Europe. It seemed to them an essential step if we were ever to sound convincing about our 'commitment to Europe'. They didn't like being the recipients of the nagging criticism of our 'negative' attitude. Superficially, membership of the ERM sounded to them to have worked for France and Italy – the massive currency alignment which these two countries had been obliged to make despite their membership could be explained away as transitional, and anyway seemed to have come to an end. They probably thought British membership would be good economics as well as good politics. In any event, Geoffrey Howe needed no persuading. He had always been interested in membership while he was Chancellor – he just hadn't decided to make a major issue of it with Margaret Thatcher. He had already made common cause with Nigel Lawson.

Neither raised the matter in Cabinet – they would have found a distinct majority against them, as well as incurring Margaret

Thatcher's disagreement. In Geoffrey Howe's later account, he said they wanted a specific commitment to join, or they would resign.

There was a European Summit in July 1989 at Madrid. Neither British membership of the ERM, nor Economic and Monetary Union, was on the agenda. Margaret Thatcher was as convinced as ever that we should not join the ERM, as she had been constantly for years. She saw all the pitfalls and drawbacks, and none of these was in any way changed or ameliorated in July 1988. The only new factor was the ominous sign of the reappearance of inflation in Britain, which itself had been caused by the very similar policy of shadowing the DM.

On the morning she was due to fly to the Madrid Summit, Nigel Lawson and Geoffrey Howe called on the Prime Minister at Number 10 jointly and alone. They confronted her with an ultimatum. They told her that they would both resign then and there unless she agreed to commit us to join the ERM by a fixed date. That this 'ambush' took place was confirmed by Geoffrey Howe in his resignation speech two- and-a-half years later. It was an act calculated to leave her with very little time or scope for manoeuvre.

She could have accepted their resignations and gone to Madrid without a Chancellor or a Foreign Secretary in place. There would have been the mother and father of a political row. It would have been more than she could take. Yet she was determined not to give way. On the aeroplane, she worked up the three famous Madrid 'conditions' with the help of her staff. They were based on some ideas that Alan Walters had had in doing some contingency thinking earlier. Geoffrey Howe and Nigel Lawson for their part had no alternative but to accept them, despite not having got what they wanted. She, for her part, had not given in to them, nor agreed to join the ERM then and there. She bought herself more time. The three conditions were that we would join the ERM when:

1. We had made much more progress with reducing inflation to the levels of our European partners;
2. Much more progress had been made with completing the Single Market in the Community;
3. All overt and covert exchange controls had been removed by our major European partners, and there was complete freedom of capital movements.

It was arguable that these three conditions would never be achieved – indeed, they would certainly take a long time to achieve. Thus, she bought some time. Also, the fulfilment of the conditions was subjective; she alone would be able to say whether or not she thought they had been achieved. By these means, she must have judged that she had got the better of the two. They had also demonstrated just how little enthusiasm they had for resignation by accepting these conditions, which at best meant a long delay before their demands were met, and at worst that she might never declare that the conditions had been fulfilled. She had called their bluff, for the time being at least.

Nor did the ploy achieve the objectives which they sought. They had consistently argued that a decision to join the ERM would have given us those good European credentials which would have allowed Britain to persuade her partners to drop the plan for EMU. In fact, neither ERM nor EMU was ever on the agenda at Madrid. Margaret Thatcher interrupted the agenda to make her concession on joining the ERM when the three conditions were met. She was offered nothing in return, and certainly not the abandonment of EMU. Thus, the Madrid ambush was not only a shameful episode, but it also failed to achieve its objective of killing EMU. Indeed it was received by other heads of government with total lack of interest. It shows how unwise is the thinking that by joining in the spirit of the Community, we can influence its decision on matters of vital concern to us. The Franco-German axis is not interested in Britain's concerns. Concessions to them merely whet their appetite for more.

Margaret Thatcher was furious and with considerable justification. The two of them had come to the decision that they wanted to join against her contrary view. It was not a collective decision to join taken in Cabinet. They had forced their policy on her by an ultimatum. If a large majority in the Cabinet had been behind them, such a strong-arm approach might have been easier to justify, but the method they had used could never have been justified. She was put in the position of risking losing her two most senior ministers, at a time when she simply could not get others in place in time to take up their jobs and when she was due to be out of the country for two days at the Summit.

The Madrid ambush did not get into the public domain for quite a long time. One journalist published a half-accurate account of it soon afterwards, but it was such an astonishing story that it was not believed. I heard about it soon after and was horrified. The whole incident left me feeling resentful and annoyed. This major change in policy had taken place behind the backs of the Cabinet; I was far from happy with the Madrid conditions, which were reported to the next Cabinet by Margaret Thatcher as a *fait accompli*, with no account of how it was that they had come about. It was the only time as a Cabinet Minister that I felt Cabinet had been bypassed and the conventions of cabinet government not observed. It was not Margaret Thatcher who had failed to observe the conditions, but it was those who were later to pray her conduct of cabinet government in aid of their resignations.

Later, when Nigel Lawson, and then Geoffrey Howe, resigned, I was amazed by their strictures of Margaret Thatcher on the subject of cabinet government. Nigel Lawson said in his resignation speech, 'When differences of view emerge (between Prime Minister and Chancellor), as they are bound to do from time to time, they should be resolved privately and, where appropriate, collectively.' He never tried to resolve these differences 'collectively'. Geoffrey Howe said in his resignation speech, 'Cabinet government is all about trying to persuade one another from within.' Over ERM membership, he never tried to 'persuade one another from within.' They both knew they had no chance of doing so. They had just decided together to try to force her hand. Margaret Thatcher had a much better sense of respect for the Cabinet than either of them ever had.

As I have said, the concept of cabinet government is itself a difficult one. In reality, the Prime Minister is the head of the executive, as symbolized by her also being First Lord of the Treasury. Other Cabinet ministers are hired and fired by her, in order to spread the great burden of decision-taking over a wider number than just one person. The Cabinet forms a useful forum for discussion, as well as providing a collective executive, rather than an executive of just one person, as in the United States. But the responsibility for governing the country is the Prime Minister's and she alone must be allowed to take the ultimate decisions which are important.

Geoffrey Howe and Nigel Lawson had no right to force their point of view upon the Prime Minister, let alone by the method they employed. If they were unhappy as members of the Cabinet with the policies being pursued, the right course for them to have taken was to resign. Threatening to resign is a different thing: it is an abuse of the position of a cabinet minister. To use it as a weapon in the day-to-day conduct of business is to apply an unfair pressure. Actually to resign is totally honourable if the issue is of sufficient importance, and one feels sufficiently strongly about it. If they both felt so strongly about the ERM, they should both have resigned, rather than employ the tactics of Madrid. But to use the threat of resignation in order to get one's way, as it were unilaterally, is the opposite of how to behave in Cabinet. Even when, in the event, they got only a quarter of a loaf, they did not actually resign. They showed they had not really intended to resign and that their threats had not been genuine: it looked as if they were trying to bounce the Prime Minister and the Cabinet.

No wonder Margaret Thatcher was annoyed. Could she ever trust either again? The fascinating question is why she tolerated their presence in the Cabinet any longer; when, against her better judgement, she had allowed Nigel Lawson to carry on despite his conduct of economic policy over the past year. The answer must lie somewhere in the range between her being just a little too tolerant of the weaknesses of human beings and her fear of being lampooned by the press as a vindictive and overbearing bully – 'bossyboots' all over again. I think the totally misleading caricature of her dreamed up by the press as a ruthless bully who sacked anyone who disagreed with her was beginning to have its effect. Caricature it was, but she was frightened of being seen to live up to it. She decided to bide her time.

Relations between the three of them were never cordial again. The relationship between Nigel Lawson and Margaret Thatcher remained in private one of deep and mutual hostility, although in public they each tried to put on a show of concord. For both this was a considerable feat of acting and, on the whole, the outside world was taken in by it. But in private there was neither concord, nor agreement on policy. Nigel Lawson continued to shadow the DM, in defiance of her wishes, and with predictable results.

In July 1989 came the annual reshuffle of ministers. Those dreaded events used to take place in September, after the summer holidays. In 1989 she wisely changed the time from September to the end of July. This saved the possible victims from having to spend the two holiday months in fear, and enabled the new ministers who were favoured to master their briefs before work started in earnest in mid-September. It also cut the press out of their usual holiday amusement of doing their own reshuffles – very effectively, indeed, in 1989, when they were taken by surprise, and to a lesser extent thereafter, by reducing the open season for this particularly pleasant sport for journalists, although unpleasant for the victims. She disliked sacking people intensely; indeed, she disliked the whole business of reshuffles and tried to make it no more unpleasant than it had to be, with some success.

I was sent for early on the morning of 24 July and she moved me from the Department of the Environment to the Department of Trade and Industry. I was content to leave DoE. I had been there three-and-a-half years, and although I had really enjoyed it, I wanted a change of scene. I had been under continuous and vexatious flak from the press, and for both my sake and the Government's, a new face was needed there. The Department of Trade and Industry did not seem a particularly onerous assignment – so much had already been done there – but there were certain things left to do which interested me and I had the pleasure of returning as Secretary of State to the department from which I had resigned as a Parliamentary Under-Secretary in 1972. It also brought me closer to the two subjects which were of the greatest concern and interest to me: the economy and Europe. Indeed, I think Margaret Thatcher wanted me to become more involved in areas outside my own department, and particularly those two, where she was in much need of support. In the Department of the Environment I had had to stick very much to my brief, not least because the workload had been so high.

I imagined that it had been a rather limited reshuffle until after lunch when I heard that Geoffrey Howe had been moved sideways to become Leader of the House and John Major had taken his place as Foreign Secretary. She had left Nigel Lawson in place as Chancellor. I immediately saw what she was doing. She was at last starting to dismantle the duumvirate who had so transgressed at Madrid. Geoffrey Howe's position had seemed the weaker of the two, and he was thus the easier to move. Too little, too late, I thought, but at least it was a step in the right direction. It was now Geoffrey Howe's turn to be angry; an anger which smouldered for months before exploding much later, with considerable consequences. The ERM disagreement and the Madrid ambush were beginning to shape the destiny of things to come.

Nigel Lawson was still in post, but was now isolated in the higher echelons of power where things really mattered. John Major, the new Foreign Secretary, worked very closely with Margaret Thatcher over

European policy, in the brief time he held the post.

Over the winter of 1988–9 the boom continued unabated, despite the high interest rate of 14 per cent. The inflationary momentum was remarkably persistent. The consequence of the growth of M3, fuelled by the interest rate cuts of 1988, had been to unleash massive extra demand which could not be met by domestic production. Imports started to rise dramatically. At the same time, and for quite different reasons, invisible earnings began to fade away. The trade deficit became of extreme concern. It rose to about £1.75 billion per month. It was true that some of these imports were of capital equipment needed to modernize industry, but the bulk were of consumer goods which British industry simply could not produce. Moreover, the deficit had to be financed by capital inflows: at least half of these inflows were 'hot' money, much of which found its way into the banking system, and was duly lent on to fuel extra consumption. Demand thus kept receiving extra boosts from this external source. M3 went through the roof, and even M0 kept obstinately refusing to come back within its target range. High interest rates were proving remarkably ineffective against this persistent inflationary pressure. Inflation refused to take a downward course.

The economy in the summer of 1989 was like the weather in late July. It gets hotter and hotter, the pressure becomes intolerable and yet no thunderstorm breaks to relieve it. The boom continued – wages, prices, and particularly house prices, all continued to grow, despite the black shadow that high interest rates cast upon the future. In fact, no thunderstorm broke, the boom continued until September, and then once more seemed to be gathering momentum. There was continuing pressure on the economy, and continuing tension between Number 10 and Number 11 Downing Street.

At the end of September, the pound began to fall below DM3.00. British inflation did not seem to be abating, rather accelerating, British ULCs were growing too fast, and the markets decided the pound was overvalued and began to move it down. Nigel Lawson was quite open about his determination to defend the DM3.00 parity, and employed massive intervention in order to keep the pound up. Investors helped themselves to the Bank of England's cash as the pound nevertheless moved on down relentlessly. Nigel Lawson's policy was not only failing to cure inflation, but the markets were in open challenge to the value he had decreed for the pound. In defiance, he decided to 'give priority to exchange rate stability.' He raised interest rates one more point to 15 per cent on 5 October.

I was horrified. Mortgage interest payers were aghast. Industry was stunned. The press turned against him. The *Daily Mail* (of all papers) went into open revolt with the headline 'Lawson Must Go'. In its inside pages, Andrew Alexander wrote a number of devastating articles chronicling the whole series of policy mistakes which had led up to this extreme and unnecessary extra squeeze. Monetarists in all the journals regirded their loins to point out the errors of putting exchange rate stability above domestic stability. In 1988 the result of doing so had been to increase the money supply when no increase was called for; in 1989 it was to reduce the money supply when it was already in heavy retreat.

There is a remarkable paradox here. In 1981, it was the wets who had protested vehemently at further downward pressure on demand, while the monetarists who had supported it were proved right in that it had succeeded in reducing inflation. In 1989 and 1990 it was the monetarists who protested against further downward pressure on demand and the wets who supported it, because they believed that DIY membership of the ERM was a sufficiently desirable policy objective in order for us to be seen as more 'European'. It cannot have seemed so desirable to those who later lost their jobs unnecessarily.

The Conservative Party was on its way to Blackpool for the Party Conference the weekend following. There was no way I could see Nigel Lawson until he arrived to make his speech to the Conference on the Thursday. He only came to Blackpool at the last moment. As soon as I saw him, I told him that I was most unhappy and wanted an urgent talk with him. He made a brave speech at the Conference, reaffirming his policy and invoking the virtue of not giving way to siren voices calling for abating the war against inflation. It was a Chancellor's unhappy and unpopular lot to stand out against the faint hearts for what he knew to be right. We should admire him for his courage and tenacity. Inflation was public enemy number one, and he was prepared to fight it, whatever the sacrifice. He got away with it – it was an impressive performance. The audience clapped his courage, but not with the zeal which he used to inspire in earlier years. The trouble was that he was not by then fighting inflation, but fighting to defend a sterling parity of DM3.00. He was invoking the call for sacrifice in aid of an objective that those who were at the coalface didn't share at all.

After Nigel Lawson's speech, I met Bruce Anderson of the *Sunday Telegraph* in the car park – we were both looking for transport in a wet, cold gale that was sweeping in from the Irish Sea. 'What did you think of Nigel's speech?' I asked him. 'Magnificent,' he replied. 'I am advising my readers to buy Lawsons.' A week later he had to write in his column, 'When I recommended buying Lawsons last week, I hadn't realized that the stock was about to be suspended.'

I think that was a truer comment than Bruce Anderson realized. The directors of 'Lawson' had, as it were, been trading close to the margin of insolvency. There was no political capital left when his critics moved to point out the inconsistency between pursuing an economic policy directed at shoring up the exchange rate, rather than the stability of the domestic economy. He was being relentlessly attacked by a large section of the press. It must have been a very daunting period, especially for one who carried such great responsibilities. He had staked his huge reputation on the premise that the exchange rate mattered most. He had run the British economy on that basis for several years. He had even thrown down the gauntlet to his Prime Minister on the issue; he knew she didn't agree with him. It was a colossal gamble – a huge and reckless adventure upon which he had been engaged. He had pressed on, regardless of her opposition, regardless of informed comment, regardless of the results. Suddenly he realized that failure was staring him in the face. One has to salute his courage and his quality of fortitude in the face of adversity. Some might call it his stubbornness.

When I finally got to see him in London a few days later, he seemed very down. He barely argued against my fears and criticisms; he was used to my views and I suppose I was to his replies. But he didn't defend his position robustly. Indeed, I suppose there was little for him to say: Perhaps he was very close to deciding upon resignation by then. I began to feel it was insensitive to pursue my deeply-held concerns further and the subject of our conversation turned to other things.

The day following, the Prime Minister returned from the Commonwealth Heads of Government Meeting in Malaysia. She was tired after a very short night's sleep in the aeroplane. I happened to be with the two of them for a while. Nigel Lawson was very low indeed by then and said very little.

The next day – 26 October – he demanded to see her, and insisted upon resigning that very day. She wrestled with him to stay, but to no avail. At 6.00 pm his resignation became public and John Major became Chancellor in his place.

The story holds no surprises when the sequence of events and the economic policy decisions are recounted. Nigel Lawson knew the economy was going badly wrong, and he knew he was entirely and solely responsible. He had too little support, from both above and below, to carry on. It was a logical, perhaps honourable, thing for him to resign. But that wasn't the reason he gave. He blamed Margaret Thatcher's decision to reappoint Alan Walters as her economic adviser. He claimed that Alan Walters had just published an article critical of his policy and that he was talking critically too at City lunch tables. He disagreed strongly with the sort of advice which he knew Alan Walters would give the Prime Minister. He said it was impossible for the Chancellor to work with a Prime Minister who had such a special adviser.

In fact, Alan Walters hadn't even returned to Britain. He was still in the United States. The offending article had been written many months ago, but it had been dredged up by the press and represented as new. He probably did say too much at City lunches: few of us can say that we have never given our real view of economic policy at a City lunch table. The real reason for the deep enmity between the two men must have been their diametrically opposite views on economic policy: but that was already the case between the Chancellor and his Prime Minister, whom Alan Walters was advising.

Nor can there be any excuse for a departmental minister to insist that a Prime Minister does not appoint a particular adviser. It was none of his business. 'Advisers advise. Ministers decide,' she kept pointing out. Nevertheless, once again he tried to bully her. He demanded that she stand Alan Walters down, or he would resign. Whether he thought she would back down, or whether he knew she wouldn't, and he was just looking for an excuse over which to resign, is not for me to judge. But in truth, she couldn't have met his request without making herself look humiliated and impotent. He must have seen that.

Whatever the truth about this, Nigel Lawson left office over Alan Walters's appointment. The irony was that Alan Walters resigned two hours later when he heard the news. He just couldn't stand getting mixed up in this sort of political row.

Was the Government badly damaged by these traumatic events? They made excellent press copy and the papers had a field day over Nigel Lawson's resignation. The political pundits thundered away about the Prime Minister's overbearing ways and her haughty refusal to do everything Nigel Lawson had wanted. The *Guardian* enjoyed it even more than the others. 'Politically and managerially it is her mess. Unless the Cabinet as a whole has the resolve to insist that she must pay for that, accept the basic disciplines of the team approach, they are putting their jobs and the continuance of Conservative rule in pawn,' its editorial stormed. Even many who had been critical of Nigel Lawson's economic policy suddenly turned their fire on Margaret Thatcher for reasons which were not clear to me. Nobody made the point that to challenge a Prime Minister to sack her adviser was a fairly brazen piece of cheek. No one drew attention to the impossible position he had put her in. The chance to turn the fire on Margaret Thatcher was irresistible and they didn't try to resist it. I doubt if it had much effect on the electors. They were concerned about the cost of their mortgages, the effect of the squeeze on their businesses, and the prospects of holding their jobs. They didn't much care about squabbles in high places; but they did want a change of economic policy.

In the short time she had, she decided to move John Major from the Foreign Office to the Treasury, and to make Douglas Hurd Foreign Secretary in his place. John Major was clearly the front runner for any possible succession, and she was right to give him the chance to occupy what is perhaps the most important position in the Government after the Prime Minister. He had already shown great promise; promise which was certainly later fulfilled. He was popular in the Party and his appointment was rightly welcomed.

John Major more or less continued his predecessor's economic policy and managed to persuade her to join the ERM. As a result an intense recession set in. A mysterious series of breakfasts was held between John Major and Douglas Hurd. the *Financial Times* reported on 18 June 1990 that: 'Mr Hurd and Mr Major had had private breakfasts at the Foreign Secretary's London residence at No 1 Carlton House Gardens and lengthy meetings at No 11 Downing Street. The aim has been to nudge Mrs Thatcher sufficiently far in the direction of a commitment to EMU to prevent Britain from being consigned from the start, to the slow lane in Europe. In the background, Mr Nicholas Ridley – this year as last – has been trying to pull her in the opposite direction. The Trade and Industry Secretary opposes membership of the ERM as well as any move beyond that towards EMU.' Once more the campaign to persuade her to join the ERM had started. History was repeating itself, and all over that wretched ERM! This time they succeeded. By then she must have felt she could no longer go on fighting and risking and daring for what she knew was right.

In the end she gave way, but she placed conditions upon her acceptance, to which I shall come later. By 1990, however, the economy was in a real mess. She alone was held responsible, although it was not her fault.

10

THE END

By the start of 1990, the political situation was deteriorating. Interest rates at 15 per cent were beginning to have their effect, first on those with mortgages, and later on small businesses, with the whole commercial and industrial sector coming under pressure by the summer. The only bright spot was exports, which rose steadily, owing to a low sterling level keeping our exporters competitive. At the same time, inflation was still rising because of the time lag before the squeeze worked. Both the disease and its cure were hurting at the same time. The public was disenchanted.

The Community Charge became a major issue of concern from March onwards, when the first councils began to make their proposed charges public. As the spring advanced, the protests came thick and fast. The extreme left tried to cash in on these protests by organising 'anti-poll tax' demonstrations, the biggest and most notorious being in Trafalgar Square on Saturday, 17 March. Other, smaller, demonstrations took place outside town halls up and down the country during the following months. In most areas, but particularly in the north of the country, the resentment at the bills which came from councils through the letter boxes was considerable.

I was no longer at the Environment Department, but I was horrified at the level of the poll tax bills which most councils were sending out. My own Gloucestershire County Council came up with charges £100 higher than I had expected. The story was repeated all over the country. Certainly inflation, the need to cover for non-payers, and the cost of setting up the machinery of collection, had been underestimated. But on top of that there was a savage increase by many councils in order to show up the Community Charge in as bad a light as possible – it was a double blessing for them: it gave them more money to spend. The more they demanded from their charge payers, the more they could blame the Government for the resulting bills. I received a bit of retrospective criticism for not having secured a larger government grant from John Major in July 1989 – but, in truth, it was a considerable increase over the grant the year before, and I had had a big fight to secure even that amount. Nor did we know in July 1989 that in the new year actual charges were to come out around £100 higher than was expected.

My successor, Chris Patten, when it became evident how high the charges were going to be, did indeed obtain over £300 million more from the Treasury; but he used it to cushion the impact on those who would have to pay more than they had in rates, rather than to improve the rebate system, which was never designed for such high levels of charges.

But I will not go over all that again. I remain convinced that the level of the charge in 1990 was too high for those at the lower end of the income scale and the rebate system was inadequate, rather than that the principle was wrong. There were also a great number of detailed issues that needed to be ironed out, particularly on second homes and bed and breakfast, both of which I always found difficult to justify.

The Community Charge, for all these reasons, had soured the political atmosphere, and at a time when the much more expensive costs of servicing their mortgage were hurting home owners very much. The average mortgage had risen in cost from £250 to £410 per month, a far greater increase than anyone had to pay in switching from rates to the Community Charge. The combination of the two for many people was the obverse of economic success. It represented a major reduction in their standard of living. Some people benefited, of course, but they kept quiet. The retired living in a large house with savings at the building society were much better off. But many lost from both. Young married couples, buying on a mortgage a house which had had a low rateable value, lost on both counts. The interaction of the two events – the interest rate squeeze and the high levels of Community Charge – produced many more losers than gainers; as a result there was a deteriorating political situation. Add to this the growing fears of recession and lost jobs, and it is not hard to see the seriousness of the situation into which the Government had fallen.

How this situation had arisen, indeed why it all went wrong, was discussed in the previous chapter. But it landed the Prime Minister in a position where she was fighting on two fronts – a deteriorating economic situation, together with a local government finance charge which compounded the problems of the losers, without too much enthusiasm coming from the gainers. I remain convinced that one or other of these situations would have been manageable, but both together were a major political hazard.

The other factor still causing some unrest at the time was the Health Service Reforms. Although the worst of the protests were past, the doctors' campaign had rattled Tory MPs and their constituents were still finding plenty to complain about in the service they were receiving. It was that awkward period in time between enacting a reform, and the advantages thereof becoming apparent to the public.

Inevitably Margaret Thatcher was held responsible. Her personal popularity ratings in the polls was at a very low point in the autumn. There always had been a large number of people in the country who disliked her: particularly in academia, the press and in artistic and intellectual circles, let alone in the Labour Party. To these were added many one-time Tories who were suffering from the burdens of their mortgages and Community Charges. The single most vital electoral attribute of the Tories – that they were seen as much the best party at managing the economy – suddenly became questionable. Historically, there seems to be an almost direct relationship between the interest rate and the popularity of a government. Over a long period, the higher the interest rate the less popular has a government been in the opinion polls, and vice versa. The interest rate was high, and had been so for a long time, in 1990. The blame for all this was laid at Margaret Thatcher's door where, technically at least, it belonged.

Many members of the Tory Party in the House of Commons began to wonder whether they could hold their seats in the next election if she were still the leader. Some of their supporters in their constituencies were openly critical of her. To the group of permanent dissidents who formed the original 'wets' were added new recruits from all wings of the Party. In addition, over the eleven years she had been in power, the number of sacked ministers and would-be ministers who had never been promoted, had grown at a steady rate as reshuffle followed reshuffle. There were thus present within the party in Parliament the original squad of dissidents, augmented by those with thwarted ambitions, and a growing number who believed a change of leader was essential if they were to hold their seats.

They were probably wrong. What was needed to win the next General Election was to have the pressure taken off both individuals and businesses, so that economic growth could be resumed, unemployment could fall, and interest rates could come down as inflation went into sharp retreat. Those were the successes which would have ensured victory. Moreover, they were bound to take time to achieve, and they would have to be seen to be real, not just predicted. There was just time to achieve all this before June 1992, by which date the election had to be held. My own view was that Margaret Thatcher would have been able to win a fourth victory if the economy had been in good shape by then. I doubted whether she (or anyone else) would have been able to win if it wasn't. There will never be any chance of my being proved right, or wrong. But what was needed was fortitude and a steady nerve – both of which proved in due course to be absent.

There was also, for the first time, an air of instability within the Government itself. George Younger left the Cabinet to become Chairman of the Royal Bank of Scotland. He was followed by David Young, who left in July 1989, eventually to become Chairman of Cable and Wireless. At the beginning of 1990, both Peter Walker and Norman Fowler left too, in order to 'spend more time with their families' – but also to further their business interests. Although in every case I think they all genuinely felt that after a long stint in government it was time to do other things, it gave the impression of a government from which senior figures were peeling off successively. My own resignation in July of 1990, although for quite different reasons, no doubt strengthened that impression. That was the main reason why I regretted leaving the Government at that time. It also reduced the supporters of Margaret Thatcher within the Cabinet by one, and she certainly was in need of them.

The press always made me one of their chief targets for attack and criticism. Partly, I think, they saw me as a strong supporter of the Prime Minister, and for that reason alone I was a prime target. It was partly because I dealt with highly contentious policy issues, like the Community Charge, water privatization, and, worst of all, planning and greenery, while I was at the Department of the Environment. Another of my failings was that I never leaked or gossiped. Mainly the press just disliked me – a feeling which I reciprocated heartily.

They appeared particularly to dislike me because I was alleged to be an aristocrat and had gone to Eton and Balliol. This should have made me into a patrician type of wet, but instead I was a strong Thatcherite. The charge is that Eton and Balliol are supposed to provide a superior education and that it is unfair that some should have these advantages. But I never saw the logic of criticizing me simply because I was alleged to have had a good education. They also invented two other myths – one, that I was an expert at embroidery, and the other that I was very rich. Neither, alas, is true. My tendency to speak my mind clearly and to use phrases all too colourful on occasions gave them the opportunity to compile a sort of charge sheet of my crimes, which were constantly paraded in the gossip columns.

At the Conservative Local Government Conference on 4 March 1989, Margaret Thatcher used an unfortunate phrase in an impromptu speech. She said that 'Water privatization had not been handled well or accurately.' I was sitting there, and saw inevitable trouble. I knew exactly what she meant, as she explained to the press immediately afterwards. She meant that the media had not put the arguments properly before the public. Inevitably, it was taken as a criticism of me, although it was not meant as such, and was merely a slip of the tongue. Later, on Channel 4 News, she sought to put the damage right in her usual forceful terms. 'He has done more as Secretary of State of the Environment than almost any of his predecessors. The volume of work he has done is terrific. He's done more to improve the quality of water.' But it suited the press to let it stick on my charge sheet, along with the embroidery and the wealth.

In June 1990 the Editor of the *Spectator* asked to do a profile of me. He wanted a long interview. He assured me that he wanted to help, and to write a supportive piece. I read two profiles he had written – one of Michael Heseltine and one of Chris Patten. They were both

extremely offensive and at first I thought I would refuse to see him. On being assured that he really wanted to be helpful, however, I reluctantly consented. In the event, he turned out not to be helpful at all. He published words of mine, about Germany and Europe, which were indeed extreme. Although I knew his tape recorder was on, it never occurred to me that he would publish verbatim my conversation at the end of the interview since he had assured me he wanted to be helpful. He added a totally unfair cartoon which wrongly suggested I had compared Herr Kohl to Hitler.

What I can only call this disgraceful piece of sensational journalism appeared on Thursday 12 July when I was travelling in Eastern Europe. The media went wild with righteous indignation and joy. Here was a splendid chance to get me out, and the pressure for me to resign began the moment the journal was published. I had a full day of visits arranged with Hungarian ministers. We were mobbed at each call by a pack of television and press hounds. It was essential to complete my programme, despite the row going on back home; I was due to leave for London the next afternoon.

Margaret Thatcher was naturally annoyed to be put in this position, but was as supportive as she could be. I 'withdrew' the offending remarks, but that went nowhere to placate the mob. She held the position until I got back late the next evening, the flight being five hours late.

My Parliamentary Private Secretary, Steve Norris, met us at Heathrow and whisked us off in his car into the night at breakneck speed, shaking off the convoy of pressmen trying to follow us. We had arranged to go to the house of some kind friends in the country in order to avoid the hordes of press that were surrounding our own house. We spent two days with these kind and understanding friends, and the press never found us.

I discussed the situation with Margaret Thatcher by telephone on the Saturday morning. I had already told her, in June, that I did not intend to stand at the next election. We both agreed that we could have battled it out, but that it wasn't worth the indignity and the stress of doing so in order for me to continue in office for perhaps only a few months. That she would have backed me if I had asked her to I have no doubt. But I had reached a point where I couldn't stand the constant personal criticism any longer, and I was content to resign.

I was by then satisfied with my political career. I had been in Parliament 31 years, 13 of them as a minister. I had fought throughout for the sort of policies I believed in, and had had the good fortune to see them put into effect and to succeed. I didn't feel there was any further position of challenge or great interest that I was likely to be offered in the Government and there were many things I wanted to do outside it. The only thing that troubled me was leaving the Cabinet at a time when Margaret Thatcher needed all the support she could get. I pressed her to appoint a strong supporter in my place. She did – she appointed Peter Lilley as Secretary of State for Trade and Industry.

Thus did one more cabinet minister leave office, strengthening the impression of instability.

The dominant issue in the autumn of 1990 was Economic and Monetary Union in Europe. Earlier in this book I have traced the events and set out the arguments, and I will not repeat them now. The Delors Plan for a Single European Currency was pressing very heavily upon the Government all that autumn. It looked as if we were again outnumbered in the Community 11 to 1. No other member state then showed much interest in the British Government's plan for a 'hard ECU'. There was a chorus in favour of joining, first, the ERM and later the Single Currency Plan, among sections of the City, industry and the press. The Liberal Democrats were in favour and the Labour Party was trying to climb laboriously onto the bandwagon. We were hectored daily in speeches by Jacques Delors and Leon Brittan. 'The train was leaving and we had to be on it,' Sir Geoffrey Howe told us, although no one bothered to tell us where the train was going.

Within the Cabinet, a few seemed content that we should allow ourselves to be borne along by this pressure, and join, perhaps in exchange for some minor concessions. There was a suggestion that we should agree all the arrangements for EMU, but make it clear that we would leave it to Parliament to decide when Britain should participate. The basis upon which Parliament was going to be invited to consider the matter was not clear. Would the Government be neutral, and leave it to a 'free' vote? That would be tantamount to the Government having no policy – impossible on such an important issue. Would the Government extend the Whip in favour of it? That would be contrary to the Government's policy. Would the Government Whip against it? If that was the plan, there was no point in presenting the question to Parliament at all. No wonder this idea got short shift from Margaret Thatcher. It was decided to concentrate on selling the 'hard ECU' idea – which was for some a diversionary tactic, for others a possible way of reaching a single European currency without coercion. It also provided a focus around which an uneasy unity could be gathered within the Government. Among the other members of the Cabinet, there were a few committed opponents of joining the ERM, and more who were against the single currency. There was a soggy majority who appeared not to mind very much either way.

Margaret Thatcher herself believed passionately that the disadvantages of a single currency would make it a disaster for Britain, and I agreed with her strongly. After my resignation, I took advantage of my freedom to concentrate in a series of articles and broadcasts on explaining why. My remarks on Germany and Europe, which were the cause of my resignation, had attracted a huge groundswell of popular support. The letters came by the thousand. Newspapers conducted polls, revealing levels of support for my views of 80 per cent or 90 per cent. Even in Paris, Amsterdam and Copenhagen, there were reports of support in such polls of between 60 per cent and 80 per cent. I realized that, by a slip of the tongue as it were, I had said something with which very many people strongly agreed. To my own astonishment, I had suddenly become a populist. The irony is that if I had said it in more diplomatic language, the public probably wouldn't have understood what I was saying. The crudity of my phraseology was both the cause of my censure and the call to arms for a large number of British people. There was no doubt that the majority of the people were strongly behind Margaret Thatcher's determination not to allow Britain to join a single currency.

The same was true of the parliamentary party, but to a lesser extent. The usual group of wets, Thatcher-haters and malcontents were in favour of a single currency, many at least partly because she was against it. But there was a healthy majority behind her point of view. So the line-up on one of the crucial issues in November 1990 was a determined Prime Minister, a Cabinet in which she probably did not have a majority behind her, a parliamentary party more robust than the Cabinet, and a Tory Party in the country which very solidly agreed with her. This should have been a position of great political strength and was certainly not an unusual position for Margaret Thatcher to find herself in; it was the sort of situation in which she usually triumphed.

However, another crucial decision was taken in early October 1990, on the eve of the Party Conference. At the beginning of September the Chancellor, John Major, had begun dropping hints that he might soon join the Exchange Rate Mechanism. Two of the three Madrid conditions – that exchange controls should be abolished throughout the Community, and that progress should be made with completing the Single Market – had virtually been met by that time. But the third condition, that our inflation rate should have come down until it was much closer to the average for the Community, had in no sense been met. John Major promulgated a new definition of inflation – the 'underlying' rate of inflation. This excluded the Community Charge and mortgage interest from the calculation of the rate. Even on this measure, it was doubtful whether the condition had been achieved, but nevertheless, he argued, all the signs were that it soon would be. I always thought the Madrid conditions were irrelevant and non-sensical. They were a fudge based on some work by Alan Walters at the time, to allow Margaret Thatcher to survive the ambush of Geoffrey Howe and Nigel Lawson. The real dispute was about whether to join or not, and I was a convinced opponent of our joining. So I was not happy with the hints that John Major was dropping.

Margaret Thatcher confirmed to me in September that she had decided to give way to the Chancellor and Douglas Hurd, who had put heavy pressure on her once more. I regretted not still being in the Cabinet for one reason only: as a member of the inner group on these matters I might have been able to stiffen her resistance. As her opposition to joining, since Madrid, had been conditional, and her conditions were not far off being met, I suppose she could no longer deploy the argument of principle. The press, much of the City and the Confederation of British Industry (CBI), were all demanding early entry. The CBI were fatuously arguing for an entry rate of DM3.00 to the £. In the event, we joined at DM2.95 to the £, and the CBI regretted it immediately! Most businessmen that I met at the time would have preferred DM2.60 or DM2.65.

All the pressures, together with the fact that she had accepted the principle at Madrid, must have forced her to conclude that she must allow entry even against her better judgement. But she agreed only subject to a condition – that there should be a cut in interest rates at the same time.

She knew that what was necessary to start bringing the voters back to the Tory fold was progressive cuts in interest rates. Retail sales were falling heavily. The money supply figures were well below their target range. The markets were signalling that interest rates could start to come down, but the Bank of England and the Treasury had been resisting the signals. So she drove a bargain with John Major that he could enter the ERM, and at the same time announce a 1 per cent cut in interest rates. There could be no better time to do this than on the eve of the Party Conference.

As I have said, membership of the ERM is harmless if domestic monetary conditions are given priority over the Exchange Rate. I believe Margaret Thatcher always wanted to put the domestic economy first, which was why she was able eventually to accept ERM membership despite her doubts.

The annual Party Conference in October is an opportunity for a political party to improve its standing in the voters' eyes. Ministers receive the undivided and unedited attention of the media and their speeches are actually broadcast live on television. The 1986 Conference had had a major influence on the electorate's decision to return the Tories again in 1987.

In 1990 the Conference was at Bournemouth. The Friday evening before it started, John Major had announced the decision to join the ERM and the 1 per cent cut in interest rates which accompanied it. This was meant to be a great boost for the Conference. But it wasn't – the enthusiasm for the ERM was not shared by the party workers, and the interest rate cut was too small to cheer up the mortgage holders. Ministers were more on the defensive than the offensive at Bournemouth.

One of the main concerns was, in fact, our European policy. The Party, particularly the Young Conservatives, was getting uneasy about the apparent drift towards getting entangled in some sort of federal union. Michael Heseltine and I both made 'fringe meeting' speeches on the subject of Europe. It was interesting that I drew a much younger audience than he did. But in the main debates on the conference floor no brave whistling in the wind, no assault on the Labour Party, no listing of the achievements of the last ten years, could assuage the fears felt by the party faithful that the electorate were in a highly critical mood. The party faithful knew what they were up against on the doorsteps and no amount of brave talk could overcome that. It was an upturn in the economy that we needed. The situation required keeping one's nerve till better news came through.

Margaret Thatcher understood that there was no relief for hard-pressed businessmen and mortgage payers in joining the ERM. What they wanted was lower interest rates. Joining the ERM implied, nay required, that interest rates be raised to defend the pound when its value reached the bottom of the band – 6 per cent below DM2.95 – or DM2.82. Both the markets and political good sense were signalling that they should be lowered progressively. The evidence of recession – rising bankruptcies and lay-offs, falling production and falling order

228

books – in the autumn were clearly showing that to raise interest rates to defend the value of the pound would have been to overkill, and disastrous both industrially and politically. This was a prime example of the objection of principle to the ERM which Margaret Thatcher and I both saw from the beginning: the inconsistency of using interest rates for two different and incompatible ends – one to defend the value of the pound, and the other to keep the money supply on target. If conditions signal that interest rates should be put up for one purpose, but down for the other, which purpose is to prevail? As to the answer, I repeat the quote from Karl Otto Poehl, 'Interest rates should be set according to domestic monetary conditions and the exchange rate should be left to go where it will.' I entirely agree with him, although that quote makes me wonder whether he is so keen on the ERM.

Some thought there was one further mistake: we joined the ERM at too high a parity – DM2.95. On expectations that there were large benefits to be had from membership and that investors could not lose their money through a fall in the pound after joining, the markets moved the pound up, at one point to over DM3.00. The true market value at the time was no more than DM2.60, around which the pound had hovered in August.

Moreover, British ULCs were rising at about 9 per cent, whereas German ones were hardly rising at all. In due course the markets were bound to adjust the pound downwards to compensate for this discrepancy. To keep it up when it was bound to go down was perverse! It was also very bad for industry and the trade deficit. British industry was put at a competitive disadvantage both for exporting and for displacing imports. It added to the depth of the coming recession. The combined burden of too high a rate for the pound and too high interest rates was not necessary for monetary policy reasons. It had a quite unnecessarily savage effect on jobs, production, exports and investment. Would that the Government had followed Herr Poehl's policy of 'letting the exchange rate go where it will.'

In the event, and at the time of writing, the pound was apparently moving up against the DM in the ERM. In fact, what was happening was that the pound was falling against the dollar, but the DM was falling even more steeply against it. Thus the pound appeared to be gaining ground against the DM, although in fact it was only losing less ground against the dollar than the DM. The German currency came into question because of the huge costs of German unification, together with their large expenditure on Eastern Europe, Russia and the Gulf War. Why such events in Germany should have any effect upon British economic policy is beyond my comprehension, but in the summer of 1991 we were saved from having to face the awkward dilemma by the severe fall in the DM against the dollar.

There was one further bad effect of this decision. It signalled to the Commission and our Community partners that Britain was weakening in its resolve to reject EMU. Although ERM and EMU are totally different things, Eurofanatics saw the one as a stepping stone to the other. Jacques Delors bragged that the British always stalled over everything, but belatedly came into line in the end. They would in due course come into line over EMU just as they had caved in over ERM. Leon Brittan actually said: 'This is good news for Britain and good news for Europe. It should mean a clear commitment by Britain to a successful completion of the first stage.' That was the very inference I feared would be drawn.

Although joining the ERM was not meant to give such a signal, and Margaret Thatcher made clear at the time that it implied no such thing, it was most certainly taken as one in Brussels. This signal played a crucial part in the events which were to follow.

There was a European Council meeting over the weekend of 27–29 October 1990 in Rome. Chancellor Kohl and President Mitterrand had earlier got together as usual and concocted a plan to force the pace of EMU. The Italian Presidency was prepared to abuse its position as chairman of the meeting to assist them. They put on the agenda the setting of the date of 1994 for the start of Stage II of the Delors Plan. As I have said, they refused to allow the much more urgent and much more important subject of the Community's failure to make progress over agriculture in the GATT Uruguay Round negotiations to be discussed at all, although Margaret Thatcher had specially asked for it to be a top priority.

Judging that Margaret Thatcher would always come round in the end, after the recent British decision to join the ERM, they decided that it was safe to humiliate and isolate her over both issues. She was, of course, right: there were only six weeks left of the Uruguay Round negotiations and a successful outcome was of crucial importance. It was the Community that was mainly at fault. To refuse even to discuss the issue not only showed how little influence Britain had in the Community, even in the aftermath of joining the ERM, but also showed the Council's totally wrong priorities. European centra

ization was more important than free trade. They ganged up against Margaret Thatcher in order to set rigid timetables for a system of centralized power in Brussels. The ERM decision had shown that she could safely be ignored. They came out, and unfortunately with great discourtesy, in their true colours. They couldn't have cared less about free trade and Britain's justified concern for it; they wanted the British economy controlled from Brussels and they thought the ERM decision had shown that they would inevitably win in the end.

Margaret Thatcher was very cross, and justifiably so. She had been treated disgracefully. She behaved with dignity, but did not mince her words at the press conference which followed: 'Community leaders were living in cloud cuckoo land in fixing a date for Stage II . . . without first deciding its substance. It seems to be putting the cart before the horse. People who get on a train like that deserve to get taken for a ride,' she said.

On 30 October she made her traditional statement in the House on the Council. The statement was merely a record of the discussions and what had been decided, but in answering the questions that followed, she warmed to her theme of the true awfulness of what had happened and the importance of the issues at stake.

Neil Kinnock asked the first question: he heaped abuse on her in a random fashion, but mainly for not agreeing to what she had been told to do by others. In reply she said: 'It sounded as though he would agree, for the sake of agreeing, and for being Little Sir Echo and saying "Me too".' In replying to him she went on to use words which were to become famous later on: 'The President of the Commission, Mr Delors, said at a press conference the other day that he wanted the European Parliament to be the democratic body of the Community. He wanted the Commission to be the Executive, and he wanted the Council of Ministers to be the Senate. No, no, no.'

It was one of her finest performances. The Tory Party were delighted, with the exception of the Eurofanatics. The talk of the tea room was how robust and effective she had been. The doubters rallied. At last we had a clear policy towards Europe with which most could agree. She had shown the leadership for which they longed once again. The Labour Party were repulsed. Paddy Ashdown, the leader of the Liberal Democrats – and an open advocate of joining the single currency – asked a question about 'weakening our voice in Europe' and was put down in no uncertain fashion: 'Oh dear, it seems that there must be quite a lot of late parrots in cloud cuckoo land, judging by the Rt Hon Gentleman coming out with that stuff,' she said.

At that time, in both the parliamentary party and in the country, there was a feeling that the Government was being pushed relentlessly and inevitably towards caving in to Delors and getting sucked into the single currency. The phrases being used were still, 'It is inevitable' or Neil Kinnock's 'It will happen in the end'. To those who were opposed to EMU on good logical and political grounds it all seemed like unnecessary and unconditional surrender. On 30 October, Margaret Thatcher re-established her leadership and her authority over this dangerous slide, despite the rough handling she had had in Rome. But that was not good news for her enemies within the Cabinet and the Party.

The storm clouds gathering over Margaret Thatcher's leadership were dimly discernible in October, but the statement of 30 October seemed to dispel them. I confess to not having myself anticipated what was to come so soon. I was deeply concerned about the contrary economic policy which the Government was pursuing. The ERM decision seemed to me a major strategic mistake. But to me it signalled trouble to come next year, or even later, not next month. In retrospect, it is easy to see that in the vaults of Parliament there was by now a gunpowder barrel waiting to be ignited. But it was hard to see at the time.

The National Health Service reform row had sapped the confidence of the weaker brethren. The economy was entering deep recession, unnecessarily. On top of that, the decision to join the ERM at too high a rate had threatened further agony on top of the already ample economic agony around. The electors were suffering financially; and all this came on top of the Community Charge. Margaret Thatcher was seen as the authoress of all these woes; she wouldn't listen, it was said, she didn't care. The Iron Lady rode roughshod over everyone's objections. It was not for one moment realized that it was some of her ministers who were riding roughshod over her objections. On top of it all, she had thrown down the gauntlet at those nice Europeans who would save us from inflation, from high interest rates and from all our current economic woes. The voters told their concerns clearly and urgently to their MPs in letters, at wine and cheese parties, and at surgeries. The MPs accepted that the blame lay with Margaret Thatcher. That was the gunpowder.

I met no one who realized that the gunpowder was there. I certainly didn't, nor did Margaret Thatcher or her political advisers. There will doubtless be some who claim they did, with or without hindsight. The press didn't. In fact, the press was giving Margaret Thatcher and her

Government a slightly less than usually rough time. The prospect of war in the Gulf had brought some people back to her support, remembering her resolve and able conduct of the Falklands War. She was also picking up support from many, often Labour, voters for her stand against the European single currency. The Party's rating in the polls was higher than in the summer. I suppose it should have been realized that her position was hanging in the balance, but I don't know anyone who did.

The fuse was lit on 1 November – four days before the traditional day for parliamentary explosions. Geoffrey Howe suddenly resigned. He had been a successful Chancellor for four years and a tireless Foreign Secretary for a further six – loyal and constant for a long time.

In the July 1989 reshuffle, however, Margaret Thatcher moved him out of the Foreign Office to become Lord President of the Council and Leader of the House. He saw it as a demotion; it was, in fact, the only move she could make to begin to dismantle the duumvirate who had plotted the Madrid ambush and were still undermining her European policy. She still did not feel able to move Nigel Lawson, although his popularity was beginning to wane and some of his chickens were coming home to roost. I don't think that she wanted to sack Geoffrey Howe; after all he had been a faithful senior colleague for ten years. Yet she knew that he and Nigel Lawson were both still determined to get their way. She decided that Geoffrey Howe was the weaker of the two politically and moved him out of the Foreign Office. She first asked him to be Leader of the House. She suggested he might become Home Secretary if he did not want that position. Douglas Hurd was then Home Secretary. Geoffrey Howe lost no time in telling the press this, causing Douglas Hurd the maximum offence, but at the same time Geoffrey Howe turned it down. In the end she moved him two steps sideways and one step down, to be Leader of the House – a typical knight's move.

Geoffrey Howe was furious. I think that he had strong aspirations to be Prime Minister himself, seeing himself as her natural successor. At one time – around 1986 – he might indeed have inherited her job if it had become vacant. But it didn't become vacant, and as time went by it looked less and less likely that it would, or that he would be seriously considered by the Party for it if it did. It is said that he had refused the Lord Chancellorship when she cast a fly over him in 1987 – when Lord Hailsham finally retired – in order to stay in the Commons, poised ready to bid for occupying Number 10. To be demoted at that stage in his career was indeed a snub. He tried to salvage what he could by demanding that he be made Deputy Prime Minister, a request to which she acceded, although there was no job involved, merely a title. She saw to it that it didn't lead to a position of power. But there was another problem: Geoffrey Howe did not have a house of his own. He had sold his house in London when he became Chancellor in 1979 and moved into Number 11 Downing Street. When he became Foreign Secretary, he moved from there into the flat above Carlton Gardens, the traditional grace and favour residence of the Foreign Secretary, in 1983. In addition, he was allowed to retain Chevening – traditionally the perk of the Chancellor – which he had used since 1979. Chevening is a large Georgian country house in Kent, very suitable for weekend house parties.

But there were no such houses available for Lords President of the Council, or even for Deputy Prime Ministers. So Geoffrey Howe had no suitable London house. He made a public outburst about this. He demanded, and was eventually given, Dorneywood for his weekends, from which the unfortunate Nigel Lawson had to depart. He also secured from Margaret Thatcher a grace and favour London house at the Royal Army Medical College near the Tate Gallery, into which a senior army officer was about to move, even after his wife had chosen the carpets and curtains. These events were far from edifying. The press paid him the doubtful compliment of dubbing him 'Sir Geoffrey Houses'.

The Leader of the House's job is not to be compared to being Foreign Secretary in terms of interest or importance. He chaired a number of cabinet committees, arranged the business of the House and had to spend long hours there trying to massage the Government's business through without too many late nights. He had no policy work and was far away from those concerned with European policy. European policy remained his chief interest and his main disagreement with Margaret Thatcher and his colleagues in the Cabinet. He became more and more frank, both in private and in public, in calling for membership of the ERM, and in a more qualified way, for some accommodation over EMU too.

Margaret Thatcher, for her part, had always felt resentful at the behaviour of Geoffrey Howe at the time of the Madrid Summit. She never, I suspect, felt able to trust him again, and she wanted him to play no part in the formulation of European policy: that is why she had moved him out of the Foreign Office. I think she found him more pedantic and crotchety as his discontent grew.

His discontent and his dislike of Margaret Thatcher must have been gathering pace behind his unflappable, unemotional exterior. He could by then see no future for himself in the Government. He was out of favour and had missed the boat for the succession. But instead of leaving in a dignified manner, he chose to use the occasion of his resignation to vent his bitterness and his frustration upon his leader personally, although he had worked with her so closely for eleven years. After the success of her statement in the House following the Rome Summit, perhaps he saw the European issue slipping away from him. The policy content of his resignation was minimal, as I shall show. But even when a resignation is over policy, my view is that one should state one's differences of policy, but not make them into a personal attack. I feel justified in saying that, since I never attacked Ted Heath at the time of my resignation. I criticized his policies amply. It was he who later tried to turn the whole affair into a personality clash.

On 1 November Geoffrey Howe resigned. My first thoughts were that his departure was for the best, because the European issue could not be fudged any longer. It was better out in the open. Margaret Thatcher would win the debate – she had huge support in the country. All this was before Geoffrey Howe's resignation statement, which he made during the Queen's Speech debate twelve days later on 13 November. Indeed, during those twelve days the atmosphere was calm. But the fuse was burning away and reached the gunpowder barrel the day he spoke, on 13 November. Guy Fawkes Day was eight days late in 1990.

Meanwhile, a quite separate story was unfolding at the same time. Ever since he resigned in January 1986 over the future of Westland Helicopters, Michael Heseltine had been waiting for his opportunity to bid for the leadership. Both Michael Heseltine and Geoffrey Howe were passionately ambitious to become Prime Minister. But they went about it in totally different ways. In the Tory tradition there are two ways to reach the top job. One is to be the loyal and long serving second-in-command, effortlessly moving into the top job when it becomes vacant. That was what Anthony Eden did, and what Geoffrey Howe set out to do. The other way is for a would-be leader to remain out of office, standing for some great issue of principle; and to wait, remote, lofty and unsullied in the wings, until the party realized that he had been right after all and called him to command. That was what Winston Churchill did and what Michael Heseltine set out to do. But unlike Churchill, he was not standing on a great issue of principle. 'Power is the name of the game,' he once said to me many years ago. Perhaps he was relentlessly pursuing power for no other reason than that he desperately wanted to have it?

The trouble was that Westland Helicopters' future was not a great question of political principle. One was left at the time with the vague impression that his resignation was about whether we should be keener on Europe or on America.

Since his resignation he had been trying to cultivate the image of standing for an alternative political philosophy to Margaret Thatcher's. He also sought to add to his appeal by a determined and time-consuming effort to speak in almost every constituency, in order to become the darling of the Tory workers. He sought to woo every Tory MP into supporting him when the opportunity came. He wrote political books and pamphlets – none of them receiving any great praise or interest. The main policies that one could identify were that we should play a much more active role in Europe, that we should intervene in and subsidize industry and that public money should be spent more liberally on social causes. He was a brilliant self-publicist and a very effective speaker to a mass audience.

Michael Heseltine was hovering around in October, wrestling with his judgement as to whether to take on Margaret Thatcher at the annual opportunity for challenging the leader which the Party's rules afford. He wasn't wrestling with his conscience, only pondering his chances of success. He had always said he wouldn't challenge her while she remained Prime Minister, only when a vacancy occurred. He had been careful always to add 'in any circumstances which I can foresee', so it wasn't the prospect of going back on his word which troubled him. What troubled him was whether he could win. I suspect he was almost sure he wouldn't and had already made up his mind not to challenge her.

There was much talk of 'stalking horses'. A 'stalking horse' was a nonentity challenger who was merely put up to test the level of her support. Sir Anthony Meyer was the first stalking horse and had challenged Margaret Thatcher in October 1989. No one, least of all Sir Anthony Meyer, expected victory, but if her support had been inadequate to prevent a second ballot taking place, then others – the real challengers – could come in on the second ballot. In the event, Margaret Thatcher got 314 votes, Sir Anthony Meyer 33 votes, with 27 abstentions. There was no second ballot. She had won easily, but she said to me at the time, 'I think that is good enough for me to carry on.' She was, I think, a little more disconcerted by the 1989 result than was generally realized. She always wanted to feel that she had a really strong and solid base of support in the parliamentary party.

One cannot be sure, but I think it is likely that another stalking horse would have run in 1990 if Michael Heseltine had not run. There was much talk of it; some names were even mentioned. I think Michael Heseltine had more or less decided to let the opportunity pass, by putting forward a stalking horse again just to test how strong Margaret Thatcher's support was. He reiterated his pledge not to stand against the incumbent, with the same conditions.

On 9 November he made what seemed at the time to be a serious error. He wrote to his constituents saying: 'The Tories could lose control of the nation's destiny unless the Cabinet faced up to Mrs Thatcher and asserted its collective judgement on European policy.' 'The collective wisdom of the Cabinet was needed,' he added. After this remarkable epistle he departed for a tour of the Middle East, a move which Bernard Ingham described as 'lighting the blue touch paper and retiring out of the country.' Of all people, he should have been the last one to talk of the 'collective judgement of the Cabinet,' remembering his defiance of Cabinet over Westland. His letter was no doubt inspired by Geoffrey Howe's resignation, which had taken place a week earlier. It was, however, before the resignation speech which was made three days later. I do not suspect collusion, merely opportunism. I believe there was no great love between Geoffrey Howe and Michael Heseltine and that they were operating entirely independently. The two sagas merely unfolded at the same time.

Michael Heseltine's letter to his Henley constituents was seen as a direct challenge to Margaret Thatcher. Nor were his constituents overjoyed with it. They held an early meeting of the Party Officers on 11 November and sent back a remarkably stuffy reply, reaffirming their faith in the Prime Minister. 'This Association supports the leadership of the Party,' they said.

The press went to town over these events. The headlines concentrated on the Henley Conservative Association officers. The editorials turned against Michael Heseltine. 'Put up or shut up,' they demanded. *The Times* even said he must, 'Throw his cap into the ring or stuff it down his throat.' There was a general demand for him to stop hovering about, to put his candidature to the test, and if he was beaten, to stop playing the game of the Young Pretender, even leave political life. Nearly everyone, including Michael Heseltine, thought he would be beaten. He was in a dilemma. He had been smoked out. He could no longer keep shadowing Margaret Thatcher from behind her left shoulder, always ready to step into her shoes if she faltered. He must have felt he actually did have to put up or shut up.

Events moved so fast that he had to live with this nightmare for only two days. On 13 November Geoffrey Howe made his resignation speech in the House of Commons. It was interpreted as a devastating attack on the Prime Minister. First, he said he had decided to resign, not just on the matter of her 'style', but on the matter of 'substance'. He went on to criticize her 'style' – he said: 'It was remarkable – indeed, it was tragic – to hear my Rt Hon Friend dismissing with such personalised incredulity, the very idea that the hard ECU proposal might find growing favour among the people of Europe, just as it was extraordinary to hear her assert that the whole idea of EMU might be open for consideration only by future generations. Those future generations are with us today.'

Taking his cue from a recent Mansion House speech in which the Prime Minister had declared herself ready to battle on, despite 'some pretty hostile bowling', Geoffrey Howe continued in the same metaphor, with the unconvincing analogy: 'It is rather like sending your opening batsmen to the crease only for them to find, the moment the first balls are bowled, that their bats have been broken before the game by the team captain. The tragedy is – and it is for me personally, for my party, for our whole people and for my Rt Hon Friend herself, a very real tragedy – that the Prime Minister's perceived attitude towards Europe is running increasingly serious risks for the future of our nation.'

On careful analysis, it was difficult to find the differences of substance, by which he meant policy disagreement. Indeed, he seemed to go out of his way to support her reservations about what was happening: 'I do not regard the Delors report as some kind of sacred text that has to be accepted, or even rejected, on the nod. But it is an important working document. As I have often made plain, it is seriously deficient in significant respects. I do not regard the Italian presidency's management of the Rome Summit as a model of its kind – far from it. I do not regard it as in any sense wrong for Britain to make criticisms of that kind plainly and courteously; nor in any sense wrong for us to do so, if necessary, alone. As I have already made clear, I have, like the Prime Minister and other Rt Hon Friends, fought too many European battles in a minority of one to have any illusions on that score. There is talk, of course, of a single currency for Europe. I agree that there are many difficulties about the concept – both economic and political. Of course, as I said in my letter of resignation, none of us wants the imposition of a single currency.'

There was a discernible nuance throughout his remarks that he personally would be content for Britain to go forward to joining a European single currency, but he jibbed at saying so. Indeed, the qualifications I have quoted above could only create a feeling of ambivalence. It would have been more convincing to have said he was in favour, while the Cabinet was not with him. Under these circumstances, the correct thing for him to have done was to resign fairly and squarely on his policy disagreement with his colleagues, but to refrain from personal attacks on the Prime Minister, as cover for his reluctance to speak out. He must have known that his views were far from popular.

There are two other passages in his speech which bring out two of the vital themes in this book. Neither was seen as very important at the time, but to me they were crucially more significant than his difficulties with style and substance over European policy.

First, he said, 'Indeed, the so-called Madrid conditions came into existence only after the then Chancellor and I, as Foreign Secretary, made it clear that we could not continue in office unless a specific commitment to join the ERM was made.' Here was the first public admission of the Madrid ambush, but expressed as an act of statesmanship, for which we should thank him, rather than an undercover ultimatum. This remark of Geoffrey Howe's justifies all that I say in Chapter 9.

The second remark came right at the end of his speech: 'Cabinet government is all about trying to persuade one another from within.'

The obvious inconsistency of these two remarks had evaded Geoffrey Howe's normally keen legal mind. They were in stark contradiction. He never once 'tried to persuade' his Cabinet colleagues about the desirability of joining the ERM. He never told them about the Madrid ambush, nor would they ever have agreed to it if he had. They never liked the Madrid conditions, but they were a *fait accompli* by the time they heard about them. Geoffrey Howe and Nigel Lawson operated throughout without the authority of a collective Cabinet decision on the subject of the exchange rate and the ERM. It was galling to be told that 'Cabinet government is all about trying to persuade one another from within,' when he had failed to do so informally, and had never tried to do so formally. The truth is that it was he and Nigel Lawson, who refused to operate the normal conventions of cabinet government. And, what is more, they were both wrong in expecting concessions about EMU from the eleven in return. Pity poor Margaret Thatcher sitting on the front bench having to listen to this and keep her silence!

Geoffrey Howe's resignation speech had a profound effect. Some saw it as the venomous outpourings of a bitter man. Some saw it as the revelation of the truth; the good and faithful servant finally driven to breaking point by the tantrums of his leader. The press, naturally, tended to take the latter point of view. I was abroad that day and only got to the House after the speech was over, so I didn't hear it. But there was certainly a mood of consternation and alarm. It probably made little, if any, difference to the way people were subsequently to vote. Those who had become opposed to Margaret Thatcher continuing in office saw it as a justification of their views: those who supported her dismissed it as sour grapes. The media saw it as a political event of immense importance, and made the most of it.

I was astonished by what he had said and the damage he had caused. Over all the years I had known him, I had never seen him behave emotionally, let alone vindictively. Behind that calm exterior, the resentment must have been building up, but it seemed totally out of character for him to let fly. I could no longer maintain the great respect for him I had always had.

Whatever the impact of the speech on colleagues, it certainly had an important effect on Michael Heseltine. The political explosion for which he had been hoping and waiting for so long suddenly took place. It gave him a way out of the dilemma; he could now challenge the Prime Minister on the basis of the discontent felt by and the charges brought by, the resigning Deputy Prime Minister. The fact that Geoffrey Howe had expressed his strong criticisms, even if they had been justified, was not a sufficient excuse for Michael Heseltine to seek to put matters right for Geoffrey Howe by trying to knock out the leader. It was true that Geoffrey Howe had concluded his speech with the words, 'The time has come for others to consider their own response to the tragic conflict of loyalties with which I myself have wrestled for perhaps too long.' But that sounded like an invitation to other ministers to resign, although none did. It was not an invitation to Michael Heseltine, who was suffering no conflict of loyalty, but it was enough for him to take it as one.

Crucially, Geoffrey Howe's last words enabled Michael Heseltine to square his conscience and justify the impending challenge publicly. It was enough, in his eyes, to constitute 'circumstances' which he could not have 'foreseen'. He gaily broke his pledge not to stand against her on these flimsy grounds. He had himself proposed and seconded for the leadership contest two days later, by which time nominations had to be in for a challenge to take place.

Even at that time, few realized the seriousness of the situation. It was generally thought that although Michael Heseltine would get a lot of votes, Margaret Thatcher would beat him easily, and there would be no need for a second ballot. She only had to secure a majority plus 15 per cent of those eligible to vote for this to occur, that meant 206 votes. The whole business was handled without taking it seriously enough; no one at the beginning realized how risky the situation had become. Moreover, Margaret Thatcher made two vital mistakes, both perhaps born of her failure to appreciate the dangers that lay ahead.

It is the leader's prerogative to agree the date upon which any challenge takes place with the Chairman of the 1922 Committee, Cranley Onslow, under the Party's rules. This was done before Geoffrey Howe resigned, and the date of Thursday, 15 November agreed for any nominations to be in. Any actual ballot would take place on Tuesday, 20 November. Margaret Thatcher knew she had to be in Paris at the Conference for Security and Cooperation in Europe (CSCE) from 17–21 November. She thus agreed a date which guaranteed that she would be out of London for nearly the whole of the 'campaigning' period. She must have judged that others could do the campaigning for her, but thought that the advantage of her almost, as it were, 'presiding' over an international conference when the Cold War was to be declared over and done, was so great that it would be a major plus in her campaign. How could anyone dream of voting for a stalking horse when the true leader was abroad, signing a treaty bringing the Cold War to an end, an achievement for which she was in large measure responsible? She did not, of course, know when she agreed the date that Geoffrey Howe was to resign and that it was Michael Heseltine who was to stand against her. But it was a serious error, because she was not in London to try to bring the waverers round to support her.

The second mistake was to appoint a weak campaign team. George Younger had led her campaign a year earlier against Sir Anthony Meyer and she asked him to do it again. Other members were Norman Fowler, Norman Tebbit, John Moore and Michael Jopling, assisted by Michael Neubert, Gerry Neale and Ian Twinn, together with her Parliamentary Private Secretary, Peter Morrison. Five of them were ex-Cabinet ministers, most of whom were playing virtually no part in the life of Parliament and the Party. They probably did not know large numbers of MPs, and they were seen as rather remote retired grandees of the past. George Younger himself was already busy with his work for the Royal Bank of Scotland. His appointment made it difficult for him to be too much involved on behalf of Margaret Thatcher. In any event he was in Edinburgh and was not in London during much of the crucial period. John Moore was abroad at the time he was appointed – he read of his appointment in the newspaper and came hurriedly back to London where he did his best. Norman Fowler considered he had been asked merely to stop Michael Heseltine standing and retreated from the fray after he had failed.

Moreover, this ill-judged team set out merely to canvass, rather than to persuade. Nor did they canvass everybody – many MPs said afterwards that no one from the Thatcher team had approached them. The figures they came up with proved to be over-optimistic. It was really necessary to have canvassed every member of the Party thoroughly, and to have got Margaret Thatcher to see every doubter personally. But they didn't do this and she was in Paris. I reported for duty to help on several occasions, but I was told there was no need. All was in hand and Margaret Thatcher's situation was said to be adequate, although not marvellous.

The atmosphere in the House of Commons was very far from reassuring, however. Arriving back in London on 19 November from the weekend, I was horrified at the apparent apathy of her campaign team, and worse still, the smell of disintegration which was obvious after talking to only a few people. The only group who were taking it seriously were some members of the No Turning Back Group, young turks who passionately believed in Margaret Thatcher. They really were working on the doubtfuls and had a horribly long list of them. I gave all the assistance I could. For the rest of my time, I fell back on accepting every invitation I could get to broadcast and go on television in order to promote her cause against Michael Heseltine's. This was of little use, of course, since the electorate was the parliamentary party, not the viewing public.

Perhaps, however, her absence abroad and the poor campaign that was fought on her behalf and in her absence, were not the only cause of the inadequate vote Margaret Thatcher received on 20 November. There were deeper forces at work. But a good campaign might have produced those two extra votes that were necessary to stave off the second ballot. What probably had most effect on the doubters was a public opinion poll showing that the Tories would be 1 per cent ahead of Labour if Michael Heseltine became Prime Minister, while she was trailing 11 per cent behind Labour at the time. Many Tories in marginal seats were simply concerned about who would be the most likely leader to secure the continuation of their political careers – an understandable, but not an edifying, preoccupation.

Michael Heseltine had promised 'a fundamental review' of the poll tax, which meant nothing, but gave hope to those MPs feeling most vulnerable from this problem. If he had had a better alternative to the poll tax, he could have told us what it was. The poll tax had been continuously under 'fundamental review' for the last five years and all the answers were the same. Apart from tinkering, nobody actually proposed a better system at the time. In the end, Michael Heseltine had to endure an undignified four months while the Cabinet proved how difficult it was to find a better answer; the problem of doing so will be with us long after this book is published! But the 'fundamental review' pledge had its effect in the four days that mattered.

It may also have had an effect on some of those few members of the public who were polled to give their views on the leadership contest. Some of that magic sample – 1,000 or so – selected at random by MORI, might have been fed up with high mortgage rates, or high community charges, or simply cross with Margaret Thatcher about some problem to do with their job or their business. Yet these fleeting reactions by this unknown and tiny selection of people at that precise moment of time may well have sealed her fate. They gave what seemed like a clear national answer – Michael Heseltine could win the next election and Margaret Thatcher could not. Many doubting Tory MPs must have been influenced by it.

In fact, it was pretty meaningless. It was the economic problems they faced which worried the respondents. I doubt if they were very interested in Margaret Thatcher's 'style' in dealing with the Europeans – and if they were, they would have been on her side. They expressed their deep, and entirely understandable, concern about the problems which Margaret Thatcher appeared to have brought upon them. The fact that these problems were not going to go away with a change of leader did not feature in their responses. Being the victim of instant polling is an opportunity to vent one's current grievance, not to make a considered judgement as to who would be the best leader. I think this view was confirmed the following week, when the pollsters reported that John Major and Douglas Hurd both had a roughly similar hypothetical lead over Labour to that of Michael Heseltine. One poll even naughtily suggested that John Smith had a better chance of winning the General Election for Labour than Neil Kinnock. Unfortunately for them, the Labour Party did not have an instant opportunity to vote on the issue. But the Tory Party did.

My view was that the chances of winning or losing the General Election were affected very little by who would be the leader. It would be decided by the success of policy between then and the election and by the electorate's view of the contenders and their programmes at that time. Margaret Thatcher's record in winning elections had shown how unwise it is to make snap decisions based on a few adverse public opinion polls. Twice, under her, the Tories had been at the bottom of the polls, and twice she had gone on to win the election.

Perhaps Margaret Thatcher made a third mistake. She had been concerned as to whom to ask to propose and to second her. I had counselled getting two backbenchers to do it – one senior and one younger. But she decided to ask the two most senior members of her Cabinet – the Chancellor and the Foreign Secretary – to do it. They both agreed. But that put them out of the running in any contest, both in the first ballot and, if there were to be a second ballot, in that too. Many MPs did not want to be presented with only the very limited choice of Michael Heseltine or Margaret Thatcher – they wanted there to be an opportunity for others, particularly John Major and Douglas Hurd, so they could vote for the one they wanted. They wanted all the horses to be allowed to run in the race. Since both Douglas Hurd and John Major were debarred, so to speak, from standing by having proposed and seconded her, there was no possibility for their supporters to vote for them. A number of MPs therefore probably voted for Michael Heseltine in order to achieve a second ballot, in which the other two could stand. It was a difficult calculation: they didn't want Michael Heseltine to win, yet they wanted a second ballot. In the end, they achieved this result only too effectively. This error, if error it was, came back with renewed emphasis when it came to the second ballot. It would probably have helped in the first ballot, however, if these two contenders had been seen to be free to stand, whether or not they had actually chosen to do so.

Peter Morrison took the results of the team's canvass suggesting a more than adequate majority to Paris on the afternoon of the first ballot, and they waited together in the British Embassy for the results to be telephoned through. The canvass had over-estimated the size of her vote by some 26 people. It must have been most unpalatable news. Peter Morrison said afterwards that he had been lied to by 26 colleagues, but he didn't know which. Margaret Thatcher won 204 votes to Michael Heseltine's 152, with 16 spoilt ballot papers. The situation was much worse than she had expected and a second ballot was actually required. It must have been a very grim moment for

Margaret Thatcher; she probably knew it was the end. She must have felt bitter and betrayed. Nevertheless, with her iron courage, she continued with the long evening of entertainments at Versailles laid on for the heads of government by the French.

That evening they opened the champagne bottles in the Berlaymont – the building where the European Commission lives. But throughout Britain there was a sense of shock, a sense of loss. Even her opponents felt the gravity of the hour. For her supporters, it was almost more than they could believe; they hadn't expected it. For me, it was one of the saddest moments of my life. I felt my whole life's work, and the achievements of the decade, were hanging by a thread. At that moment, when I heard the voting figures, it seemed as if all we had striven for was being contemptuously dismissed by lesser men and for unworthy reasons.

If two more people had voted for Margaret Thatcher rather than for Michael Heseltine, there would have been no second ballot. She would have won. Surely she must have felt that two extra votes could have been won by a little extra effort, by her campaign team trying a little harder, or, ruefully, by her being in London to take part in the campaign herself? Or in some other way could it not have been done? To be so near, and yet to miss, is agony – perhaps the same agony that Jim Callaghan felt on the night of 29 March 1979, when his Government was defeated by one vote in a Motion of No Confidence, and the General Election which followed ushered in Margaret Thatcher as Prime Minister.

And yet? Without a second ballot, she would have been able to remain Prime Minister, but she would have been gravely weakened. If in her victory over Sir Anthony Meyer a year earlier her vote had been 'good enough for me to carry on,' would 104 fewer supporting votes than she got the time before have been 'good enough'? We shall never know, but she might have been so damaged that the first ballot was in fact a fatal result, whether or not she had received those two extra votes. She would never have wanted to continue without robust support; she was too much of a democrat.

A contingency plan had, quite rightly, been made that if her vote was higher than a certain minimum number she would immediately announce that she would stand in the second ballot. If it were less, she would immediately resign. She declared her intention to stand straightaway. This was wise. She could not have left the matter open for more than a very short length of time: rumour, speculation and pressure would have gathered pace inevitably and the situation would have become chaotic. It gave her time to come home and digest the situation and ponder it. Nevertheless, she was even blamed for coming to too hasty a decision, and for 'not consulting' her Cabinet colleagues. This was a ridiculous criticism, but it apparently annoyed some backbenchers that she had decided so quickly. Michael Heseltine did not hesitate for a moment to declare his candidature for the second ballot – no consultation was expected of him. There was jubilation in his camp that he had forced her to a second ballot, and he would most certainly enter it. To complicate and aggravate the situation, Neil Kinnock put down a Motion of No Confidence – a motion which always has to be taken early. It was decided to debate the No Confidence Motion on Thursday, 22 November, two days later.

That evening, there were many telephone calls between London and Paris which bore further bad news. The message they contained was: 'She cannot win.' Thus the campaign began very early indeed to persuade her that the cause was hopeless and that she couldn't win. Almost as soon as the votes were announced, the 'she cannot win' movement got under way. She asked John MacGregor, the Leader of the House, to canvass the views of all the members of the Cabinet, and report them to her when she returned to London the next day.

On the morning of 21 November, the signing ceremony for the Treaty took place in Paris, after which she returned to London at midday. She had to make a statement in the House that very afternoon on the CSCE Conference, a major undertaking in itself. The following day she had to speak in the No Confidence debate; a major speech had to be prepared within the next 24 hours. All this came on top of the need to grapple with the immediate situation over the leadership issue.

She handled the statement on the Paris conference with her usual skill and sang-froid. It is not easy to make statements in the House and face an hour or more of questions afterwards. Any googlie may be bowled – one has to be totally in command of all the facts and arguments, one must never lose one's cool, and one must think up the necessary repartee on one's feet. For a Prime Minister, the stakes are even higher, because one slip of the tongue can cause a major diplomatic incident, or a major domestic row. Add to these hurdles the emotional stress of her leadership being in jeopardy, and one can see what an exceptional performer she was. The stamina, the self control, the grasp of detail, the patience, to go through that ordeal with flying colours was remarkable; but it was a feat to be outdone the very next day.

That moment is one I will never forget. She was announcing to the

House the official end of the Cold War – perhaps the most important event of the whole decade. It was something for which she had worked and striven all her life; and she had contributed greatly to achieving it by the method she had calculated was most likely to succeed, 'peace through strength'. In a way, it was the crowning achievement of her career, but she had to announce the result with the handles of the daggers of Michael Heseltine, Geoffrey Howe, and Nigel Lawson visibly sticking out of her back. She did it as if they were not there. But they were there. Both Geoffrey Howe and Nigel Lawson announced over the course of the next weekend, after Margaret Thatcher had resigned, that they would vote for Michael Heseltine in the second ballot, as if to emphasize the point that they had both played a major part in bringing the present peril upon her. They were not content to leave the 'credit' to Michael Heseltine, though I doubt if either of them really wanted to see him as leader. By that time they seemed to want to proclaim in public that they had started the engineering of her downfall by the Madrid ambush.

On Wednesday, 21 November, the atmosphere was even worse than before. This time her supporters were openly abandoning her cause. They were not merely fighting ineffectually for her, they were not fighting for her at all. Even senior supporters of hers looked grim and flashed a list before me of names of MPs who claimed to have supported her on the first ballot, but who would become defectors next time round. I suspect many of them were defectors first time round. Many were ministers who had voted against her on the first ballot, although they told the canvassers that they were loyal (for obvious reasons). Despite her impressive performance in the House, the ground seemed to be sliding from under her feet. Weak men were panicking, and it appeared that even strong men were being borne along the wave of pessimism. The 'she cannot win' campaign was well and truly under way. I was very concerned by the one-sided way in which her erstwhile supporters saw the situation that Wednesday afternoon. That list of defectors acquired a certain certification of authority; the same sort of authority as had been afforded to the MORI poll the week before on the question of who was the most likely leader to win the next election. It was not the result of a systematic canvass, which might well have shown some transfers in the opposite direction. Nor had Margaret Thatcher even started to talk to any backbenchers to try to win them round. It was as if her supporters were hoisting the white flag even before battle had been joined. They were telling everyone it was hopeless.

Another factor was working strongly against her. She had telephoned John Major from Paris on the fatal evening of the first ballot and asked him to propose her for the second ballot, as indeed she asked Douglas Hurd to second her. In both cases a reluctant assent was given. Both men feared that Michael Heseltine would win the second ballot and wanted to stand themselves. Both wanted to be Prime Minister and neither wanted Michael Heseltine to be. By agreeing to propose and second her, they effectively ruled themselves out of the contest. To do both credit, they let their loyalty prevail over their personal ambitions. But many Tory MPs wanted to be able to vote for one or other of them and they were effectively frustrated if their candidate was unable to stand. Indeed, it was clearly wrong, once there was an open field, for two favoured horses to be prevented from running. By asking them to nominate her in the first instance, and then again in the second, she had effectively blocked them. In retrospect, she would have been wiser to have chosen two backbenchers and to have made clear that any member of the Cabinet could enter his name if he so wished. She immediately came under pressure not to stand herself, after all, in the second ballot, so that Douglas Hurd and John Major would be free to stand. By then, that was the only way to release them.

I saw her briefly myself that evening and begged her to start seeing the defectors straightaway. She replied that first she had to see every member of the Cabinet. She too had heard of the crumbling of the support of the senior figures on whom she thought she could rely. John MacGregor had canvassed the Cabinet in the morning and reported to her when she returned. His report was encouraging. On Peter Morrison's advice, she resolved to see each one separately. Her advisers believed that if she could ask members of the Cabinet to come out in her support publicly, the Party would rally behind her. One after the other that evening they trooped into her room in the House of Commons, to see her alone and face to face. It was not as John MacGregor had told her. Her opponents said she couldn't win and, moreover, they would not vote for her. Her supporters said they would vote for her but that she couldn't win; and so she should stand down. Only a small minority urged her to fight, said she could win, and pledged their support. They were, I believe, Peter Brooke, Kenneth Baker, Cecil Parkinson, John Wakeham and David Waddington. Later, no doubt, she discussed the position with her husband. That evening she came to the final conclusion that she must resign.

She told John Major of her decision late that night, in order to give him, her preferred candidate, as much notice as possible. She told the Cabinet next morning, virtually breaking down in the process. 'It's a funny old world,' she is said to have begun. She told the world immediately afterwards. She went to the Palace and told the Queen she would no longer contest the second ballot. So ended one of the greatest premierships in our history.

Was there a plot? Did her supporters suddenly see a chance to profit themselves by unseating her, and gang up ruthlessly to take it?

There was much talk of the 'Catherine Place Conspiracy'. There was certainly a gathering on the night of the first ballot, at the home in Catherine Place of Tristan Garel-Jones, a notorious wet, an ex-Whip and a recently appointed junior Foreign Office minister. He had recruited a number of colleagues after the vote on Tuesday evening to come back to his house to have a drink and discuss the situation. Among those present were several Cabinet ministers, including Norman Lamont, William Waldegrave, Malcolm Rifkind, Chris Patten and Tony Newton.

It seems that it was at this gathering that it was mooted, and eventually accepted, that Margaret Thatcher could not beat Michael Heseltine at the second ballot. Either Douglas Hurd or John Major was judged able to do so, but they were effectively barred by their having nominated her. So she had to be persuaded to stand down – it seemed the only way of stopping Heseltine. Her supporters were horrified at the thought of a Heseltine victory – to prevent that was the top priority. So they persuaded themselves that they must prevail upon her to stand down. Cabinet ministers who I thought were loyal to her were actively pressing her to stand down. I couldn't believe it. She had never had a chance to try to persuade the party, there had been no fight at all; and yet, here were even her loyal lieutenants laying down their arms. They spread the fatal message to Tory MPs the next day. They certainly spread it to me. They spread it to her when, one by one, they went to see her the next evening.

Was that a plot, or was it a meeting of realists, facing up to a situation that was irretrievably heading for disaster? It was not a deliberate conspiracy to engineer her downfall; but it was remarkable how quickly some people came to the conclusion that 'she cannot win'. Tristan Garel-Jones and Peter Lilley had come to that conclusion within minutes of the votes being declared and the visitors to Catherine Place were assured only three hours later that there was no doubt about the inevitability of defeat. There had not been enough time to canvass the party. The question to which we will never know the answer is whether the 'she cannot win' campaign was genuine or deliberate. Could the defectors have been won round, if a serious effort had been made to do so? Was it true that she couldn't win the second ballot? Many people in the Party did not agree with the instant judgement of Tristan Garel-Jones and others, nor its endorsement at his gathering. Some in her Cabinet believed she would win and urged her to fight, as did many in the parliamentary party. Groups of would-be callers came through the night to Number 10 to try to persuade her to continue, and a final group came at dawn the next day. But she had made up her mind; she saw no point in seeing them. She wanted to be alone; the battle was over. From then on, it would be memories; memories of the great days, of the great crusades, and of the great achievements. Bitter memories too, of that fateful day, and of her betrayal by those whom she had brought to her Cabinet table.

When she left for the Paris conference, she had an apparently unassailable position. No one really believed she would be beaten. There was certainly a great under-estimation of the threat, there was even some complacency; no one predicted that she was about to fall. Four days later she fell.

For my part, I pass no final judgement on the conduct of her colleagues. I have simply tried to tell the story. She always evoked strong feelings in other people; her supporters were intensely loyal and her enemies intensely critical. Over the leadership contest, her true supporters urged her to fight all the way, her enemies, of course, did their utmost to defeat her. It was those who turned because they believed the battle could not be won who sealed her fate. We shall never know whether they were right or wrong and therefore whether they betrayed her or gave her wise counsel. Each of us must make our own judgement.

Even if she had entered the second ballot and won, it would have been a very marginal victory. The size of the vote against her would have been very uncomfortable to live with. There were underlying causes of discontent and a feeling of the need for a new mood, and a new style, which were the reasons why she had lost so much support. I will discuss them in the next chapter. Her premiership must, in any event, have been drawing near to its end. But if she had won at least she would have been able to go in her own time, in her own manner and with dignity.

There was revulsion throughout the Party and the country, indeed the whole world, at the brisk and brutal way she had been dismissed.

There remains a large amount of resentment in this country at the way she was treated in the Party. Even her enemies were shocked by the sudden and merciless way her own Party treated her. For one who had done so much for the fortunes of the Party to be forced to resign overnight by those whom she had brought to high office seemed like medieval savagery. I for one, who experienced the old system of choosing the leader in operation in 1963, regret that we ever changed it. The Chief Whip, the Chairman of the 1922 Committee, and a few grandees of the party – the 'men in grey suits', as they were called – could make it clear to a leader that the time had come to stand down after canvassing the parliamentary party. It was just as effective as the public challenge and those public voting figures, but it left the leader free to leave with dignity.

It was the Party that threw dignity to the winds. Margaret Thatcher most certainly retained her dignity. On the afternoon of the day she announced she would resign, she had to answer questions and then respond to Neil Kinnock in the No Confidence Debate. She was still Prime Minister. She had had but the bare minimum of time to prepare. She was under stress. The Government side of the House gave her a tumultuous welcome. Many even who had betrayed her stood up and cheered her, a sight which sickened me. But she conducted herself with a courage which was amazing. She set out the achievements of her Government over eleven-and-a-half years in a way which combined confidence in her achievement with defiance of her critics. 'Should we be censured for our strength?' she asked. 'Or should the Labour Party be censured for its weakness?' She was even capable of humour. When the subject of an independent European Central Bank was mentioned, Dennis Skinner interjected, 'She is going to be the Governor.' 'What a good idea!' she came back immediately. 'I had not thought of that. But if I were, there would be no European Central Bank accountable to no one, least of all national parliaments.' The House collapsed in merry laughter. It was a great speech, watched throughout the nation on television. Many of the public must have thought the Tory Party was mad.

Five days later a second leadership ballot was held. On this occasion, the Party gave John Major 185 votes, Michael Heseltine 131 votes, and Douglas Hurd 56 votes. Michael Heseltine and Douglas Hurd immediately withdrew from the contest. John Major was the new Prime Minister. Margaret Thatcher tendered her resignation to the Queen at 9.45 am on Wednesday, 28 November. The Thatcher era had come to an end.

The Tory parliamentary party never looks back. It is ruthless and cruel. Few that evening spared a moment to regret both the fact and the manner of her going, let alone to permit themselves a tear. There was much unconcealed pleasure at the clever way they had got her out. The talk was all of who would be promoted and who would be sacked, and who would have which job. There was no collective move to honour or salute her publicly, although many individuals will have paid her private tribute. The Tory political machine just moved on instantly to the new leader, the new Government. We all knew the proclamation: 'The King is dead, long live the King.' There can be no more than the smallest interval in the exercise of power at the top. That must be right. But there are such things as dignity, honour and respect. The Tory Party has much to learn about how to deploy these virtues when it changes leader. It is a very cruel animal.

So cruel, indeed, was the procedure which allowed a Prime Minister in office to be challenged in midstream and publicly, that there was a move to change the rules in this respect. A committee was set up to study what might be done. I believe there must be better ways of doing these things – the old way, the 'men in grey suits' even, was better than this. When I put this view to Margaret Thatcher after she had resigned, but before John Major had been elected, she joked, with her indomitable spirit, 'No, Nick, they shouldn't change the rules by which I was brought down. I may need those rules myself later on!'

Margaret Thatcher lives to fight another day – but her private hurt must have been very grave indeed, although she never showed it. General de Gaulle, on suffering a similar fate at the hands of the French electorate in 1969, retreated immediately to his country home. 'What other consolation can be sought,' he said, 'when one has faced history?' Margaret Thatcher had certainly 'faced history'.

11

AN ASSESSMENT

IN THAT IMMORTAL last speech which Margaret Thatcher made as
Prime Minister on 28 November 1990, she set out her Government's
economic achievements: 2 million more people in jobs since 1979;
income tax down from 33p to 25p in the pound; no surcharge on
savings income; 400,000 new businesses set up since 1979. She
claimed her 'stewardship of the public finances had been better than
that of any government for nearly fifty years.' I can add more facts: £28
billion of National Debt was repaid; taxes were cut dramatically; the
nation enjoyed sustained economic growth as a result of her stewardship; she brought about 35 per cent real average increase in the
standard of living in Britain. It was an astonishing achievement when
one remembers the failures resulting from the years of fudging which
preceded her. Many critics pick on that word 'average' and claim that
the 'gap between the richest 10 per cent and the poorest 10 per cent has
widened substantially,' to quote the words which the Liberal
Democrat MP Simon Hughes used, when he interrupted her during
that last speech in the House. Her response was devastating: 'He
would rather have the poor poorer provided the rich were less rich,'
she said. In fact, although the gap has certainly widened, at every level
in society there has been a substantial increase in everyone's standard
of living, with pensioners 37 per cent better off in real terms on
average.

It was a truly remarkable record of achievement, set out in a speech
of indomitable spirit. I was reminded of some words of Abraham
Lincoln's many years ago: 'You cannot bring about prosperity by
discouraging thrift. You cannot strengthen the weak by weakening
the strong. You cannot help the wage earner by pulling down the wage
payer. You cannot further the brotherhood of man by encouraging
class hatred. You cannot help the poor by destroying the rich. You
cannot establish sound security on borrowed money. You cannot keep
out of trouble by spending more than you earn. You cannot build

253

character and courage by taking away man's initiative and independence. You cannot help men permanently by doing for them what they could and should do for themselves.'

Margaret Thatcher had followed those precepts to the letter and as a result she had transformed the nation's position. It is too easy nowadays to take these achievements for granted and to forget the failures of the 1960s and 1970s when we were the 'sick man of Europe'. Many people have long forgotten how much less well off they were in 1979.

Much of the economic achievement will remain and is unlikely to be reversed by any government in the future. That is what is so unique about Margaret Thatcher's record. She forced the Labour Party to abandon, one by one, the basic policies of socialism. She forced them to abandon unilateral nuclear disarmament. She made capitalism popular as well as successful. No socialist now dare advocate more power for the trade unions, more nationalization, or penal taxation. The successive reforms of trade union law are unlikely to be reversed in principle; the trade unions are now far more responsive to their members' wishes, and a far less disruptive force in industry. The industries which have been privatized are likely to remain so. The Labour Party talk of renationalizing some of the utilities if they ever regain power, but that would be going against the grain and the popular mood. Privatization became popular under Margaret Thatcher. The example we set of the advantages of privatizing the whole of industry is one that has been followed by the rest of the world; I doubt if that will be reversed here, even by a future Labour government, when everyone else is pursuing it hard abroad. Margaret Thatcher's Government got rid of a large number of taxes and distortions in the tax system aimed at discriminating against one group or another: the rates of direct taxation were also dramatically reduced. Though a future Labour government would certainly increase taxes, they suggest it would be only for the better off. Even for the rich, I very much doubt they would seek to go back to the penal levels and the discriminations of the 1979 tax regime. I believe the same holds true for the major reforms of Corporation Tax which Nigel Lawson carried out. Margaret Thatcher has simply ended the era of penal taxation for its own sake.

By the end of her time, she had forced the Labour Party to accept the basic tenets of the market economy. One by one they had had to accept selling council houses to their tenants, shares in companies for employees, an end to state subsidies for ailing industry, and even an

254

open trading environment. She forced the political debate in Britain onto the ground of who can best run a market economy in Britain; it is no longer about whether we have a market economy or a socialist one.

The example of her strength and her style galvanized many people in Britain. She changed attitudes throughout society, partly as a result of the example of her formidable character, and partly as a result of the successes she achieved. She made it possible for people who showed effort and initiative to enrich themselves. She made it possible for millions to own their own houses, to own shares, and to start their own businesses. For the first time since the war, there were sufficient incentives to motivate people. To prosper became no longer anti-social; it was actively encouraged by the Government. In place of a work force largely employed by big companies, fighting for wage increases with the help of their trade unions, she presided over a blossoming of small companies and self-employment, with people winning better livings from the market by their own efforts.

Much of this transformation will persist. The tragedy was the squeeze of 1988–91 which brought down so many of the new small businesses. It seemed to tarnish the good image of striking out on one's own. The habit of starting a small business or going self-employed was still a tender plant, some would-be entrepreneurs will have been put off from starting up by the last few years. Nevertheless, the same basic economic climate which encouraged starting out on one's own is still with us, and as the current recession eases, we should see a resurgence of this vital development.

Thus I believe most of the supply side reforms will stick – even if we were to suffer the misfortune of having a Labour government. The element in the mix that is essential, but which is always at risk, is reasonable levels of taxation. I have an uneasy feeling that direct taxation in Britain will creep up over the years ahead, perhaps dangerously close to the point at which incentives are blunted. If they do, tax evasion will set in again, and many good people will go overseas to establish their businesses. Higher taxation can actually mean lower tax yields. It requires determination of the order shown by Margaret Thatcher to keep expenditure low enough to maintain tax levels close to our present ones. I hope and pray her successors will be strong enough to secure this.

All these are solid achievements which are likely to endure, not least because to reverse them would be extremely unpopular with the electorate. The other major element which played a part in the industrial recovery which Margaret Thatcher undoubtedly brought about was sharpening up competition – both within the domestic economy through competition policy, and externally by pursuing an unashamedly free trade policy. The policy of privatization contributed to this, as did the strengthening of the competition laws. Many would say that there is still more to be done (although increasingly, competition is a policy coming under the control of the European Community). Nevertheless, she succeeded in sweeping away much of the protection and the cosy restrictions operated in many industries and professions.

In a world that now seems to be going increasingly protectionist, her free trade policy may turn out to be a less enduring feature of the business environment. The European Community is partly to blame for this. The difficulties Margaret Thatcher experienced in opening up the Single Market in the Community demonstrates its instinctive dislike of open markets. The blatant pursuit of protectionism in motor cars, electronics, transport and other areas made her despair. The part the Community played in wrecking the Uruguay Round was unforgivable. All this caused her to look for ways of securing open markets and keeping them open by other means than just relying on membership of the Community. Towards the end of her long experience of the Community, she began to talk more and more of the need for some sort of Atlantic Free Trade Area, embracing all those nations who wanted to practise genuine free trade. She was particularly keen to maintain a close trading relationship with the USA. Perhaps she remembered Winston Churchill's last admonition to his Cabinet the day he retired from being Prime Minister: 'Man is spirit. Never be separated from the Americans.' She could have said the second sentence at least herself when her turn came to resign.

Had she survived a few years more, I believe she would have begun to make overtures in that direction. My experiences of the Community make me despair of ever seeing a European market completely open both internally and externally. The difficulty with Margaret Thatcher's dream of a wider free trade area embracing North America is that it could, and would, be effectively frustrated by the Commission itself, who have the responsibility for trade policy. It would indeed be a paradox if the once so-called 'Common Market' sought to prevent one of its members engaging in a genuine free trade agreement. There was more work still for Margaret Thatcher to do in this vital area of world trade policy. It is an opportunity which I hope her successor will pick up. I fear we may be entering a period of renewed protectionism, which can only result in reduced economic growth.

In relation to the dependency culture and state provision of welfare, health and education, in fairness Margaret Thatcher's achievements were less dramatic. She started too late: reforms in this area take a long, long time to work through. Although what she did will turn out to be beneficial, she fell between two stools. Either a Government must provide State services, paid for by the taxpayer, of a quality which people find acceptable; or it must put in place private sector methods of provision, giving competition and choice, which must be seen to work better. The latter in no way precludes making such services free at the point of consumption.

I am sure that Margaret Thatcher does not believe it is possible to provide free public services of a quality that will satisfy almost everyone – so that even the rich prefer to use them. That appears to be the aim of some members of the present Government. I do not believe it is possible. The point can be vividly illustrated by taking the analogy of housing. If council housing were made so good that nobody wanted to own their own home, how much would that cost? Nor would it be desirable, because it would remove choice from people in deciding in which house and where they want to live. For these sorts of reasons, I suspect Margaret Thatcher does not believe it is desirable, let alone possible. But then, she ought to have put in place alternative methods of provision based on the private sector which gave the people both choice and the quality of service they wanted. Her steps in this direction were too late, too hesitant, and not radical enough: 1983 was the year of her opportunity – she should have then had in place a strategy for the reform of health, education and higher education that would have at least transferred the operative provision of these services to private enterprise. Much work and study is necessary for such an alternative system to be successful: but I am convinced it can be done. It requires separate management, even leading to separate ownership of different schools and hospitals, while keeping the services basically free to the customer at the point of delivery. Such a solution would be vastly superior in respect of the quality and efficiency with which the services are provided. By 1987 it was too late, and the ground work had not been properly done. The extraordinary thing was how much was actually achieved in those few weeks before and after the 1987 election in terms of policy making: the changes in education are bearing fruit already; housing will be a longer haul. As I write, some self-managing hospital trusts set up under the

Health Service Reforms are beginning to tackle the problems of overmanning, bureaucracy and inefficiency in their hospitals. Improvement through better management has just begun to come through.

But by 1990 nothing like enough of the fruits were apparent for Margaret Thatcher to be able to claim much credit for rejuvenating the public services. Just as privatization was not a popular slogan in 1979, because it had never been tried and shown to work, so choice and efficiency in the public services was unpopular in 1990 because they too had never been tried and shown to work. The present Government's avowed intent to improve the public services is not so much a repudiation of Thatcherism, as a decision not to embark on the last great Thatcherite reform, to complete Margaret Thatcher's last piece of unfinished business.

I do not blame her for this: she could not have fought on more fronts than she did. She fought, and won, primarily on the economic front; she also fought and won on the European front, and she was immensely successful on the international front. To criticize her for not undertaking a great struggle on the social front at the same time would be mean and unfair. Perhaps part of the reason was that she did not have the people in place whom she could trust to work out the necessary reforms. She had to do too much herself.

All this brings us back to the persistent weakness in her political position. She never really had enough true supporters, particularly in high places. She always felt the need to placate important factions in the Party by liberal representation in her Cabinet; and, as a result, she didn't get enough people who were both able and agreed with her aims into the places in Government where it mattered. She tried to do it all herself with her authority as Prime Minister. She just couldn't do everything. In fact, it is amazing now much she did succeed in doing. Although she got the reputation of pushing everything through that she wanted to, the Iron Lady was in fact more malleable when she had to be. What were not malleable were her political beliefs.

Perhaps also the political mood in the country in 1983 was not favourable to such a programme. The scale and pace of change would perhaps have been more than the country could take if these reforms had been added to the supply side reforms which were working their way through the system at that time.

During her premiership, Margaret Thatcher acquired an almost legendary reputation abroad. She soon came to be seen as the first post-war Prime Minister who had tackled Britain's economic problems and led the country back to prosperity. Tales of the success of her industrial relations policy, her monetary policy and her privatization policy crossed all the oceans and began to be copied from Moscow to Brazil. It was as a worker of economic miracles that foreign heads of government first looked forward to meeting her.

They soon realized, however, that she was interested in more than economics, and she began to acquire a reputation as a leader of great firmness and directness. It was the Russians who first christened her the 'Iron Lady'. This was in response to a speech she made in 1976 – long before she became Prime Minister – in which she described the Soviet system as 'a failure in human and economic terms.' She did not resent her new title at all – she made capital out of it. She was very resolute over defence, and believed strongly in deterring the then still belligerent Russians with both conventional and nuclear arsenals. She was the first European leader to accept the stationing of cruise missiles in her country. She maintained and modernized Britain's own nuclear weapons. The policy of deterrence through strength eventually paid off – perhaps mainly because the Russian economy started to collapse just at the same time as the Americans 'upped the ante' with their immensely expensive Star Wars programme. She was totally justified in claiming at least a share of the credit for the ending of the Cold War.

She developed close relationships with both President Gorbachev and President Reagan. This enabled her to participate in international affairs with far more authority than would have otherwise been the case. Indeed, world politics for much of the 1980s were dominated by Gorbachev, Reagan and Margaret Thatcher. Britain wielded an influence under her far greater than our economic strength or our military power justified. In my early days I remember seeing photographs of Churchill, Roosevelt and Stalin sitting together at the Yalta Conference and carving up the post-war map of Europe between them. I felt proud that such a small country as Britain ranked equally with the two superpowers. For years since I thought that that was something we would never see again – but it actually came to happen once more under Margaret Thatcher. This time it was Gorbachev, Reagan and Margaret Thatcher who settled the peace after the end of the Cold War.

It also enabled her to fight and win the Falklands War without harassment from either of the superpowers. This in turn enabled her to establish with great clarity that big states must actually be prevented from invading their smaller neighbours. The principle had to be enforced again when Iraq invaded Kuwait. She was influential in stiffening President Bush in August 1990 to send troops to the Gulf and to make sure he meant what he said when he told Iraq to leave Kuwait. She is reported later to have warned him: 'Don't go wobbly.' The victories in the Falklands War and the Gulf War were largely due to her resolution.

She closed her speech in the No Confidence Debate – the last speech she made as Prime Minister – with these words: 'There is something else which one feels. That is a sense of this country's destiny; the centuries of history and experience which ensure that, when principles have to be defended, when good has to be upheld and when evil has to be overcome, Britain will take up arms. It is because we on this side have never flinched from difficult decisions that this House and this country can have confidence in this Government today.'

She resisted sanctions against South Africa at successive Commonwealth Conferences and kept the European Council more or less in line with her policy of persuasion, rather than sanctions, against South Africa. Again, she was vindicated by the obvious moves which Prime Minister F. W. de Klerk has since made to unwind apartheid without unleashing a bloody civil war.

She became a heroine in Eastern Europe. It was an extraordinary feat to have an ever-closer relationship with President Gorbachev at the same time as she was encouraging the resistance movements in those countries in thrall to the Soviet Union to demand their independence. Perhaps by then President Gorbachev knew, and even welcomed, the fact that the satellites were going. None the less, she did it and she will always be welcomed in Eastern Europe for the spirited support she gave the people there on the eve of their emancipation. The leaders of the Eastern European countries were all invited to the Conservative Party Conference at Bournemouth in October 1990. They made their assessments of her contribution to the liberalization of their countries in emotional speeches to the Tory faithful. The Hungarian Prime Minister talked of her 'extraordinary role' in recognizing the revolution in Eastern Europe and 'encouraging the Western Allies to see the direction and significance of the event'. It was all rich tribute, richly deserved.

Eventually, the worker of economic miracles became one of the most powerful and well-known leaders in the world. Few abroad could understand why she was suddenly unceremoniously turned out by her own Party in November 1990. People still ask with amazement why it was done. I find it hard to answer the question. Almost single-handed, with the aid of Sir Charles Powell, she had implanted her will, her sense of morals and her strength of purpose on numerous international situations.

Looking back over her eleven-and-a-half years, she gained far more ground for the British concept of Europe than the Commission did for theirs.

She saved the taxpayers many billions of pounds by her long-sustained battle to get our contribution to the Community budget made fairer. She used the Single European Act to forge ahead with opening up the market of Europe to something resembling a free market, against the dogged resistance of the protectionists. She achieved some limited reform of the indefensible Common Agricultural Policy, although she had not by the time she resigned succeeded in getting the Community to adopt a position which would allow the GATT Uruguay Round to succeed. Given more time, she might have done so – who can tell. It is a task which her successor should pursue relentlessly.

She succeeded in looking after the interests of the British people in these respects. She cannot be held responsible for what may, or may not, come next, but during her long stewardship Europe was, in fact, steered decisively in the direction in which she wanted it to go. Those in Europe with the opposite convictions made very little progress, despite the fact that she was outnumbered by 11 to 1 most of the time. She certainly was attacked for her 'stridency', although I would claim she did no more than state her position clearly. She defended herself on this score in an interview in *The Times* on 19 November 1990 by saying: 'Had I faltered, or taken some of the easy short-term ways out, we would have neither the success, nor the international reputation we have. Yet when a woman is strong, she is strident. If a man is strong, gosh he's a good guy. Some of the things that have been said to me . . . but never mind.' She certainly was strong, and she achieved her purpose, which I believe was greatly to the nation's benefit.

The great threats hanging over Britain in 1979 had been swept away – domination by the trade unions, rampant inflation, industrial decline, takeover by Brussels, the Cold War, the nuclear threat. The nation began to sense this, and the mood of the country began to change towards the end of her prime ministership.

Many said that she had become 'out of touch'. I would prefer to put it that the mood changed in a way that perhaps she didn't welcome; perhaps she didn't quite believe it had. She certainly didn't want to change her style of government, and her answer to the question, 'Why should I change my policies?' would surely have been an equally emphatic, 'I will not'.

There are many ways of describing this alleged change of mood in the country. A friend from the north of England put it to me that the people there had worked and striven and tightened their belts for ten years: now they wanted to stop making sacrifices and have an easier life. How a 35 per cent real increase in the average standard of living can be described as a sacrifice I do not know, but it is typical of the mood that there had been enough change; the time had come to enjoy the rewards. It was time for a rest.

Socialists described the new mood in terms of the public being fed up with the 'cuts' and wanting to see more spent on the public services. Again, how real increases in spending on the public services of the scale I have described in Chapter 4 can be described as 'cuts' I know not. But again, what matters is what people believe. The new generation of Tories see the need to provide a 'classless society', by which I think they mean equality of opportunity, although the opportunities for all had increased greatly under Margaret Thatcher. In response to opinion polls, people appeared to want higher public spending, more done by the State, and less choice left to the individual. But that wish didn't seem to be entirely borne out when it came to paying the Community Charge, which is mainly raised to pay directly for public spending on social provision. All this evidence seems to suggest that the British people wanted a rest from radical change, and they wanted the State to do more for them. Again, I suspect they would have been horrified if they thought they would have to pay for it through higher taxes. Her attempt to get direct contributions to the public services through the Community Charge is evidence of this.

Another way in which the situation appeared to have changed is that we seemed to be experiencing another wave of Puritanism, not unlike the one ushered in by Prince Albert and the Puritan revolution itself before. 'Puritanism' means to me an evangelical campaign to prevent others engaging in 'sin'. One does not necessarily have to give up sin oneself, but it can be awkward if one is a Puritan who is caught out sinning. It is a particular affliction of the British – from which the French, to their eternal credit, have never suffered – that they want to stop other people doing many of those things which they enjoy. The French glory in making their lives as enjoyable as possible: I sometimes wonder whether the lobbies in Britain don't glory in trying to make other people's lives as unenjoyable as possible.

We seem now to have another surge of Puritanism upon our hands. Our society is becoming more and more 'caring', but less and less tolerant of other people's desires. War is waged against those who like to drink a little – either they are abusing their health, or they are alleged to be engaging in 'alcohol abuse.' Now there is a campaign against the motor car, on the grounds that it causes pollution (although nothing like as much pollution as is caused by burning coal, which the Puritans find acceptable). The other charge against the motor car is that it causes congestion – which is true but, of course, evidence of how popular and how vital it is to nearly everyone in their daily lives. They say there is no point in building more roads – all that will happen is that the traffic will expand to fill them. That is evidence that demand exceeds supply. It is rather like saying that we should not build any more houses – all that will happen if we do is that the homeless will fill them up and the market will demand more. Mobility is vital in a modern economy – we should seek to provide roads, not frustrate the motor car.

Many of my favourite foods have lately come under withering censure from some quarter or another: beef, veal, battery eggs, butter, salt, soft cheese, chips – one after another they are attacked. We are told we must eat less fat, less cholesterol, fewer calories and all the rest of it. Growing numbers of people want to ban this, that or the other blood sport, although blood sports are part of traditional British country life and give many people both exercise and enjoyment. Women who wear fur coats are spat at, car drivers are forced to wear seat belts and motor cyclists are forced to wear helmets for their own protection, not that of the general public. I hardly dare mention smoking; smokers, of which I am one, are treated like outcasts, although they do no harm to anyone but themselves, many now complain of passive smoking.

The strange thing about this new Puritanism is that it is not directed at upholding the interests of society as a whole; rather, it is a crusade to stop others doing what they want or taking risks with their own lives. It is intolerant of both the weaknesses and the harmless desires of other people. Surely we can perfectly well be allowed to decide for ourselves what we eat, drink, wear and do in our spare time? In my opinion, the new Puritanism is an attack upon the personal freedom of others. It is also selective, in that other dangerous activities – like hang gliding, skiing and motor racing – are apparently acceptable. Prejudice is replacing logic.

Margaret Thatcher could not have found either of these two alleged new public moods too congenial. She believed so strongly in letting people keep their own money to spend on what they wished, and in letting people do as they wished with their own lives, exercising their freedom under the law. I am sure she would have ignored both these moods had she continued in office. I think she would have been right to do so. The British tend to give the canvasser, the pollster and the politician the answer that they think he would like to hear. They feel they have to say things which chime in with the current political mood, although at the same time they rely on the politicians to take no notice of what they say. Nearly everyone in Britain in fact wants to pay less income tax, poll tax, VAT and National Insurance contributions – few really want to pay more. The vast bulk of the population enjoys eating, drinking and spending its time on pastimes of its own choice: and many aspire to partake in hunting, shooting or fishing, and many women aspire to wear a fur coat. Puritanism suits the British – it enables them to sound virtuous – but only so long as it doesn't remotely affect their prosperity and their freedom to do as they will under the law. They rely on the Government to defend their rights, whatever they may say. Perhaps Margaret Thatcher's greatest achievement was that she knew this, that she had that unique certainty and determination not to be pushed off course by the current fashionable political mood. Despite the efforts of the intellectuals, the Opposition and the media to set her up as 'Iron' or 'uncaring' or 'out of touch' or 'refusing to listen', each time she went to the country she came back with a resounding win. It was as if the people saw her as the Iron Lady who was necessary to protect them from the do-gooders, the Puritans, high public spending and the higher taxes that come with it. As an air hostess said to me a few days after she resigned, 'She was too good a leader for us.'

There emerges from all these themes the picture of a leader with vision – and vision of what is right for the British people, one who understood what they want and one who had the strength to fight for that against all odds and however isolated she might have seemed.

In domestic politics, in international affairs, and in Europe, she had these clear, devastatingly simple, concepts about what was right and wrong, what the people wanted, and what was in the national interest or against it. She would brook no opposition, make no compromise, give no quarter, in her determination to achieve those goals she identified as the correct ones. The fact that she was isolated in Europe, or the Commonwealth, or the international community, or even in her own Cabinet, may have delayed, but never weakened her determination to achieve what she believed to be the right policy.

Keith Joseph's role in the phenomenon of the Thatcher years should not be underestimated. He articulated the intellectual case for what she believed in her gut feelings. She took it from him, and she did it. Keith Joseph's biographer, Morrison Halcrow, summed it up well: 'Both Margaret Thatcher and Keith Joseph had the courage of their convictions; but in a sense, it was he who provided the convictions to match her courage', he wrote. The courage lasted to the end, and beyond. It will surely be remembered long after the end of her life.

Pervading it all was her style. Margaret Thatcher's style, which was so much derided, and the butt of so much criticism by lesser men, was the outward expression of that determination, that inner self-confidence. She was in power by democratic election, she had made her purpose clear, she was benign, and she knew what should be done. How essential, therefore, to do it with style, with quality, with a flavour of civilized grandeur. Medieval kings and 18th century aristocrats used ostentatious wealth and pomp to impress the ignorant peasantry, and to make them feel that they should look up to superior beings like themselves. She took the best out of this and rejected the worst. She took the style and the quality, and rejected the ostentation and the pomp. She was thus not guilty of Belloc's famous charge:

> The accursed power which stands on privilege
> (And goes with women and champagne and bridge)
> Broke – and Democracy resumed her reign:
> (Which goes with bridge, and women and champagne.)

There was never a hint of corruption against her, despite her eleven-and-a-half years in office. The one real crisis in her career – the Westland affair – may have been mishandled, but it is impossible to sustain any worse charge than that in my opinion. She was never guilty of peculation or nepotism; there was nothing gross or pompous about her conduct of affairs. She went for quality in everything – in conversation, in entertaining and in her relaxation, which was political discussion with clever people. She read a lot, she kept up with thinkers, scientists, artists and entrepreneurs. She added the qualities of humility and charity: for her there was always time to care about life's casualties, in an individual sense rather than in a public relations sense.

She went for quality in the way she led the Government – she wanted a Government of quality. Some would say she believed in 'meritocracy' – government by people with merit. In truth, her ideal was closer to the true meaning of the word 'aristocracy', which the

Oxford Dictionary defines as 'the government of a state by its best citizens'. She wanted both herself and her Government to be numbered among the 'best citizens'.

All this left her critics with little of substance to throw at her. They could only try to assassinate her character by developing the 'Iron Lady' theme – she was bossy, she rode roughshod over people, she wouldn't listen, she was determined to get her own way. Such criticisms were in fact only an acknowledgement of the strength of her character and her determination. She brought an unusual mixture to the highest office of quality, incorruptibility, radicalism, and determination, while opening up to her critics no valid line of personal attack. But that didn't stop them from trying. She had all the qualities of a great leader.

So how will her era be regarded in the history books? When all our generation is dead and gone, there will be no one trying to justify himself or her; nor will there be enemies carrying on a vendetta against her. But the balm of impartiality which time brings also buries with it what life felt like at the time: the emotions and passions of the age. We read that Mary Tudor was a 'bad Queen' or Elizabeth I was a 'good Queen' – but we learn little about what they were like, or what life was like in either reign, nor whether the monarch brought about decisive change in the nation's character or achievements. History certainly relates events, statistics record economic performance, letters and documents are preserved for posterity to tell us what happened. But the impact of individuals on the course of history can never be accurately assessed by historians, try though they may. Certainly we believe it was Henry VIII who personally broke Rome's domination over England – an early and unsuccessful attempt at imposing European union upon us! We also believe Wellington was a vital personality in our success in preventing Napoleon's attempt to do the same thing; and that Churchill frustrated Hitler's attempt.

I have tried to describe what life was like close to Margaret Thatcher. My experiences convince me that she personally changed the course of history in the 1980s. She was instrumental in bringing the Cold War to an end. She changed the direction in which Europe was moving on both sides of the Iron Curtain. She helped lay the foundations of a new world order, and she transformed the British economy.

In the domestic arena there are many great figures who have had a really dramatic effect upon social and economic conditions in Britain. There are so many who could lay claim to have done so; I mention only

Wilberforce, Burke, Gladstone, Peel, Lloyd George, Attlee. I believe history will place Margaret Thatcher in that same category. But no other British Prime Minister achieved so much both at home and abroad. Most of her predecessors were famous wartime leaders or distinguished peacetime leaders: she was one of the few who were both. Impartial historical analysis should give her a very high rating in the roll of honour of our great Prime Ministers.

There is also the quality of leadership to assess: Margaret Thatcher was certainly a leader of the highest order. Political leadership has been described as the ability to stake out a radical agenda of action, to be able to succeed in mobilizing public opinion behind it, and then to carry it through as well. On this basis, she ranks alongside very few – perhaps only Gladstone.

Such people rarely occur. Not only is it very unusual that someone comes upon the scene who combines all the qualities needed to galvanize this complex, civilized, conscience-stricken democracy of ours, but the timing has to be right. There has to be the opportunity and the people have to want it to be done. Margaret Thatcher would never have succeeded in the 1950s or 1960s – perhaps we had to get to the degradation of the 1970s before the time was right for her. We are all fortunate that in our hour of need someone of the quality required was to hand, and willing to serve.

I return, finally, to the threats which overhung the nation in 1979. Mythical figures in medieval history were alleged to slay dragons – though I have never understood what these dragons were and how they can have existed in real life. They must have been symbolic of some evil, some oppressor, some tyrant. Perhaps the best analogy, therefore, is that the nation was oppressed by many dragons in 1979, and that Margaret Thatcher came forth to slay them. After she had slain them, the nation no longer had need of her. Normal, humdrum government has been resumed. We shall miss her style of government.

INDEX

consensus, government by, 3, 24, 25, 54, 55, 78, 75–6
Conservative Party, 6, 9; Backbench Finance Committee, 5, 7; Conferences (1986) 228, (1987) 125, (1990) 154, 214, 226, 228, 260; and Europe, 151; malcontents in, 25, 26, 31, 35, 38, 49, 175, 221, 226; 'men in grey suits', 251, 252; 1922 Committee, 23, 52, 241, 251; No Turning Back Group, 242; policy groups, 3, 15, 16, 136; ruthlessness of, 251, 252; traditional policy of, 54–5, 79, 221; 'wets' in, 14, 24, 25, 29, 101, 162, 172–6, 214, 221, 226, 249
Conservative Philosophy Group, 20
Constitutions, British and US, 27–8, 30
Cope, John, 12
Crawshaw, R., 10
credit boom, see housing
Cripps, Sir Stafford, 3
'cuts', see public expenditure

Daily Mail, 113, 214
de Gaulle, General Charles, 159, 252
de Klerk, F.W., 260
Delors, Jacques, 145, 146, 230, 231–2
Delors Report, 145, 146–52, 160, 225, 230; alternatives to, 149–50; objections to, 147–9
dependency culture, 15, 17, 79–101 passim, 257
Depression, the (1930s), 165, 170, 200, 202, 204
Deutschemark (DM), 'shadowing' the, 74, 75, 201–4, 207–8, 211
Douglas Home, Alec, 173
Dryden, 104
du Cann, Edward, 9

Ecology Party, 103
Economic Dining Club, 20, 39
Economic and Monetary Union (EMU), 143, 145–7, 151, 153, 158, 171, 208, 225, 230, 232
Economist, The, 38, 67
economy, the: demand management, 6, 86, 118, 165–6, 168, 170, 173, 202,

206; free market, 3, 22, 255; legal infrastructure of, 57; recession in, 229, 232, 255; service sector, 56, 61; 'social market', 6, 7, 78–9, 80, 102; supply side policies, 6, 20, 54–5, 56, 64, 70–1, 72, 75, 83, 86, 255, 258; upturns in, 21, 38, 71, 168, 187, 190–1, 196, 228
ECU, hard, 150, 160, 225, 238
Eden, Sir Anthony, 81, 235
education, 78, 79, 82, 92–4, 257; egalitarianism, 12, 19, 32, 80, 81, 202
Elections, General: (1955) 3; (1959) 3; (1970) 4; (1974) 6, 66, 119; (1979) 10, 13, 20–1, 22, 24, 28, 86, 164, 245; (1983) 38, 39, 40, 68, 86, 185; (1987) 31, 33, 64, 83, 86, 88, 91, 94, 95, 96, 126, 196, 257; the next, 97–8, 221
environment: conservation, 113–15; Control of Pollution Act, 112; 'green' issues, 103–18; 'green' parties, 103–10, 112, 113, 115; HM inspectorate of Pollution, 112; London Conference on the North Sea, 112; protection, 57, 63, 90
Europe, Eastern, 31, 43, 44, 146, 152–5, 156, 224, 260
European Commission, 54, 114, 137, 139, 141, 142, 146, 154, 159, 160, 230, 231, 245, 256
European Community: British objectives, 136, 137, 140, 145, 160-1, 228, 261; doctrine of 'subsidiarity' 142; environmental issues, 106–15; finance, 138–40, 141–2; foreign policy, 143–5; Franco-German axis within, 136–7, 140, 145, 154, 209, 230; future structure of, 136, 140–1, 143, 151; the Irish in, 141, 148; opponents of, 20, 136, 142; regional policy, 148; Single European Act, 137, 142–4, 261; Single European Currency, 137, 146, 225–6; Single Market, 55, 73, 142–3, 256; Summits, 139, 145, (Madrid) 160, 208–11, 212, 216 (Rome) 157, 159, 160, 230, 232, 238; Treaty of Rome (1957), 137, 138, 142, 148

INDEX

Medium Term Financial Strategy
(MTFS), 182–4, 188, 189, 194
Merrison, Sir Alec, 95
Meyer, Sir Anthony, 236, 241, 245
Middleton, Peter, 183
Mitchell, David, 62
Mitterrand, François, President, 145,
158, 159, 230
Monckton, Sir Walter, 14
monetarism, 6, 7, 24, 163–8, 170,
182–4, 188–9, 206, 214
Monopolies Commission, 56
Moore, John, 35, 36, 40, 61, 96, 98,
186, 241, 242
Morrison, Peter, 241, 244
Murdoch, Rupert, 70

National Debt, 206, 253
National Health Service (NHS): 65, 78,
82–3; cost of, 95, 96; doctors in, 96–
7; policy, 95–7; reforms, 45, 86, 221,
232, 258
nationalization, 2–3, 4, 15, 54, 60, 62–
5, 76, 120, 180–1, 254
National Rivers Authority (NRA), 64,
111
NATO, 144, 155
Nature Conservancy Council (NCC),
113, 114, 115
Neale, Gerry, 241
Neave, Airey, 9
Neubert, Michael, 241
New Left Review, 68
Newton, Tony, 12, 249
NIMBY, 117, 118
Norris, Steven, 224
Northern Ireland, 9, 34
Nott, John, 24, 33, 162
nuclear power, 105, 109, 113

Observer, 28
oil revenues, 169
Onslow, Cranley, 241
opinion polls, 21, 26, 86, 221, 233, 242,
243–4, 247, 262, 264
Opposition, the: Conservative, 11, 12,
13, 179; Labour, 6, 11, 13, 23, 25,
34, 41, 52, 95, 101, 129, 131, 264

Page, Jack, 40
Parkinson, Cecil, 12, 39, 186, 248
Patten, Chris, 36, 91, 111, 112, 131,
175, 220, 223, 249
pensions, 79, 85, 86, 99–100, 171, 187,
253
permissive society, 19
Peyton, John, 9
Pirie, Madsen, 8
Plaza Agreement, 199, 200
Poehl, Karl Otto, 38, 149, 151, 152,
195, 201, 205, 229
Poll Tax, 32, 85, 94, 103, 119–35,
219–21, 232, 243, 262; alternatives
to, 126–8, 134; Community Charge
Reduction Scheme, 132; Green
Paper, 125; levels, 130–1; protests
against, 131, 135, 219; rebates 130–
3, 135; in Scotland, 125, 131 see also
rates, domestic;
Potter, Beatrix, 113
Powell, Charles, 41, 43, 51, 260
Powell, Enoch, 3, 20
Pravda, 58
Prices and Incomes Bill (1973), 5–6
Prices and incomes policy, 6, 65, 66
Prior, James, 9, 14, 23, 29, 64, 65, 163,
173–5, 176, 180; *A Balance of Power*,
174
privatization, 3–4, 6, 14–16, 40, 44, 45,
56, 58–64, 103, 177, 187, 222, 223,
254, 258; advice to USSR, 58; and
customers, 60, 63; and shareholders,
64
protectionism, 57, 73, 137, 143, 157,
256–7, 261
public expenditure; control, 6, 167; the
'cuts', 66, 83–5, 92, 96, 97, 101, 262;
increase in, 83–5
public sector, 78–9, 82–6, 258
Puritanism, 32, 262–4
Pym, Francis, 23, 173–5

Question Time, Prime Minister's, 11

rates, domestic, 32, 88, 119, 127, 128;
history of, 119–20; rebates, 121;
reform of, 122–5; Resources
Equalization, 121; in Scotland, 119,
123, 124, 127, 128; see also Poll Tax

273

handbag of, 35; as hostess, 31–3; as 'Iron Lady', 17, 19–20, 232, 258, 259, 264, 266; lectures Russians at airbase, 43; and loyalty, 1, 6, 17, 36, 41, 42, 45, 52, 53, 224; moral views of, 17–19, 91; myths about, 39, 98; and Party leadership contests, 1, 9, 10, 24, 35, 232–3, 236, 241–50; and pay, 19; political beliefs of, 13, 17, 18, 19, 79, 81, 179, 264–6; probity of, 17, 23, 39, 51, 52, 265; public support for, 226, 233, 235, 251, 264, registration of, 1–2, 247, 248–9, 251, 252, 256; and retirement plans, 39; and scientific issues, 90, 115, 118; as Secretary of State for Education, 6, 11, 41, 92; Shadow Cabinet of, 11, 26; and social policy, 79–80; 'special interests' of, 45–6, 47, 86, 92, 93, 96, 110–11; style of, 8–9, 10, 23, 26, 31, 159–61, 238, 243, 255, 265; unpopularity of, 221, 232; and U-turns, 176; verdict of history on, 266–7; and Victorian values, 18–19; as world leader, 258–60, 266

Thatcherism, 2, 10, 13, 80, 258

Thomas, George (Viscount Tonypandy), 33, 34

Times, The, 172, 237, 261

Trade Union Acts, 64–5

trade unions: Democratic Mineworkers, 69; militant, 65–70; pay bargaining, 21; picketing, 21, 65; power of, 3, 21–2, 55, 60, 81, 82, 85, 172, 254; reform of, 14–15, 55, 64–5, 72, 95

Twinn, Ian, 241

Tyler, Wat, 68

unemployment, 4, 79, 165, 167, 170–2, 174, 194, 206

United Nations, 106, 144

Unit Labour costs (ULCs), 192–4, 195, 201–2, 213, 229

USA, 27, 30, 45, 47, 54, 62, 73, 145, 155, 157, 195, 198–200, 210, 256, 259

USSR, 43, 58, 64, 152, 154, 230, 259, 260

Waddington, David, 26, 248

Wakeham, John, 26, 162, 248

Waldegrave, William, 123, 124, 249

Walesa, Lech, 32

Walker, Peter, 23, 35, 68, 175, 222

Wallace, Euan, 61

Walters, Alan, 5, 7, 8, 165, 167, 190, 201, 208, 216, 227

Webley, Simon, 8

Weinstock, Lord, 14

Welsh Nationalists, 21

Westland Helicopters, 46–50, 52, 235–6, 237, 265

Whip, Chief, 25–6, 251

Whips Office, 33

Whitelaw, William, 9, 10, 24–5, 26, 33, 46, 174

Wilberforce Committee, 66, 67

Wilson, Harold, 11, 34, 66

Winter of Discontent, 14, 19, 21–2, 24, 65, 163, 172

Yalta, Treaty of, 155, 259

Young, Lord, 57, 58, 59, 222

Younger, George, 50, 123, 125, 222, 241